The Reflective Teacher

Case Studies of Action Research

NEERAJA RAGHAVAN

Contributing Editor

VINEETA SOOD

Orient BlackSwan

ORIENT BLACKSWAN PRIVATE LIMITED

Registered Office
3-6-752, Himayatnagar, Hyderabad 500 029, Telangana, India
Email: centraloffice@orientblackswan.com

Other Offices
Bengaluru, Bhopal, Bhubaneshwar, Chandigarh, Chennai, Ernakulam, Guwahati, Hyderabad, Jaipur, Kolkata, Lucknow, Mumbai, New Delhi, Noida, Patna

First published 2016

ISBN 978-81-250-6045-1

Typeset in Adobe Caslon Pro 10.5/13 *by*
Bookcraft Publishing Services (I) Pvt Ltd
Chennai 600 004

Printed in India by
Yash Printographics
Noida 201 301

Published by
Orient Blackswan Private Limited
160, Anna Salai
Chennai 600 002
E mail: chennai@orientblackswan.com

Contents

Foreword

'You can never step into the same river twice.' This oft-quoted and apt comment by Heraclitus (535–475 BC) still provides a meaningful insight into so much of our learning. In terms of this wonderful, helpful and informative book, the quote can guide us in our understanding of professional development.

One interpretation of the Heraclitus quote is that you can never step into the same river twice because the *river* is always changing. The world of twenty years ago has certainly changed to become the world of today. Technology has changed with the growth of the internet and its uses. More people have access to computers, to email and to social networking sites. People now turn to the internet to purchase goods, to see what cinema is playing locally or to watch a movie at home. The schools and the purpose of schools has shifted as we demand that all students receive more education than in the past regardless of whether they reside in a rural village or a booming metropolis. The economy has changed over this same time frame with enormous wealth created for some in our society. Alongside these economic changes, we have different interpretations of the meaning of social justice. India has changed in twenty years and the world has changed. There is more migration and travel in international trade which makes new demands on education.

A contrasting interpretation of the Heraclitus quote is that you can never step into the same river twice because *you* are always changing. Over a span of a teaching career, the teacher has changed. When first placed in a classroom, the teacher may struggle with all aspects of teaching. I like to remind my pre-service teachers that the first year in the classroom is similar to driving into oncoming traffic. Over the years, teachers improve their **content knowledge**. The facts and theories that they learned in college grow in meaning as they teach and this firmer foundation allows teachers to learn additional content. Teachers also improve their **pedagogical knowledge**. They learn that teaching is not merely telling the students which pages to read in a book. Teaching is not explaining what you know to the student. Teaching is exploring what the students know, how the students explain things and then trying to understand how they reached these conclusions. Teaching is helping the students to accept that there may be alternative ways of explain these same things that are superior to the initial way in which they explained them. Teachers also change as they experience teaching and find ways in which to improve their **pedagogical content knowledge**. The techniques to use in teaching history, science, math and literature have some commonalities, but each discipline has its own set of approaches that are unique to the discipline and that experienced teachers learn over the course of their career.

This book helps us to better understand a specific approach to professional development. All teachers experience their own education from the age of five to eighteen and then move on to college where they may receive education related both to subject matter as well as teaching. Following this immersion, teachers must take additional courses in order to receive certifications to allow them to seek employment as a teacher. Calibrating this education, one can see that the bulk of experience is the 12–16 years as a student contrasted with a year or two or three learning how to be a teacher. For a teaching career that may span an additional thirty years, there must be something else – professional development.

My personal interest in this book stems from my own experiences in teaching and leading professional development workshops. My teaching career began as a Peace Corps volunteer teaching Math and Science in a small village in Nepal very close to Janakpur and with a large Maithili language presence similar to our neighbours in Bihar, India. After many years as a high school teacher, science coordinator and professor in the United States, I have attended and led professional development workshops. Over the past three years, it has been my privilege to work with teacher leaders supported by the Azim Premji Foundation in India. Parts of this book are based on the reflection of some teachers who have benefited enormously from the work of the Foundation. In a somewhat parallel effort, Wipro has funded a Science Education Fellowship program in the United States which I oversee.

The Wipro Science Education Fellowship (Wipro SEF) is a two-year Science teacher-leadership program which aims to address the needs of improving STEM teaching and learning. Broadly, it focuses on the three pillars of reflective practice, adult learning and leadership. It is guided by much of the same research that this book summarises and articulates. This book builds on that research base and helps bridge that research with the practice of teachers learning how to improve their teaching.

As stated, 'The book is intended to serve a readership of teachers, teacher educators, students of graduate and post-graduate programmes in education, NGOs that work in the education sector, researchers and Heads of Schools. It is envisioned that the second section will meet the needs of the reader who would like to learn largely about practice, while the other two will be of greater interest to those who also wish to ground this practice in theory.'

The literature and quotes throughout the book help guide us in understanding the theories of Dewey, Schon and others. I was particularly struck by the careful articulation of the intent of 'action research' and how it leads to 'reflective practice'. The theoretical models were valuable in their own right. The teacher snapshots brought the theoretical structure to life. The book allowed me to be part of a conversation with the teachers as they describe their instruction and the lessons learned from this instruction. This section of the book was equally satisfying. The authors took one final step in the third section of the book where they provide an overview of the research and how it manifests in the instruction and in the professional development models. In this regard, we have come full circle. They have made sense and brought meaning to the research field of professional development.

The authors have also helped me to relate Heraclitus's words with with those of T.S. Eliot's. 'We shall not cease from exploration, and the end of all our exploring will be to arrive where we started and know the place for the first time.' And for this, I am grateful.

Arthur Eisenkraft
Distinguished Professor of Science Education; Professor of Physics;
Director of the Center of Science and Math in Context (COSMIC)
University of Massachusetts Boston; Boston, Massachusetts, USA

ACKNOWLEDGEMENTS

This book is the outcome of action research work that was voluntarily undertaken by the teachers of Azim Premji School, Dineshpur, facilitated by members of Azim Premji Foundation and anchored by me during my tenure as Professor, Azim Premji University. The Principal, teachers and the Azim Premji Foundation permitted us to publish their work in the form of this book, and they are gratefully acknowledged for this. Given the nature of sporadic interaction of facilitators with teachers, none of this work would have turned out as it did but for the sustained anchoring of the project by the Principal, Deepak Dixit. This is also acknowledged with thanks.

The video-taped interviews with each teacher at the end of the study were produced as a set of eight short films available with the Azim Premji Foundation. The interviews were transcribed and translated into English by Usha Kumar. Her enthusiastic approach to the work contributed to the way in which the subtitles finally turned out, and the transcribed documents have also been referred to for much of the compilation contained in this book.

Sneha Kumari meticulously coordinated the entire project and followed up with the film editor, the transcriber, the contributing editor as well as the team of facilitators, for which we thank her.

Several people gave generously of their time to review different versions of the manuscript, as the book evolved into what you now hold in your hands. Prof. S. Rajashree of Azim Premji University carried out a meticulous and thorough review of the very first draft of the manuscript, which resulted in a far better second draft. She invested considerable time in this effort and we are extremely grateful to her for this. Shri S.C. Behar gave much of his valuable time to read through the manuscript and made extremely useful suggestions. We thank him deeply for this.

Many others offered very useful feedback. Dr Maria Athaide's enthusiastic and painstaking reading of the manuscript (twice!) was heartwarming indeed. G. Gautama (KFI, Chennai) and Dr Sindhu Mathai (APU, Bangalore) gave detailed and valuable feedback.

Sneha Titus willingly offered her efficient editorial assistance to Section II, and this made a big difference to the way the Section turned out. I acknowledge with gratitude the insightful inputs of the contributing editor, Vineeta Sood, who helped me greatly in stepping back and looking at the project I had been so much a part of.

All the photographs in the book (unless otherwise mentioned) were taken by the facilitators. Photographs appearing on the front cover and pages 1, 75 and 185 were taken by K. Natarajan, Rishi Valley School. We are very grateful to them for sharing these with us.

Every effort was made to incorporate all feedback – for any gaps that persist, I claim sole responsibility.

Neeraja Raghavan

SECTION I

BACKGROUND

1. Reflection and Action Research: What, Why, How?

A classroom in a school can be regarded as a potpourri of several elements: youth, freshness, vitality, regeneration. Thirty or forty pulsating young minds, a teacher, lessons to learn and access to books – at the very least.

Why, then, does teaching–learning frequently turn into a mechanical and repetitive process?

What drains it of the vibrant life that is inherent in the elements that it contains?

Unwittingly – and sometimes, even with awareness – the same lessons are transacted in more or less the same manner, year after year. In the daily rush to 'cover the syllabus', conduct mid-term tests and administer end-of-year examinations, teachers are often hard-pressed to find the time to address their own professional development in a regular, consistent manner. Sporadic workshops are sometimes organised by managements of schools, on topics that are seldom aligned with the unique and specific developmental needs of each teacher. Further, the impact of such workshops on altered practices, understanding or beliefs of participating teachers is hardly ever examined.

Therefore, it is often only the degree (or diploma) in education acquired by a teacher that serves as the source to dip into for ideas, resources and strategies to meet ongoing, everyday challenges. However, in the words of Donald Schon (1983), any professional frequently encounters situations that are characterised by 'uncertainty, instability, uniqueness and value conflict'. A teacher can therefore hardly expect to resort to a formula or established method to tackle these daily dilemmas. Indeed, there are no readymade answers for questions that spring from uniqueness, uncertainty and conflict.

> *Psychology is a science, and teaching is an art; and sciences never generate arts directly out of themselves. An intermediary inventive mind must make the application, by using its originality.*
>
> ***William James (1899)***

Such situations call for *reflection*.

Reflection is necessary for meeting most of life's unexpected challenges. It is a rare person who does not draw upon the quality of reflection in order to handle day-to-day problems encountered in one's personal life. Indeed, it has often been found that a crisis perforce triggers deep reflection. Rich biographies have been written of turning points in people's lives, caused by unexpected events (sometimes catastrophes) which caused them to step back and reflect. Further, the development of this quality (in any individual) moves along a continuum – there are no easily quantifiable (or measurable) milestones which a person developing this quality may have definitely 'crossed'. In a sense, becoming reflective is an ongoing journey, with no claim possible of having finally 'arrived'. While the authors of this work hold such a view, the reader is referred to contrasting views of researchers – Yost et al (2000) who recommend frameworks to evaluate levels of reflectivity, and Latour (1988) who argues that it cannot be ranked in orders of discourse. Even as we agree that ranking may not be meaningful, in a later chapter (see page 63), we do refer to a framework of teacher reflectivity proposed by Stanley (1998), for the sake of identifying the location of these teachers on the path of reflection.

Few would disagree, then, that a significant percolation of this quality of reflection into one's *professional life* as well would render it that much more effective. Particularly in work such as teaching, where the chances of operating repetitively from habit are high, the importance of consciously inculcating a reflective quality cannot be underrated.

This begs the question: What are the various ways in which reflection can be developed/enhanced?

Ways of Enhancing Reflection

We do not plan to provide a comprehensive description of the array of methods used by teacher educators. An overview of various methods that can be used has been given in Lock, Conderman and Morin's (2004) easy-to-read summary. Journals (Powell 1985), portfolios (Guba and Lincoln 1985), self reports (Pak 1985), collaborative diary-keeping (Brock, Ju and Wong 1991), autobiographies (Gore 1993), case studies (Chambers and Clarke), peer coaching (Costa and Garmston 1994), group discussions (Fazio 2009), peer feedback (Richards and

Lockhart 1991) and video- and audio-recording of classroom processes (Pak 1985) are only some of the methods that have been successfully tried out.

In the following study, **action research** has been used as a way of enhancing reflective thinking in the teacher. Opportunities that everyday issues throw up for learning and reflection are often missed in the rush to cover content and prepare students for the end-of-year examinations. Action research helps teachers grasp such opportunities and exploit them for their own benefit.

Action Research

The choice of this route was, to begin with, based purely on pragmatic considerations. Given how busy each teacher in this school was (and indeed are in most schools), it was felt that the chosen route should be as non-intrusive as possible. Since teachers could not be expected to set aside time for regular and sustained discussions with their facilitators or peers, all the methods which necessitated the sustained physical presence of another (classroom observations, video- and audio-recording) in the teacher's class were ruled out. The team from the Foundation also did not want to make demands on the teacher's time after school hours. Action research, by its very nature, fitted this requirement best. Organically, a teacher could work through his/her dilemma even as (s)he taught the lessons. At best, the documentation step would call for out-of-class time, but even this is not a daily need.

As the study developed, it became increasingly clear that this method would be appropriate for various other reasons as well (see pp 10–13).

By identifying an ongoing dilemma that disturbed the concerned teacher, action research was initiated. Facilitators worked with teachers to run through the framework of action research (described later in this chapter), so as to use the identified problem as ground for rich learning.

Action research offers a route to tap into the fertile soil of daily practice, so that a teacher can identify and examine assumptions and beliefs, re-examine practices and alter them to suit a unique context. Slowly, as action research is conducted by a teacher, the process of reflection begins to *consciously* unfold. What's more, this does not demand a separate time slot or budget, happening 'online' as it does.

Schools for the marginalised sections of society can make as much use of this method (of awakening reflection in their teachers) as can elite schools, for there is no need to allocate a separate budget or time. Teacher professional development can thus be built into a teacher's workday in an organic manner, without fragmenting it into sporadic workshops or training programmes that may add little to the lived experience of a teacher. Instead of budgeting for (and relying on) external experts to enhance the knowledge base of a teacher, action research reveals to each teacher the domains of learning that *that particular teacher* needs to enhance, organically. A concerned teacher will then himself seek out ways of addressing these gaps. An alert principal will use the opportunity provided by action research to encourage teachers to focus on the specific areas of capacity enhancement that emerge.

In this book we attempt to give the reader a taste of research that has been conducted in this domain, with special emphasis on the pioneering work of Dewey (1933) and Schon (1983).

Keeping the focus of the study in mind, this chapter will make an attempt to answer the following questions:

- What is action research?
- Why was action research selected as the route to enhance reflection?
- Has action research been used for teacher development?
- How objective can such a study be?
- What is meant by 'reflective practice'?
- Has action research been found to promote reflective practice?
- Has reflective practice been found to promote teacher development?

What is Action Research?

Several excellent texts are available on this subject: Mills' (2006) *Action Research: A Guide for the Teacher Researcher*, a primer by Jeffrey Glanz (1999) titled *A Primer on Action Research for School Administrators* and the classic by McNiff and Whitehead (2005) titled *All You Need to Know about Action Research*, to name a few.

Most importantly, it is critical that the newcomer to action research understands the difference between the sort of research that aims largely to broaden the scope of the researcher's knowledge and 'action' research. Unlike typical research studies which serve mainly to add to the knowledge in an existing domain, **action research sets out to study something with a view to improving it, or to solving a problem**. Thus, instead of focusing mainly on gathering information, the action researcher seeks to address a problem that is being faced in the workplace, and searches for information, methods, resources and any sort of tools that are suited to address that particular issue. It serves as a way for the practitioner to better understand her work, and employs traditional research methods to solve real problems or issues (Glanz 1999).

Historically, Kurt Lewin is said to have coined the phrase 'action research', which he described (Lewin 1952) as being 'composed of a circle of planning, executing and reconnaissance or fact-finding for the purpose of evaluating the results of the second step, for preparing the rational basis for planning the third step, and for perhaps modifying again the overall plan.'

Kurt Lewin is said to have first brought it centrestage, declaring that 'research that produces nothing but books will not suffice' (Lewin 1948).

An action research cycle consists broadly of the following steps: Plan, Act, Observe and Reflect. This can then loop back as shown below.

Reminiscent as it is of learning cycles, it is well suited to adult learning or andragogy. Andragogy has been a subject of study which is different from pedagogy. Boud (1994) emphasised the experience that

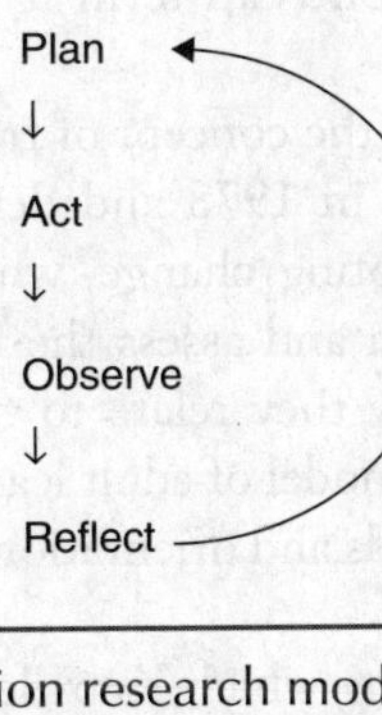

Figure 1.1 A basic action research model

Source: © Patrick J.M. Costello, 2011, 'Effective Action Research', Continuum Publishing, by permission of Bloomsbury Publishing Plc.

adult learners bring with them as being central to their learning. Since teachers are adult learners, the consideration of the principles and parameters of adult education is critical while planning any education for them.

Andragogy (Greek *andros* – adult man, and *agogue* – guide) is defined as a process model for adult learning (Knowles 1984). Facilitators consider the activities and steps needed for adults to acquire knowledge and skills, rather than adopting a content model such as pedagogy, where the *teacher* often decides what needs to be told and how to present it to the learner.

According to Knowles (1984) there are four principles of adult learning:

1. Adults need to be involved in the planning and evaluation of their instruction.
2. Experience (including mistakes) provides the basis for learning activities.
3. Adults are most interested in learning subjects that have immediate relevance to their job or personal life.
4. Adult learning is problem-centred rather than content-oriented. (Kearsley 2010).

Teachers may relate immediately to points 3 and 4; action research has as its entry point some doubt or discontent experienced by the teacher. A teacher who is puzzled or disturbed by something in his class is likely to consider any intervention that addresses this conflict as 'relevant'. Further, action research is also less content-oriented and more problem-centred. The appropriateness of action research as an adult 'pedagogy' – if one can term it so – is thus implied by the above.

Jack Mezirow introduced the concept of transformative learning to the field of adult education in 1978 and defined it as 'an approach to teaching based on promoting change, where educators challenge learners to critically question and assess the integrity of their deeply held assumptions about how they relate to the world around them.' Knowles (1980) proposed a model of adult learning which summarises the relationship between needs and orientation of the adult learner and learning.

These principles of learning which Knowles formulated in relation to adult learning are actually general principles of learning which, when applied to *any* age group, contribute to better learning.

Steps in Action Research

Let us now look at a flowchart describing the steps in action research.

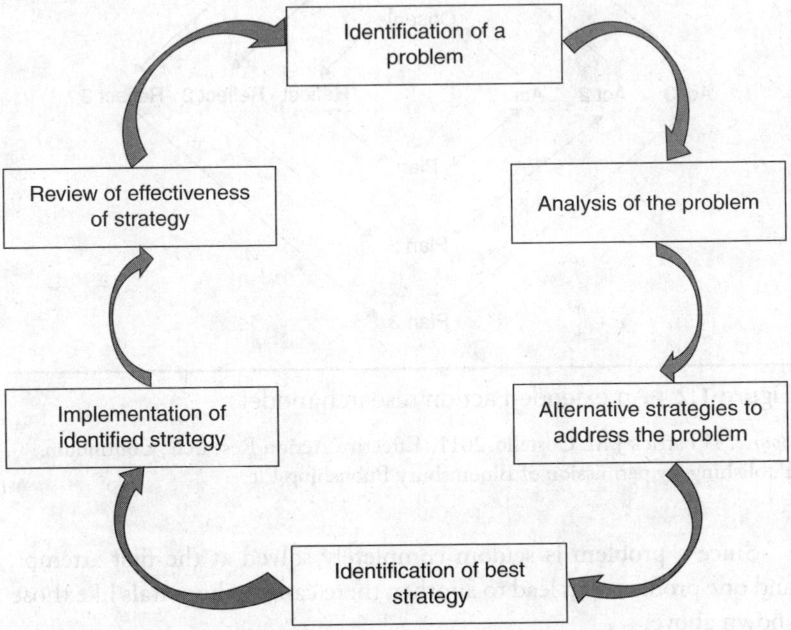

These are the steps taken by the teacher to address the specific problem that (s)he has identified in the classroom situation.

We refer to this as the *first spiral of action research*, as there is also a *second spiral* ***embedded*** in this study: that of examining (if and) how a teacher who conducted action research turned more reflective [see pages 23, 34, 188–215). Quite often, the two happen in tandem, for even as the teacher's action research pans out, his/her reflection becomes more evident.

Therefore, it is difficult to separate the first spiral from the other in a rigid or mechanical manner. In the course of this book, consequently, the reader may justifiably perceive a 'switching back and forth' between these two spirals. This has deliberately been retained so as to bring out the inevitable intertwining of increasing reflection and action research. [In the concluding section, there are guidelines for introducing greater rigour in these two spirals for those interested in conducting similar research.]

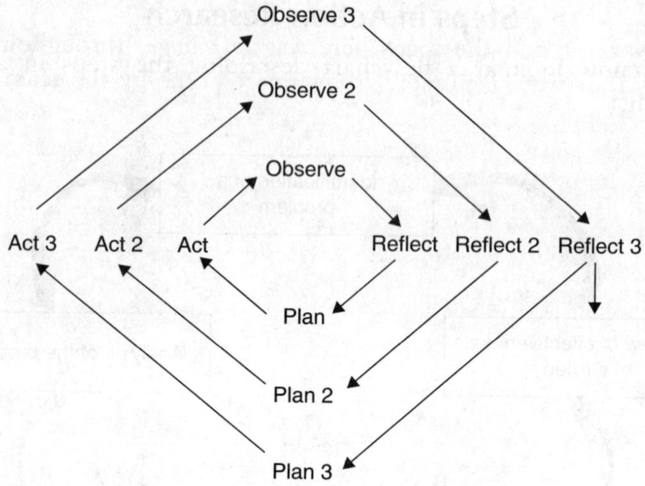

Figure 1.2 An extended action research model

Source: © Patrick J.M. Costello, 2011, 'Effective Action Research', Continuum Publishing, by permission of Bloomsbury Publishing Plc.

Since a problem is seldom completely solved at the first attempt, and one problem can lead to another, there can also be spirals like those shown above.

Why was Action Research Chosen as a Method to Work With the Teachers?

The members of the Foundation took into account the following factors while selecting action research as a means of teacher development:

- Principles of andragogy
- Teacher Education Programmes that teachers in India are usually exposed to
- Vision of the Foundation

Keeping in mind the principles of andragogy, action research seemed to fit best as, during action research, teachers identified their problems, proposed strategies, implemented them and, by and large, succeeded in solving the problem that they were facing. In the current study, the participating teachers were almost entirely in charge of their teaching as well as their own learning. Thus, *the teachers were the researchers*, and the focus here was *to change*. Throughout this process, they were facilitated from time to time by the team from the Foundation. [The process of facilitation is described in a later section (see pages 37–38).] Lieberman (1995) asserts that there may be far greater similarity between the ways in which teachers and students learn than has been recognised. Through active involvement and articulation of whatever has been learnt, people learn best – this is what learning theorists and organisational theorists proclaim, according to Lieberman (1995).

In many teacher education programmes in India, as in prevalent educational programmes for children, the emphasis is on identifying what is *not* working well and then 'telling' the teachers how to correct it. The Report of the Justice Verma Commission on Teacher Education (2012) asserted that pre-service as well as in-service teacher training has remained largely unchanged over the last fifty years. This Commission found that a mechanical application of techniques resulted from reducing teaching to a set of techniques. Consequently, there was little or no cognizance of the subject being taught, the unique circumstances of the students or the specificities of the school setting.

Usually, what is missed in such training programmes is the unique potential and strength of each individual that is brought into the teaching–learning situation. Action research breaks away from this traditional approach. As can be seen from the work described in this book, the teachers conducted the research from start to finish, relying on their own experiences, by choosing a real-life problem that they were facing in the classroom, and were disturbed by. They were invested enough in the project, being alive to these problems and naturally inclined to solving them. This motivation sprang from each teachers' connect to his/her own experience, his/her need to find a solution to the problems being faced. The adult teaching–learning process is thus, generally, dynamic, geared towards change and dependent on what the persons involved bring to the table.

With the vision of Azim Premji Foundation being the development of a just, equitable and humane society, this necessarily calls for the development of the critical faculty in the teacher as well as the learner. Thus, teacher education practices adopted by teacher educators of the organisation have to necessarily disallow 'teaching to' teachers, as an individual cannot examine social structures critically if (s)he is not reflective. The critical importance of developing reflective practice in teachers was thus an inevitable consequence of holding such a vision.

Action Research and Teacher Development

While action research has been used in a range of environments, [e.g. healthcare – Lingard (2008), Whitehead (2003); social work – McNicoll (1999); community – Ozanne Anderson (2010); management – Whyte (1991); environment – Gibbs (1982)] it was first applied systematically to education by Stephen Corey (at Teachers College, Columbia University) in the 1950s. He declared that the direct involvement of teachers and supervisors was critical for fundamental change, even going so far as to say:

> .... Our schools cannot keep up with the life they are supposed to sustain and improve unless teachers, pupils, supervisors, administrators, and school patrons continuously examine what they are doing. Singly and in groups, they must use their imaginations creatively and constructively to identify the practices that must be changed to meet the needs and demands of modern life, courageously try out those practices that give better promise, and methodically and systematically gather evidence to test their worth. This is the process I call action research. [From Glanz 1999]

Now, let us turn to the term 'teacher development'. What exactly is meant by this term?

> Teacher development can be succinctly described as teachers acquiring or adapting new knowledge, beliefs, and skills in order to change their educational practice. [Fazio 2009]

With the above definition, the question is – How (and has) action research been used for teacher development?

This was by no means the first attempt to use action research for teacher development. There is such a vast amount of work in this area, that no attempt will be made here to comprehensively review the entire domain. Presented below is a glimpse of such work, as it pertains to this project.

Action research has gained popularity in educational contexts as an effective tool for professional development that promotes inquiry, reflection, and problem-solving, resulting in action or change (Carr and Kemmis, 1986; Riel, 2010; Whitehead, 2005). Carr and Kemmis (1986) have termed action research as a 'critical educational science' and declare that 'action research provides a means by which distorted self-understandings may be overcome by teachers analysing the way their own practices and understandings are shaped by broader ideological conditions.'

More recently, action research was used by Sagor (1992) as a collaborative process to support teachers' professional development.

In a university-sponsored school development initiative, Sagor showed that collaborative action research can contribute to the development of a school culture that is conducive to school improvement. Vaino and Holbrook (2013) reported a case study whose goal was to explore the role of collaborative action research in eliciting change in teachers' beliefs. Their research demonstrated that perceived constraints, where identified, can be meaningfully addressed by teachers through collaborative action research.

Despite the popular notion of democracy in action research, there are critiques of this stance by several researchers. For instance, van Maanen (1990) observed that such projects are usually initiated by university-based researchers, who 'uneasily redefine' their relation to the teacher practitioner by terming themselves as 'process facilitators' and 'project collaborators', an act that van Maanen sees as a means of instituting a democratic tone to the relationship. It is the contention of van Maanen that despite this, the asymmetry in the relationship between facilitator and teacher remains, and this is similar to that between an adult and child. He is critical of the dependence that naturally ensues.

As will be discussed later, one of the inadequacies experienced by teachers in this study was that of receiving the sort of support that they had anticipated in ideas for alternative classroom strategies. Thus, while the asymmetry may well have existed in expectations and how they were met, an unintended fallout (which we deem positive) was that of teachers relying more on themselves and peer interactions than on the facilitators, to come up with alternative strategies.

Against this backdrop, the team who embarked upon this study intended to build upon Stephen Corey's vision of teachers and school administrators 'continuously examining what they are doing', that is, engaging in reflective practice.

As will be seen in later chapters, many of the findings cited above were reinforced through this study.

How Objective and/or Rigorous Can Such a Study Be?

This is a question that is often asked about such a study.

It can be reasonably asserted that when a person (or group of persons) is engaged in studying a situation (that is usually unique) – with a view to addressing a problem or improving a practice – the results are hardly ever going to be generalisable. No physical laws determine the end result of such investigations, and the results are also not likely to be replicable. How objective, then, can such results ever be? What are the criteria by which the value of such research will be assessed?

McQuist (1978) describes the epistemology of action research, and gives reasons for the rejection of action research by Empiricism, Logical Positivism, and Structuralism, as well as the basis for its acceptance by Pragmatism and Dialectical Materialism. Susman and Evered (1978) have, on the other hand, questioned the use of positivist science criteria for assessing the merits of action research, and have, instead emphasised the need to base the legitimacy of action research on 'philosophical traditions that are different from those which legitimate positivist science.'

McIntosh (2010) concurs by arguing that the action researcher does not see the work as 'value neutral' as is the case in scientific research. Therefore, instead of constructing change and development, these are seen as natural occurrences which are effected through personal engagement. Since the aim is 'to promote social justice through politically informed stances', access to mechanisms of power is enabled so as to bring about (and direct) the desired change.

A typical characteristic of action research is the flexibility – even fluidity – of the ends to be achieved. Often, the action researcher starts off with a certain envisioned end, but due to the uncertainty and instability of the unique situation, this takes on varying hues as the work proceeds and often uncovers new questions, even as it sometimes reveals unanticipated ends. Schon (1983) argues that when the ends are fixed and clearly defined, only then can professional practice serve as a means to that end. However, 'when ends are confused and conflicting, there is as yet no "problem" to solve.' He goes on to claim that this demands *problem-setting*, even before *problem-solving*, from the practitioner, and asks if this necessarily translates into a sacrifice of rigour. He goes on to assert that reflection-in-action can be rigorous in its own right, terming it as an alternative to the prevalent 'positivist epistemology of practice', and urges practitioners to search for another epistemology that they can bring 'to situations of uncertainty, instability, uniqueness and value conflict.'

Schon describes the values of parameters 'central to the model of Technical Rationality' like control, distance and objectivity, in the course of reflection-in-action. He asserts that these parameters 'take on new meanings in the reflective conversation', as, in such a context, the inquirer is primarily setting out on hypothesis-testing. That being so, the inquirer seeks to control these variables purely with this end in mind. However, as the inquirer's hypothesis is always linked to changing the current situation, *he enters it as part of the process* of testing. While he thus 'produces knowledge that is objective, in the sense that he can disconfirm it', he can also alter the change intended if he finds that the change achieved is unsatisfactory. An important distinction that Schon draws here (from the model of Technical Rationality) is that 'his knowledge is also personal, bounded by his commitments' to his value systems and overarching theories. Only a group of people who share these commitments, therefore, will be likely to buy into such an experiment, Schon claims.

It appears – from the chapters that follow – that this research did result in the formation of a community of inquiry within the school where this work took place. Whether this community continued to inquire deeply is a matter that remains to be seen. With the intent of triggering the growth of many more such communities, this work has been compiled herein.

McIntosh enumerates core elements contributing to the construction of reflection as given by Johns (2007):

- Practical wisdom
- Reflexivity
- Becoming mindful
- Commitment
- Contradiction
- Understanding
- Empowerment

He talks about the difficulty experienced in measuring concepts like 'practical wisdom' and 'becoming mindful' in concrete ways. He says, it is these essences of human behaviour that are very difficult to 'place within a structure', being wound as they are in a 'complex knot of experience, interpretation, values etc.' In that sense, we can say that reflection is not scientific in its approach. Johns' (2007) constituent elements of reflection are not statistically measurable, but he emphasises that they are a means to help the growth of human enquiry. Others like Carr and Kemmis (1986) have eloquently explored this question, and bring out the rejection in action research of 'positivist notions of rationality, objectivity and truth in favour of a dialectical view of rationality.'

They go on to declare that action researchers aim to improve their own practices; unlike scientists, they are not working on 'objects' that lie *outside themselves*. In other words, they study practices that *cannot* be independent of the researcher-practitioner, and consequently, these processes are not guided by universal physical laws. In addition, action researchers are not guided purely by the improvements that they wish to see in their practices, like agricultural researchers who would strive mainly to improve the yield of the crop. But they hasten to add that 'neither can action researchers accept the interpretive view of educational practices, understandings and situations.'

It would be too simplistic, the authors argue, to declare that ideas alone affect actions, and that changed ideas will *necessarily* result in changed actions. External conditions can constrain as well as distort the practitioners' understandings, and therefore without taking into account such factors, one can naively conclude that a transformed consciousness will always result in a transformed social reality. Notwithstanding the fact that transforming ideas is *key* to effecting such a change, the authors caution that it is not a sufficient cause for change.

McIntosh (2010) takes the above argument further by stating that action research, in closing the gap between the researcher and the researched upon, negates positions of power in the research process itself. It can therefore be viewed as being subversive rather than democratic.

McIntosh goes on to question whether 'quality' can always be measured, for what is 'quality' to one may not be 'quality' to another. By its very nature, action research empowers the researcher to explore the concepts of quality and value, which 'are uncovered democratically in exploration, not imposed as preordained constructs.'

Making the universally true statement that each person is unique and 'will react differently to the same diagnosis and proposal for intervention', McIntosh emphasises the need to rethink the modality of research work in this domain. He is critical of the present-day focus on throughput and output – even in human services – and expectation of automaton-type function, 'creating systematic human machinery models to achieve target. ...Such an industrial model is an easy way to function. Machines do not need to think about what they are doing; they just do it. Reflection, conversely, is hard work. It involves confrontation of ourselves and our situations, and the problems we encounter when we do this.'

It is with the above understanding that this study was undertaken, and results analysed. While the exploration of the perceived shifts in teachers' thinking and practice is detailed in Section III, it is pertinent to mention here that in the course of this exploration, each teacher in his/her own unique way, broke away from the epistemology of positivist science and examined, instead, 'the concepts of quality and value' (McIntosh 2010).

Rooted as this study is in case studies of action research (described in Section II), findings have been gleaned qualitatively. It is also important when absorbing the results in Section III to bear in mind the cautionary advice of Carr and and Kemmis (1986). In order to sustain the shifts in assumptions/attitudes that teachers experienced, external conditions would also need to be conducive to such transformation.

What is Meant by Reflective Practice?

The term 'Reflection' derives from Latin term '*reflectere*' which means 'to bend back', like the mirror bends the light back (reflects) and in the process, helps us see our own image in the mirror. Reflective practice is a similar process, and it is mental – it helps one see one's own experience with clarity. It involves skills like the following:

- To first look at one's own experiences
- To systematically look at various aspects of each experience
- To acknowledge the strengths and weaknesses of the self/others that surface through the experience
- To identify the areas that need to be worked on
- To find ways to resolve identified problems
- To implement the solutions identified
- To stay open to one's own experience at every stage
- To evolve one's refined practice from experience

In effect, the act of reflection serves as the bridge between experiences and learning.

John Dewey and Donald Schon are well known for their seminal work in reflection and reflective practice. Dewey's *How We Think* (1933) is a classic and so is Schon's *The Reflective Practitioner: How Professionals Think in Action* (1983). Dewey (1933) describes reflection thus:

> Reflection involves not simply a sequence of ideas, but a consequence, a consecutive ordering in such a way that each determines the next as its proper outcome, while each in turn leans back on its predecessors.

> ***Reflective thinking***
> *Active, persistent, and careful consideration of any belief or supposed form of knowledge in the light of the grounds that support it and the further conclusions to which it tends.*
> ***Dewey (1933)***

The successive portions of the reflective thought grow out of one another and support one another; they do not come and go in a medley. Each phase is a step from something to something technically speaking, it is a term of thought. Each term leaves a deposit which is utilised in the next term. The stream or flow becomes a train, chain, or thread.

Schon (1983) described reflective practice as intentional, systematic inquiry that is disciplined and that will ultimately lead to change and professional growth (reflection-on-action). Schon added to this the idea of a practitioner being able to *reflect on* Reflective Practice – reflect on his or her intuitive knowledge while engaged in the action of teaching (reflection-in-action). Schon examined how professionals think on their feet. He also believed that professionals learnt much more from their experience than they were able to articulate. This is what he called *reflection-in-action.* Farrell (2012) describes it as an examination of 'our beliefs and experiences and how they connect to our theories-in-use.'

He further notes

> For me, the implications of both Dewey's and Schon's work is that reflective teaching is evidence based; teachers collect data or evidence about their work and then reflect on this evidence to make informed decisions about their practice. Engaging in evidence-based reflective practice enables teachers to articulate to themselves (and others) what they do, how they do it, why they do it, and what the impact of one's teaching is on student learning.
> (Reproduced with permission from Prof Thomas Farrell [2012])

The practice of gathering evidence in a systematic manner was one of the gifts this study bequeathed upon the teachers. While none of them can be said to have been entirely ignorant of this practice at the start, it is clear that the *systematisation of evidence collection* crystallised through this study for all the teachers, some of it through the facilitation provided to them by the team of facilitators.

Returning to what researchers have to say, Farrell (2012) is inspired by both Dewey and Schon. He says, 'like Dewey, I consider reflective practice as a form of systematic inquiry that is rigorous and disciplined. And like Schon, I am interested in how teachers "think on their feet," or how they reflect in action, on action, and for action.'

Several elaborations of what constitutes reflection and reflective practice abound. Two from Osterman (1990) are given below:

> Reflection is concentration and careful consideration, and reflective practice is mindful consideration of one's actions, specifically one's professional actions.
>
> Reflective practice is challenging, focused, critical assessment of one's own behaviour as a means towards developing one's own craftsmanship. While reflection is certainly essential to the process, reflective practice is a dialectic process in which thought is integrally linked with action. It is as Schon (1987) describes, a 'dialogue of thinking and doing through which I become skillful.'

Farrell (2012) asserts that for Dewey, the cause of reflective thinking comes out of the feeling of doubt or conflict connected to teaching. He maps out five main phases of reflective thought that he considers *not* in a particular order, but rather, as fluid:

1. Suggestion: A doubtful situation is understood to be problematic, and some vague suggestions are considered as possible solutions.
2. Intellectualisation: The difficulty or perplexity of the problem that has been felt (directly experienced) is intellectualised into a problem to be solved.
3. Guiding Idea: One suggestion after another is used as a leading idea, or hypothesis; the initial suggestion can be used as a working hypothesis to initiate and guide observation and other operations in the collection of factual material.
4. Reasoning: Reasoning links present and past ideas and helps elaborate the supposition that reflective inquiry has reached, or the mental elaboration of the idea or supposition, as an idea or supposition.
5. Hypothesis Testing: The refined idea is reached, and the testing of this refined hypothesis takes place; the testing can be by overt action or in thought (imaginative action).

(Reproduced with permission from Prof Thomas Farrell [2012])

Zeichner and Liston (1996) distinguished between routine action and reflective action and suggested that for teachers, tradition, external authority and circumstance direct routine action, whereas *reflective* action 'entails the active, persistent and careful consideration of any belief or supposed form of knowledge.' 'Reflective thinking generally addresses practical problems allowing for doubt and perplexity before possible solutions are reached.' (Hatton and Smith, 1995).

With so many viewpoints, the summary that Ghaye (1998) has tabulated showing four common views of reflection, is particularly meaningful.

Table 1.1 Four of the more common views of reflection

Kinds of Reflection	Meanings
A. Reflection-IN-action	1. In a particular workplace 2. Thinking on your feet; improvisation
B. Reflection-ON-practice	1. After the event 2. On something significant
C. Reflection-FOR-action	1. For a reason or particular purpose 2. Planning what you are going to do
D. Reflection-WITH-action	1. Conscious future action 2. Action alone or with others

[Reproduced with permission from Ghaye (1998)]

Much of the above ties in neatly with the work presented herein. When the concept of action research was first introduced to these teachers, all of them quickly identified the problems that they were facing in their own teaching–learning processes. Almost all the teachers identified more than one problem and went through a process of sifting out that ONE problem that was most crucial for them to resolve. [Some of them needed to be facilitated in this step by the team from the Foundation.] The journey that the teachers made in zeroing in on strategies (that they eventually adopted) to resolve these issues, is apparent in the narratives that comprise Section II. The process of working through various steps of action research is a live example of reflective thinking in action. The process that Osterman outlines is clearly visible in the way that teachers carried out action research and engaged in reflective practice and the manner in which they grew professionally – and some, even personally. Osterman (1990) maps the process eloquently. He notes that the trigger is provided by the problem, which brings to the surface a 'discrepancy in what occurred and what was expected'. This provokes a detached examination by the practitioner of their own actions and the reasons for the same. Through subsequent reflection on the rationale as well as impact of their action choices, practitioners employ this newly gained understanding to develop alternative strategies. Thus 'through this dialectic process of thought and action, the practitioner takes an active role in shaping his or her own professional growth.'

> *To maintain the state of doubt and to carry on systematic and protracted inquiry – these are the essentials of thinking.*
> **Dewey (1933)**

[For a deeper understanding of how this process mapped out, readers are referred to Section II.]

With this background of action research and reflective practice, we now look at the link between the two.

Can Action Research be Used to Promote Reflective Practice?

The nature of action research, for Elliott (1991), is reflective. Indeed, what Schon and others term 'reflective practice', he terms 'action research'. For Elliott, action research is fundamentally about the transformation of practice. Its role is not purely philosophical, though he recognises that it has philosophical qualities. McIntosh (2010) concurs:

> There is no doubting the overlapping qualities that are required to engage in reflective action and action research. They can coexist alongside each other and simultaneously be embedded within each other as they are employed in daily working practices, but to be effective they require contexts which are transparent and supportive of allowing that which is unconscious to come into consciousness.

It is not surprising to find, therefore, that action research has been used by many teacher educators for teacher development, and by researchers to promote reflection in their practice. For instance, Perrett (2003) has described a four-month action research project, where in-service teachers experienced two cycles of action research. Perrett found that 'the teachers both displayed and reported an increase in reflection during the project and immediately after it.' Oberg and McCutcheon (1987) have described in detail the experience of teachers doing action research. They found that even though all teachers could not deem their projects to have achieved their goals, every one of them 'spoke enthusiastically about their action research projects'. They go on to add 'All the teachers learned something about students, parents, colleagues, or themselves that they had not known before.'

The experience of teachers whose work is described in this book was similar. Indeed, through their action research work, many of the teachers also corroborated the six assumptions underlying action research that have been listed by May (1993) as below:

> (a) Teachers theorise and develop theories-in-practice, (b) action research involves more than technical problem-solving, (c) a practitioner of any professional field and at any level can engage in action research, (d) research methods matter and are usually interpretive or qualitative, (e) action research can be collaborative, and (f) such inquiry can purposefully address social inequities and issues of power.

Irvin and Daniels (2002) reported a study undertaken by a school in Georgia, where it was found that teachers who were immersed in action research for several years began to take decisions based on solid evidence. They also began to look critically at data and thus knew which programmes were effective for their students.

There is thus considerable advocacy for teachers to conduct research. Berghoff et al (2011) recommended working with dilemmas, following structured protocols, and practising collaborative inquiry as means to teaching critical reflection to new teachers. Nunan (1997) has argued that teacher-research should be particularly alive to ethical issues and serve to strengthen relationships between research and practice. In the cases that have been described in this book, it is our contention that such a relationship emerges with great clarity.

How does a teacher educator bring about reflection in teachers? McIntosh (2010) asks if reflection is a skill that can be learned in some 'technical way, as a clinical procedure or an interpersonal interaction'. He reports that the learners and the researchers in the qualitative domain have been expected to 'reflect upon the experience of learning and researching and what is found through these experiences'. He also accepts that this does not often happen of its own, as people are not always naturally inclined towards reflective activities. Indeed, they are merely advised or required to reflect and provide evidence that they have done so. He further stresses the need to understand reflection in order to make it work, and not to treat even reflection as yet another 'outcome'! McIntosh (2010) asserts that questions and responses form a large part of any reflective conversation, be it internal or external. 'But asking the right questions – similar to the way in which physicians ask questions in order to make a diagnosis – is fundamental to creating the dialogue.'

McIntosh then lists out the following questions which can help the practitioner 'enable a critical distance to practice' and develop new knowledge for his/her practice:

- What is my practice like?

- Why is it like this?
- How has it come to be this way?
- What is the impact of my practice on service users?
- How can I improve what I do?

The same critical distance from practice is talked about in a slightly different way by Maurice Merleau-Ponty (2003). Merleau-Ponty notes that while sensory experience is the means by which we are aware of our existence, the process of drawing out facts requires interpretation and conclusion – which do not lie in the realm of sensory experience. He therefore suggests that 'this problem belongs to the domain of reflection and not that of the experiment as the empiricist understands it, which is also as scientists understand it when they dream of an absolute objectivity.'

Reflective Practice and Teacher Development

Re-stated below (for ease of reference) are the two spirals of research embedded in this study:

1. The first spiral consists of the specific action research conducted by each teacher, addressing the problem identified in the classroom.
2. The second spiral consists of (the Principal Investigator and facilitators) examining the extent to which *teachers become reflective*, through several indicators like teachers identifying and revisiting their own assumptions, altering some of their practices or simply becoming more aware of their own needs for capacity enhancement.

In this study, the second spiral did reveal certain tangible and intangible indicators of increasing reflection in teachers who conducted action research. While only time will tell whether significant and sustained teacher development ensued as a result of the current work, the abundant literature on this subject does connect teacher development with reflective practice.

Berghoff et al (2011) have used critical reflection to improve urban teacher development. This collaborative inquiry examines the ways in which new teachers are being prepared as critical reflective practitioners in three urban teacher education programmes. Researching individually and collectively, the research team analysed and compared pedagogical methods and programme features for preparing new teachers for urban schools. Their findings detail how each teaching method impacted pre-service teachers' capacity for critical reflection. The researchers recommend working with dilemmas, following structured protocols, and practising collaborative inquiry as means to teaching critical reflection. They also recognise the need to continually develop their own explicit frameworks for critical reflection.

Kemmis (1994) points out that the common notion is that reflection is something that is quiet and personal. What is not realised by those who hold such a view, according to Kemmis, is that the 'product' of reflection is 'praxis (informed, committed action)'. Given that a teacher's actions are of great significance, the focus in teacher training was – for long – on having them exhibit certain behaviour, recount Zeichner and Liu (2010). With the pioneering explorations of teachers' *thinking* by researchers like Schulman (1992), there was a gradual shift to educating teachers to understand the rationales for their choices and the basis of their decisions. In their comprehensive review, Zeichner and Liu (2010) begin tracing the journey in teacher education from a point where 'teaching was largely seen as a technical process to be directed by what people either in schools or universities wanted them to do and for the most part the students did not see teaching as a moral and ethical activity over which they had any control.'

They declare that Schon's (1983) publication *The Reflective Practitioner* 'marked the reemergence of reflective practice as a major issue in North American teacher education.'

Zeichner and Liu point out that even though the idea of reflective practice has been around for some time now (from the time of Dewey [1933], and as traced in Houston [1988]), it was the publication of Schon's book in 1983 that triggered a tremendous amount of work (and consequent publications) in this domain, worldwide. Indeed, they go on to claim: 'Reflective teaching quickly became a slogan that was embraced by teacher educators from every political and ideological perspective to frame and justify what they were doing in their programs and after a time it began to lose any specific meaning.'

They conclude that reflective teacher education has failed to harness true teacher development, managing, instead, to create an illusion of teacher development. In this regard, they acknowledge four main themes that undermine the potential for genuine teacher development:

1. a focus on helping teachers to better replicate practices suggested by research conducted by others and a neglect of preparing teachers to exercise their judgment with regard to the use of these practices;
2. a means-end thinking which limits the substance of teachers' reflections to technical questions of teaching techniques and ignores analysis of the ends toward which they are directed;

3. an emphasis on facilitating teachers' reflections about their own teaching while ignoring the social and institutional context in which teaching takes place; and
4. an emphasis on helping teachers' to reflect individually.

Zeichner and Liu (2010); reproduced with permission from Zeichner and Liu (2010), Springer Rights and Permissions

An important take-home point from this work, therefore, is that getting teachers to 'reflect' need not necessarily translate into their development; instead, it could well reinforce their subservient positions by invoking their compliance with issued directives.

On a more positive note, Darling-Hammond (2006) has shown that it is possible for student teachers to reflect on more than technical issues if certain environments for teacher learning are created. Loughran (1996) has stressed the need for teacher educators to model the reflection that they wish to see in their student teachers. Ulmer and Timothy (2001) examined 23 teachers' reflections through the lens of shifts in their thoughts and actions. Interestingly, they also looked at sustained shifts in these teachers' beliefs as well as practices two years later. While they did see changes, they stress that change is slow and requires constant support.

Therefore, what we have attempted to do in this work is to see how this ability to reflect (already present in everyone to some degree) can be made to percolate into the teacher's classroom.

The present study seems to suggest to us that it is relatively easy for a fairly reflective person to conduct action research; perhaps we can even extend this to state that a true action researcher will inevitably become more reflective. While it is still too early to draw such a conclusion from just this set of teachers, such a finding is not at all uncommon in the plethora of literature on action research and reflective practice.

It is therefore important that the work described herein is seen as a seed that is being sown – in soil which will need continuous tilling and watering.

2. The Unfurling

This work is an attempt to capture a process of drawing out the reflective practitioner from within the in-service teacher, through two spirals of research.

The work described here is that of teachers in a school in Dineshpur, Uttarakhand, India, carried out with some facilitation over a period of about five months (between August and December 2013). Eight teachers and the Principal chose to conduct action research on problems that they faced in their classrooms, and were facilitated in this process by some members of Azim Premji Foundation.

There are three sections in this book:

- Section I positions this work against the backdrop of research done by several others in the area of action research and reflective practice. This section also encapsulates all the teacher profiles so as to gain an overall idea of the teachers' assumptions and beliefs before they embarked on conducting action research.
- Section II is a compilation of each teacher's individual profile and one classroom observation of that teacher (collated and observed by facilitators) during the period of action research. It also contains the teacher's own documentation of the Action Research. Relevant extracts from the post–action research (video-recorded) interview that was conducted by a facilitator in Hindi (and later transcribed and translated into English) are also included. In addition, this section contains jottings from the facilitators' diaries, positioned as interleaves.

> *Action research is simply a form of self-reflective enquiry undertaken by participants in social situations in order to improve the rationality and justice of their own practices, their understanding of these practices, and the situations in which the practices are carried out.*
> ***(Carr and Kemmis 1986: 162).***

- Section III explores shifts in teachers' attitudes, assumptions and pedagogies, describes new insights gained, and connects these to the teachers' prior system of beliefs and practices against the backdrop of current research in this domain. This section also contains an overview of each teacher's work and any shifts experienced by teachers during the course of (or, perhaps, as a consequence of) action research.

The book is intended to serve a readership of teachers, teacher educators, students of graduate and post-graduate programmes in education, NGOs that work in the education sector, researchers and Heads of schools. It is envisioned that the second section will meet the needs of the reader who would like to learn about practice, while the other two will be of greater interest to those who also wish to ground this practice in theory.

Aim of the Study

The intent was primarily to enable the in-service teacher to blossom into a reflective practitioner, using action research as one way of assisting this emergence. In facilitating this, the team from the Foundation attempted to understand each teacher in some depth, observe classroom processes, facilitate each teacher's action research, offer assistance in documentation of the action research in a systematic manner and finally, draw out from each teacher the learnings derived from conducting action research.

School Where the Study Took Place

Azim Premji School, Dineshpur was set up in April 2012. It is located in the fertile Terai region; crops are grown thrice a year, and water as well as human resources are available in plenty. Even in the summer, the farmers here grow rice and other crops. With the establishment of the State Infrastructure and Industrial Development Corporation of Uttarakhand Ltd (SIDCUL) in 2002, the sprouting of industry has resulted in over 500 industries now operating in the vicinity, offering employment to skilled, semi-skilled and non-skilled labourers.

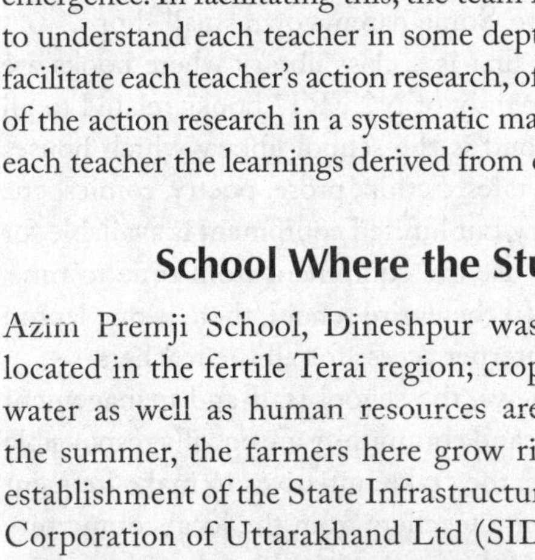

Other schools in the area: There are six government schools that are located within 7 km of this school. The infrastructural facilities, books and syllabus in this school are the same as in any government school. Like government schools in the area, this school too does not boast of a sophisticated lab, library, air-conditioned classrooms, smart classes, internet in the class, computers, etc.

Student and staff strength: At the time of writing this book, the student strength of this school is 167 (89 boys and 78 girls), in Classes I to VII. There are eleven teachers, one Principal, support staff (two cooks and one ayah [matron]) and one administrative officer.

Background of students: Students of this school hail largely (98%) from a Bengali community who migrated from Bangladesh during the 1971 war, and were given eight acres of land when the Indian government offered settlement to Bangladeshi refugees. Over time, they sold their land and took up work on farms. Thus, the students' parents work mostly as daily wage labourers, while a few of them are in government service as clerks, etc. Some parents own small shops.

There are two libraries: the first is a class library where books are kept in each class, consisting mainly of NCERT* books related to all the disciplines taught. The second is the school library which houses non-academic books like fairy tales, fiction, prose, poetry, comics, etc. At present, there is no laboratory, but limited equipment is available for students' use. The teachers also use the equipment from time to time, for classroom demonstrations. In the entire school, there is one laptop and one data card to provide Internet access for all the teachers.

As revealed through interviews, the school staff and management believe that the student, teacher and community are equally responsible for shaping the child. Therefore, they take initiatives to make frequent visits to the community. They hire teachers from the local community (as do all local schools); the only difference that this school lays claim to is in the teachers' pedagogy and attitude towards teaching/learning. Their pattern of assessment and report writing – they assert – is also different from the commonly adopted practice in many mainstream schools. Teachers write a qualitative report based on the evidence that they collect throughout the year. Teachers' lesson plans are based on keeping the child at the centre, and in the Principal's words: 'Everything we do/plan is focused on one question –"*Will it help the*

* National Council of Educational Research and Training

child in his/her learning?" Azim Premji Foundation invests heavily in teacher development programmes, as a result of which we have some of the best teachers. They are open to learning and are reflective. This very basic quality helps them to design plans and also execute them.'

Genesis of this Action Research Study

Keeping in mind the vision of Azim Premji Foundation, and against the backdrop of work that the Foundation had been engaged in thus far, the need to work in the area of reflective practice – particularly with in-service teachers – was felt acutely by many researchers. Using action research as a trigger for evoking reflective practice was an idea that, though in no way original, caught the interest of some members of the Foundation across the country. As discussions unfolded, however, potential participants in the research work needed (and demanded) clarity on details like design of the study, time invested (on a monthly basis), timeline of the study, etc. Since the Principal Investigator (Neeraja Raghavan) could not answer most of these questions with clarity – this being the first such attempt – it emerged that the study called for working with uncertainty. A few members chose to work with this uncertainty – while most others withdrew.

And it was thus – *in a comfort zone with uncertainty* – that this research study was born.

The team began to brainstorm and chalk out a plan for conducting action research with government school teachers. The aim of that study was to facilitate the emergence of the reflective practitioner from within the in-service teacher, through action research. For two years, this team made consistent (though irregular) efforts to work with the government school teachers. For several reasons, this effort did not fructify, the main obstacle being the unavailability of teachers for this study. Despite being interested in the idea, several non-academic demands on their time (collection of census data, election duty, etc.) prevented the otherwise willing teachers from engaging with this study in a systematic and sustained manner.

> *I have become certain of the need for uncertainty.*
> ***Jean MacNiff (2003:5)***

Even though that attempt did not result in a research study, it did help the team formulate a workable research design, test out some elements of that design and gain confidence in actually conducting such a study. Indeed, the team now found that they

had answers to several questions that had remained unanswered at the start of the study. For instance, the need to arrive at an optimal frequency of school visits (in consultation with the Principal) became clear. It also emerged that classroom observations would have to be kept to the minimum, so that they would not impede the teacher's functioning. The time that each member would have to invest in the study also became clearer after this pilot project.

Thus, the small research team that embarked on this project, after spending a couple of years attempting to work with teachers in two government schools, shifted their sample to teachers of Azim Premji School, Dineshpur, Uttarakhand, where it was expected – and indeed experienced – that teacher availability would not pose any such problem.

Design and Rationale of the Study

While brainstorming about the modus operandi, members drew upon the work of Dewey (1933), Schon (1983) and others. Considerable time was spent in discussing issues like: What is meant by a *reflective practitioner*? What are the indicators of *reflective practice*? The experience of the team in working with government school teachers in the past was factored in. Although excellent rubrics for teacher development like those of Danielson (2007) are available, this team preferred to organically develop a framework for collating the profiles of teachers from the teachers' own contexts. The format used for collecting Teacher Profiles is appended in the Appendix. The rationale for designing the study is discussed below. All the photographs in this book were taken by the facilitators of the study.

Schon (1983) identifies two critical elements in the steps followed by a reflective practitioner:

1. The inquirer 'draws on some element of his familiar repertoire which he treats as exemplar or as generative metaphor for the new phenomenon'.
2. Thereafter, the practitioner formulates new hypotheses, which she tests. As she tests, she also shapes the situation even as she explores it.

In so doing, Schon says the practitioner relies on four roots or 'constants'. The first of these, termed 'media', refers to the language that practitioners use while engaging with their work. Schon evokes an awareness of the unique language that is employed by each professional as they engage in their practice. The second is called 'the appreciative systems' and largely encompasses the value systems that practitioners rely on while evaluating inquiry or engaging in reflective conversation. Even without awareness, there is a constant drawing from this background value system that drives the practitioner to evaluate and reflect, during practice. The third, referred to as 'overarching theories', is quite clearly the means by which the practitioner makes sense of phenomena, by slotting them as falling under the overarching theories that the practitioner holds. And the fourth is termed 'role frames' – these are the boundaries within which the practitioners set their tasks, being bound (if they are) by their own institutional settings.

Schon hastens to emphasise that he does not mean to imply that these 'constants' are 'unchanging', but that even as they do change, 'sometimes in response to reflection', they do lend that solid reference 'from which in reflection-in-action… [the practitioner] can allow his theories and frames to come apart.' The level of engagement of (and ease of recognition by) the practitioner with these constants is directly proportional to their robustness *in the practitioner's mind.*

It was therefore felt imperative that the team explores this 'familiar repertoire', that is, the existing beliefs and practices of each teacher, in some depth. This could be done in several ways: interviewing the teacher, observing her class, examining the document that captures the entire action research and finally, interviewing the teacher so as to prompt her to reflect on her reflection-in-action. While it would certainly have been more meaningful to observe more than one classroom transaction of each teacher, it was feared that this could impede the natural flow of the teachers' work. [As discussed in the concluding section of the book, this turned out to be a severe limitation of the study.]

Therefore, facilitators decided to restrict classroom observation to just one for each teacher, while relying heavily on (a) the responses of the teacher to the Teacher Profile questions and (b) the detailed documentation that would be carried out by each teacher of his/her action research (AR documents). As it turned out, these documents were indeed very enlightening, and yet another opportunity for probing this was afforded by (c) the post-AR cycle interview with each teacher. Since this was also video-recorded and transcribed, much of the validation of conclusions drawn herein is traced back to these three tools.

Thus, the team designed the study so as to employ the following tools:

- Conducting a detailed interview with each participating teacher so as to understand the teacher's background, interests, attitudes and beliefs, so as to yield a **Teacher Profile** for each teacher (for details refer Appendix)
- Observing one classroom transaction of each teacher to see if and how the above-expressed beliefs and attitudes find expression while teaching: it would yield **one CRO** (classroom observation) for each participating teacher. [This was observed at any time during the period of action research, not necessarily of a class that pertained to the topic of action research.] During CROs, it was observed if any obvious discordance could be seen between professed beliefs (while collating the profile of the teacher) and actual classroom practice. In Section Two, each teacher's CRO – observed during the period of action research – is inserted in a box in the chapter containing the work of that teacher.
- Facilitating Action Research which will be done by the teacher, in an area of concern to him/her: this would result in structured documentation through an **Action Research (AR) Template** [see Appendix]. This document would reveal the teachers' reflection *in* action, and to some extent, reflection *on* action.
- Conducting another **interview** at the end of the study to allow for *reflection on* reflection-in-action (Schon 1983). As already mentioned, this interview was video-recorded, translated into English and transcribed.

Teacher Profile

The format for compilation of a Teacher Profile was designed keeping in mind the above, and comprised three broad domains: *Teacher as a professional, Teacher as a facilitator/views on learners and learning* and *Teacher as a reflective practitioner*. [The detailed questionnaire is in the Appendix.] The rationale for selecting these three domains is described below.

Research has shown (Hatton and Smith, 1995) that among the barriers which impede the development of reflective approaches, existing pre-conceptions about *teaching as a profession* are critical.

In India, teaching is often taken up as a profession for reasons that seldom encompass a passion for it. Many factors influence the choice of teaching as a career (if it is indeed chosen!), and the sustaining of this choice. In her study of some rural South Indian primary government schools, Sriprakash (2011) reported how the teaching profession was seen primarily as an employment opportunity, with a teaching qualification extending one's job prospects. Batra (2005) has bemoaned the decline of school teaching to 'a least favoured profession' in India, post-globalisation. She asserts –

> It has become a last resort of educated unemployed youth; part-time business people and young women seeking to find a part-time socially acceptable profession away from a competitive university education system. Yet, due to the sheer demographic demand from schools, an assurance of getting a job seems to draw many participants to teacher education courses. This, however, is more of a 'safe fall back option' than a formal career choice.

Often, teaching serves as a convenient option while the teacher awaits results of competitive examinations that hold the promise of 'privileged positions' in banking, government service or in colleges as lecturers. For many mothers/homemakers, it serves as a convenient time-slot away from home – while children are also in school – that provides some income and a longer vacation than many jobs offer. While the economic benefits of becoming a government school teacher are not insignificant, they cannot compare with a lucrative career in the private sector.

It was therefore deemed vital to ascertain *why* the teacher had taken up this profession, and if (s)he would now opt for an alternative career, given a choice. Was it merely a convenient way to earn an income? Or did it add meaning to the teacher's day and value to her purpose in life? Did it help fill the day with some activity or was it a source of fulfilment?

Further, it was felt necessary to investigate how important the teacher believed it was to be up-to-date with developments in the field of teaching and learning. This could manifest as an interest in attending training programmes, or a vivid recollection of impactful training programmes, or a hunger for reading more in a relevant domain.

The effort made in this work to trace teachers' thinking through this journey owes its origin to the work of several researchers. There is an abundance of literature on the subject of teacher attitudes and beliefs, and no claim is made in this book to review it. Dewey (1933) has connected the basis of thinking to beliefs thus: 'Thinking in its best sense is that which considers the basis and consequences of beliefs.'

As the study intended to enable *shifts in the thinking* of teachers, it was deemed critical that we should attempt to be aware of the teacher's thinking, right at the start. Understanding the teachers' beliefs appeared to be a plausible route for this. Decisions that a teacher is called upon to make must trace back to core beliefs held by her. In this regard, we quote Pajares (1992), who says 'beliefs are the best indicators of the decisions individuals make throughout their lives (Bandura, 1986; Dewey, 1933; Nisbett and Ross, 1980; Rokeach, 1968), an assumption that can be traced to human beings' earliest philosophical contemplations.'

From thought that crystallises into belief, actions stemming from these beliefs in turn give rise to personal theories of action. Teachers often hold sometimes unarticulated, but often explicit theories of effective learning and teaching. Action research needs to be understood in the light of the theories of action that lie at the root of each teacher's practice since its goal is the transformation of practice so as to improve it. In this regard, McCutcheon (1988) asserts that 'Teachers develop, through their actions, interrelated sets of beliefs and practices about matters such as how students learn, what they should learn, and how motivation occurs. These interrelated sets of beliefs and practices constitute personal theories of practice.'

Not only is the above true of teachers, it holds good for school administrators as well. Osterman (1990) mentions that Argyris and Schon (1974) 'observed that people's ideas about how things work, their "theories of action" were central to their effectiveness as leaders: to become more effective in school reform, administrators needed to learn not simply new skills, but "new theories of action".'

Intertwined in these theories and beliefs are of course, values which, in turn, determine further courses of action. McIntosh (2010) refers to MacNiff (2003) when he declares 'Learning is therefore rooted firmly in experience: the experiences are reflected upon in the light of the researcher's values and then future actions can be decided upon.'

Lieberman's study (1995) is one of many that document teacher beliefs as a way of understanding the basis of successful facilitation (by teachers) of student learning.

Questions probing the value that teachers attached to good performance in examinations, competition, ranking and class/gender equity were therefore included in the questionnaire that comprised collation of Teacher Profile. While answers to questions probing such values could well be termed rhetoric, no discordances were found between the professed value and those that manifested during each teacher's classroom observation. Dewey (1933) asserts –

> Indeed, the deepest plane of the mental attitude of everyone is fixed by the way in which problems of behaviour are treated. If the function of thought, of serious inquiry and reflection, is reduced to a minimum in dealing with them, it is not reasonable to expect habits of thought to exercise great influence in less important matters. On the other hand, habits of active inquiry and careful deliberation in the significant and vital problems of conduct afford the best guarantee that the general structure of mind will be reasonable.

Mahapatra (2004) has noted that

> 'the untrained mind of the teacher operates on the basis of old biases and prejudices collected through his own schooling and life experiences. Part of the teacher's preparation should be to examine these experiences and beliefs, analyse and reflect upon them within the precincts of the professional course.'

In this regard, it is worth noting that teachers who were recruited for Azim Premji Schools were told at the start that corporal punishment would not be allowed in these schools. As one teacher admitted, 'This shut a familiar door to us. We were forced to think of other ways of tackling indiscipline in students.'

The Teacher Profile was therefore designed to understand the following aspects of each teacher:

- Background of Teacher: age, family situation, educational qualification, work experience, etc.
- Exposure: Training received in the past, nature of reading that teacher usually engages in, etc.
- Teacher as a Professional: questions which would reveal the teacher's interest in teaching as a profession, his/her efforts to keep up to date in this domain, etc.
- Views on Teaching–Learning: questions which would elicit the teacher's conditioned/examined beliefs and attitudes to teaching and learning, like *When do you think children learn best? Least?* etc.
- Reflective Practice: questions that would draw out efforts currently being made by the teacher to adopt a reflective approach to teaching and learning.

The study began with a detailed compilation of each teacher's responses to questions exploring their beliefs and attitudes to teaching and learning. Undoubtedly, there are several pitfalls in the methodology adopted in this study. To begin with, an interview or a questionnaire may not be the best way of honestly capturing anyone's innermost beliefs, for the belief that one articulates at a given instant is often determined by several other factors like social norms, one's current frame of mind, the openness of the person one is sharing the belief with, etc. However, in this study, an attempt was made to ask questions (during the collation of each Teacher's Profile) which would reappear in a changed form later in the interview – a practice that is often used to uncover contradictions. Further, as already mentioned, while observing each teacher's classroom process, not a single observed practice was found to be significantly discordant with professed beliefs. Again, it can rightly be argued that a single classroom observation would hardly allow for contradictory behaviour to emerge. While this is undeniable, it was also found – from the AR documents and lesson plans that teachers wrote – that their sustained practice (over four to five months – the duration of one action research cycle) appeared to be largely consistent with their professed attitudes (as shared by them during the Teacher Profile interview). In their post–AR-cycle interview, many of them admitted to a shift in understanding and some even changed a few of their assumptions (see Section III.)

The Teacher Profile was compiled at the very beginning of the study, with the initial intention of monitoring change in attitudes and beliefs by the end of the study. As will be seen from later chapters, the minds of this group of teachers seemed to have already been set in motion on the paths of reflective thinking – perhaps (as some admitted) due to various workshops and orientation programmes that they had participated in at the Azim Premji Foundation. Therefore, indicators of the *impact of action research* on their thinking could not really be determined by again posing the same questions to them at the end of the short (four-to-five-month) period of action research. In fact, the shifts in thinking actually emerged from their own *admissions immediately after completing one cycle of AR* (in the video-recorded interview), rather than in response to the Teacher Profile questionnaire. Therefore, the original intent of repeating the same interview at the end of the study was dropped. Instead, the video-recorded interview that was conducted at the end of the completion of one AR cycle by each teacher allowed the teacher to *reflect on* his/her reflection-in-action, and this provided some valuable insights.

Facilitation of Action Research

Facilitating action research conducted by teachers is a common practice that has been employed by many. As mentioned earlier, van Maanen (1990) has described the nature of the relationship between the facilitator and teacher-researcher as being similar to that between an adult and child. 'As a result of the asymmetry of this relation the adult carries an unshakable responsibility for the becoming of the child.'

Had this panned out in the present study, the responsibility of the Action Research would have rested largely on the facilitators. Instead, this element of asymmetry was almost totally absent as the Principal took responsibility for the sustenance and completion of the action research cycles, right from the start. As a consequence, Lieberman's (1995) critique (see below) of such disempowerment of teachers was unwittingly taken cognizance of:

> 'Teachers have been told often enough (or it has been taken for granted) that other people's understandings of teaching and learning are more important than their own and that their knowledge – gained from the dailiness of work with students – is of far less value.'

Kumar (2008) echoes this sentiment, by asserting that the system 'lacks faith in teachers, especially in their capacity to think and take decisions.'

Very early in this work, even before engaging with teachers of AP School, Dineshpur, the team had formulated a set of do's and don'ts to guide members as they engaged with teachers in action research. Although this was developed when the study sample was different (government school teachers), it served as an indicator of the sort of planning required before embarking on such work, and also as a set of guidelines which was largely followed even during this study. From recommendations on how far to support the teacher in action research, to restrictions on when *not* to intervene, this protocol (outlined below) served as a very useful reference for facilitators as they proceeded to work with teachers.

The mechanism of facilitation was discussed in detail by the team from the Foundation; the following general principles were collectively arrived at:

- Making the Action Research Study a purely voluntary effort by those teachers who choose to opt for it
- Keeping the option open for any teacher to opt out of the study if and when (s)he wishes to
- Engaging with the teachers *without becoming prescriptive* – in a manner that allows them to explore various options to address

the problem at hand (This would entail making school visits after consulting the Principal for a mutually convenient date and time, and then spending time with the concerned teachers.)

- Acting as a liaison between the teacher and sources of academic assistance like subject matter experts who can advise on subject pedagogy, resource material like books and films, activities, games etc. that pertain directly to the problem at hand
- Refraining from directly taking a class or engaging with the children so as to aid the teacher in taking class, as this would cause dependence on the facilitator and not promote reflection by the teacher
- Helping the teacher with documenting the action research work as it progresses

As often happens in action research, the protocol that was developed could only largely be adhered to – not entirely. The main impediment in implementing it exactly as planned proved to be the scattered locations of the facilitators and the teachers, as they were spread across the country. However, as can be seen from the narratives in Section II, a certain optimal interaction with teachers was maintained through regular school visits by the facilitators.

By the end of the study, teachers candidly shared their own experience of the facilitation provided. While some of them admitted that the problem was definitely fine-tuned through facilitation, others expressed a need for alternative strategies to address the problem. Some received assistance in sourcing appropriate resources for their identified strategies from the Principal, and added that it would have been even better if such help could also have come from the facilitators. Facilitators said that they strove to help teachers zero in on the right sort of evidence for the shifts that they wished to see. [Being the first such exercise, several teachers needed help in understanding what constituted 'evidence'.] In the phase of documentation, facilitators worked with some teachers to transform their raw documents into the format required, a template of which was provided. Some teachers had adequate help in documentation while others felt the need for more assistance.

Sample Selection

In alignment with the above protocol, the sample did not truly have to be 'selected'. Instead, the invitation for participation in this study was extended to teachers after a three-day workshop on Action Research and Reflective Practice. During this workshop, teachers were introduced to the idea of action research. With animated discussion, some activities around reflection and reflective writing, teachers' interest in the study was triggered. After this, the Principal was asked to talk to the teachers and find out if (and how many) would like to take part in the study. Of twelve teachers (including the Principal), ten agreed to participate. The tenth teacher is still carrying out action research even as this book is being written, so that work will be documented in a later publication. Teacher Profiles were collated at the start of the study.

As the study panned out, the objective crystallised.

Objective of the Study

Within the broad aim of using action research as a means of drawing out the reflective practitioner from within the in-service teacher, the objective now narrowed down further. What exactly was meant by '*drawing out the reflective practitioner*'? In the second spiral of this study, considerable effort was directed towards understanding if and how the action research helped each teacher examine her prior assumptions and understanding about various aspects of teaching and learning, the subject at hand and education at large. Through an exploration of any shift in the teacher's assumptions and understanding, the above-cited research (which showed that the beliefs and attitudes of a teacher significantly affect her practices) was built upon.

Selection of the AR Problem

At the start of the study, the team of facilitators divided the work so that each teacher worked with one facilitator. However, since there were five facilitators and nine teachers (including the Principal), almost all the facilitators had to work with more than one teacher.

Following the collation of each teacher's Profile, facilitators began helping teachers identify an 'action researchable problem' in their own classes. Sometimes, this was a simple task: as all it necessitated was a clear articulation of what the teacher already had in mind, for example, Mohit Sharma started off by saying he faced the following issues in class:

1. The first problem was how to teach Hindi to those children who were not Hindi-speaking, because language is fundamental to all learning.

2. The second problem was to explore the right assessment tools to evaluate the learning level of these children.
3. The third issue was to investigate how to bring all children to more or less the same level, knowing that some children are not even able to understand the language.

It did not take much effort for the facilitator to help the teacher, Mohit, in narrowing down his focus to a single problem: 'Some children learn [Environmental studies, EVS] quickly, while others take an extraordinarily long time to learn the same things, and these are found to be the very children who have difficulty in the language.'

Having laid before them their specific areas of concern in the form of *action research problems*, teachers were then faced with the task of detailing and analysing their specific problem. This entailed a closer scrutiny: how many children were facing this issue? What were the *indicators* that these students and *no others* were facing this issue? What could be the causes of this spread in children facing this issue? Were there any links between their home situation, for instance, and their facing/not facing the issue?

By conducting this sort of analysis, teachers were already closer to identifying alternative approaches to deal with the issue, as the remedy is always linked in some way to the ailment! Listing out several alternative strategies was a step where teachers sought their peers' views, and facilitators found that this could be a very valuable intervention for subject matter experts. Shipra, for instance, found that four students in her class had great difficulty in reading English words, although she had tried making them memorise these words. Suggestions were made to her by colleagues during their weekly sharing meeting on Saturday that peer-learning could be an effective option, and suggested an activity for it. She tried this approach and found that it worked – to some extent.

> *Much reflection-in-action hinges on the experience of surprise. When intuitive, spontaneous performance yields nothing more than the results expected for it, then we tend not to think about it. But when intuitive performance leads to surprises, pleasing and promising or unwanted, we may respond by reflecting-in-action.*
>
> ***Schon (1983)***

Strategies and Review

Next, the teacher had to select the best strategy from the list of approaches, and implement it. For instance, from several identified strategies like peer discussion, playing of a word game, role play, etc., a teacher would select what seemed to be the best approach under the circumstances. A limitation of this study is that the specific criteria that were consciously or unconsciously used by each teacher in choosing the 'best' strategy were not recorded. While implementing the strategy, the teacher also had to document the effectiveness of the strategy because evidence had to be gathered to check whether it was 'effective' or not. The questions posed to the teacher for detailed documentation of this step nudge her to *reflect in action* (see Appendix). All these steps culminated in a review of the action research cycle, which was deemed complete only if the teacher had managed to address the issue first raised, by and large, with the identified students. If it was still not addressed, the action research cycle was repeated – perhaps with new strategies, or with the same strategy done in a way that factored into it the learnings from the first run.

It is important to note here that action research can never 'fail', as even the discovery that a certain strategy does not work with the particular set of students is also worthy of learning. That learning can be said to be the fruit of one cycle of action research. It so turned out that all the teachers who conducted action research in this study managed to address their identified issue by employing one, and sometimes more than one, strategy.

The team of facilitators was acutely aware that this process of reflection – if it could be deemed authentic – had to be *triggered in all* those who took part in the study: not only the teachers. So each of their school visits was accompanied by their documenting *their own reflections* in a Facilitator's Template (Appendix). These reflections of the team of facilitators find a place in the interleaves of this book, giving the reader a peep into the minds of the team who worked with the teachers.

Does the following of a stepwise process such as this ensure that action research is being done?

This brings us to another linked question:

What are the dangers of adopting action research as a means to effecting reflective practice?

Giving teachers a framework to think and work was probably the single most important step in this entire study: there was almost universal agreement amongst the teachers that this helped them structure their thinking and work very effectively. We ask the above question because frameworks, when followed with vigilance and critical thinking, can prove to be very powerful. However, like anything else, they can also be adopted mechanically: ticking steps off a list is not only very easy, it can be extremely deceptive in affording the (illusory) conviction that one has 'done the job'. McIntosh (2010) critiques the 'use of evidence-based practice as instrumentalist and which forces its users into mechanical ways of being practitioners. In so doing, something is lost to their practice because what they see and experience is not transferred to their cortex.'

Mechanical reflection is an oxymoron, no doubt, and we should guard against this in our well-intentioned efforts to bring about reflective practice in our schools. McIntosh terms this the 'proceduralisation of practices': and we call it a 'formula'. No formula can work: needless to say, in what is an effort to reach a highly fluid, dynamic and vigilant state of mind in practitioners! In conducting such research with teachers, the facilitators have to guard against establishing a distinct set of procedures that, if employed, will work to reach the end. Even this 'end' is open to revision, as can be seen by the cases exemplified in this book – Mohit Sharma, for example, relaxed his intent of getting the five children to correctly identify the animal (drawn on the piece of paper) and name its habitat, when he found that one child got it only partially right (the child named a fish a *tortoise*, but identified its habitat as *water*).

How, then, does one get around this? McIntosh puts it succinctly thus:

> Through re-positioning evidence-based practice as practice-based evidence, and by building on the concept that all practitioners can be researchers of their own practice through action research and reflective practices, I propose a move away from the pure instrumentalist practice and towards an approach that begins to develop a critique of its use.

There is thus a danger in following this stepwise process too literally. Indeed, as we have pointed out above, there is even the rather paradoxical possibility of turning 'mechanically reflective'! Action research must not be construed as simply ticking off these steps, one by one. According to Kemmis and McTaggart (1996), it is erroneous to think that merely following the action research spiral implies that one is 'doing action research'. 'Action research is not a "method" or a "procedure" for research but a series of commitments to observe and problematise through practice a series of principles for conducting social enquiry.'

The key phrase above is 'a series of *commitments*' – contrast this with 'a series of *steps*'. Checklists that get ticked off with ease impede deep reflection. McTaggart argues that Lewin has been misunderstood, even misused. While the notion of a spiral serves as a useful teaching device, one must guard against the very likely possibility of slipping into using it as the template for practice (Kemmis and McTaggart 1996).

McIntosh (2010) cautions against the 'proceduralisation of practices' when he stresses that, inadvertently, the 'establishing of a distinct set of procedures through which a practice appears to work becomes the focus'. It is all too easy to tick off steps from a checklist: however, this can hardly be said to constitute reflective practice!

If action research has to be truly undertaken, the focus has to be in the here-and-now. An overwhelming preoccupation with the end result can therefore render the entire exercise mechanical.

3. Teacher Snapshots

Before embarking on action research, an attempt was made by the facilitators to understand each teacher in some depth. Unless we know where each teacher is coming from, it is unlikely that such a study will prove meaningful.

The following teachers participated in the study:

1. Shipra Agarwal who taught English to Class IV, and felt the need to enhance their vocabulary
2. Deepak Dixit, Principal of the school, who was asked by a teacher to help him transact the content of Transparent, Translucent and Opaque objects to Class VI. In so doing, he recorded his experience of teaching children of Class VI how we see.
3. Mohit, who taught EVS (Environmental Studies) to Class IV, and had to address the issue of teaching some children whose mother tongue (Bengali) was not the medium of instruction (Hindi)
4. Narendra and Sahabuddin who team-taught Hindi to Classes V and VI, and found that the ability of some children in the language was way below the expected level
5. Neeraj who taught Science to Class VI, and felt the need to develop scientific temper in them
6. Madan who taught Hindi to Class IV and found that five of them needed help in identifying the letters, being clueless about the Hindi alphabet
7. Shakuntala and Saud, who team-taught Math to Class VI, and found that five children in the class did not know place value.

The Profile of each teacher was gathered according to the Template in the Appendix. Three broad domains (which overlap to some extent) were probed for each teacher:

- *Teacher as a professional* (where the place of teaching as a profession in the teacher's mind was gauged),
- *Teacher as a facilitator* (where classroom practices and preferred pedagogies were unearthed) and
- *Teacher as a reflective practitioner* (where the teacher's own propensity to grow and think about his/her work was explored).

The healthy attitude of the teachers to feedback brings authenticity to this section. All of them feel that children should be given feedback about their work, but add that feedback is not a fault-finding project: it should be positive and constructive; the *strengths* of the child should be the key focus. For themselves too, the teachers value feedback from children, colleagues, principal, parents, mentors and other people from the Foundation. They regard this as a learning opportunity and as one way of being supported in their efforts to enhance capacity. They kept in mind that feedback should not be hurtful and should be coupled with suggestions on how to improve teaching. They would give feedback only to those who are willing to receive it and whom they understand.

While there were similar views on most of the questions posed, there were also a few strongly deviant exceptions. Sometimes, they acknowledged that their own experience or family situation contributed to the views (or assumptions) that they held, and the honesty with which some of them admitted to holding certain prejudices was disarming. One or two teachers even admitted that their teaching experience in this school (as well as the occasional teacher development programmes that the Foundation held for them) had shaken some of their former assumptions. Presented below are snapshots of the teachers, arranged thematically.

Choice of Profession

The teachers in this school come from varied backgrounds, and not many have consciously opted for this profession. For example, Shipra studied Computer Science and that is what she would have liked to engage with as the first choice for a career. However, she became a teacher because in the cultural context of India, teaching is largely seen as a more 'acceptable' profession for women compared to other professions. The work timings coincide with the hours that the children are out of the house, and so the woman is available – for children as a mother, and for the family as a breadwinner – and can manage household chores.

Deepak Dixit, the principal, has an MBA degree and tried his hand in the corporate sector as he succumbed temporarily to societal pressures, only to realise that teaching is his calling. When he started working in the corporate sector, he says, 'Very soon, I realised that the corporate style of working is not my cup of tea and so (I) came back to the same place (education).' He attributes his affinity for the teaching profession to the 'ineffectiveness' of his own teachers.

Shakuntala is one of the few who always wanted to be a teacher. She decided that she wanted to be a Math teacher very early in life, owing to the indifference and punitive attitudes of her school teachers. Sahabuddin used to work in the corporate sector. However, while he was working there he missed the opportunity to learn new things, although he realised this only after he quit the job and started teaching. Now he finds that as a teacher, every new challenge is a new opportunity to learn. Neeraj came to like teaching as he had had an early exposure to the teaching profession at home, as his father worked in DIET.* He enjoys teaching as it gives him an opportunity to do something for children. Narendra was clueless as to what he wanted to do in life. He tried his hand at priesthood before doing his B.Ed. at the behest of a friend. He felt that teaching is a noble profession where he gets an opportunity to have an impact at various levels. Of all the teachers, only Saud, Shakuntala and Deepak Dixit opted consciously for this profession. Most of the other teachers took up this job for other reasons but eventually grew to like it.

Having taken up this profession, for whatever reason, *what kept them going*? We tried to understand this.

Motivation

Most of the teachers draw their motivation from the visible interest as well as learning achievement of their students. All admit that when children understand the subject and perform well academically, ['better than expected', in Shipra's words] it gives them satisfaction. In Saud's words: 'It is even more rewarding when you see that some of the students who generally do not understand the subject have finally understood.' Deepak derives fulfilment from helping his students understand a topic. Narendra finds that teaching is a profession where his own beliefs have been challenged and new beliefs have emerged, leading to a completely new learning which spurs him on. Shipra also experienced a significant change in her belief system. She used to focus on finishing the syllabus within a stipulated time frame. However, during action research, she found it much more meaningful to focus on whether each child has understood what she has taught. This change

* District Institute of Education and Training. DIETs have been set up in almost all the districts of all the states in the country

in her focus has yielded significant results: improved involvement, enthusiasm and learning for the children.

Neeraj draws satisfaction from learning how to help children develop greater interest in their own learning, increasing parents' awareness about the importance of educating their children and working to address social issues like discrimination. Hailing from a family where culture, patriotism and social service are esteemed highly, Mohit always wanted to contribute something meaningful to society: 'This feeling of contributing something meaningful to society through my profession keeps me motivated.'

Challenges

The teachers are quite aware of the challenges that they have to face in this profession. Each teacher experiences a personal challenge based on her own personality, beliefs and style of engagement with students. For Mohit, the challenge as a teacher has been to provide equal opportunities for learning to all students. Similarly, Shipra, Shakuntala and Narendra find it challenging to meet the diverse learning abilities of children, taking all the children along at the same time and paying equal attention to all. Madan, too, finds dealing with the diversity of children challenging, while Neeraj is challenged by keeping a balance between transacting the curriculum and ensuring learning for children. He feels the need for greater teacher autonomy to take decisions to create a better teaching–learning experience. Deepak declares that patience as well as the ability to trust the child's intent to learn are crucial issues. Both of these, in his view, can often impede teacher–student relation building and also effective learning. Saud feels that as a teacher, to have a good grasp of the subject is not enough; one must also have the skills of teaching. At the same time, the teacher should set a good example for the students, as a role model.

Investment in Professional Development

They are all greatly invested in their profession and appear to put in considerable effort towards their own professional development. They read and like to attend workshops and training programmes. While almost all teachers acknowledged the impact of working in the Foundation, with opportunities for attending workshops and meeting resource persons, three teachers (Neeraj, Sahabuddin and Mohit) could recount training programmes that they had attended with interest; none of the others experienced similar impact.

While conducting action research, the teachers also expected (and some of them sought) help from the facilitating research team. Every Saturday evening they have an internal school meeting where they discuss their problems, share solutions that they have found and thus, support each other. All the teachers acknowledged that peer interaction has been a big part of their support, as they work with the same set of children, under similar conditions. Some specifically mentioned the value of learning from their peers. (This was stated even before they participated in action research.)

Individual Efforts to Learn More and Stay Up-to-Date

Mohit is a proactive learner who enjoys gathering information from varied sources, like the Internet, videos, cartoons, audio-visual aids, TLMs (Teaching–Learning Materials), workshops, etc. Currently, he is doing some amount of reading, and visits the Azim Premji University website to widen his exposure. Both Narendra and Sahabuddin feel that other teachers and members of the Foundation as well as the school Principal can be of support to them. 'They can all help because they understand classroom processes, have experience or can find ideas from other resources.' Sahabuddin says 'there are various resources from where I gain knowledge such as reference books, NCERT,* CBSE,† State Board books, library, teacher portal (www.teachersofindia.org), training programmes, discussion with colleagues, sharing ideas, etc.' The Internet and TLMs also feature in Sahabuddin's list of resources that help him grow as a teacher. They would both like to learn more child psychology to understand their students better. Narendra is presently trying to learn 'classroom management, child psychology and content knowledge about subjects' he teaches. He feels it will help him understand children's behaviour, different types of personalities and their learning styles. Neeraj also spends time reading education-related literature on a regular basis. [At the time of the interview, Neeraj was reading books written by Giju Bhai Badheka.] Neeraj wishes to learn

* NCERT – National Council of Educational Research and Training
† CBSE – Central Board of Secondary Education

how to evolve better content-specific pedagogy techniques, and how to come up with innovative techniques and how to implement these. Madan gets a lot of support from his colleagues as they also deal with the same set of children in the same set-up and face similar challenges. Other resources from which he draws support are books and the Internet. There is also a support system in the school where teachers stay back after children leave for the day, for preparation and discussion. Though he has not received any additional training after becoming a teacher, he is of the view that attending workshops and participating in weekly discussions do add to his learning. He would like to learn good teaching strategies that capture children's interest. Presently, he is working on increasing his repertoire of activities, so that children with different levels of abilities can be taught at the same time by a single teacher. Shakuntala Chaurasia also draws her 'most important support' from colleagues: 'Discussions with them regarding teaching methods and activities, and also their views about the same set of children are very helpful.' She uses books prescribed by other Boards, textbooks of other classes, activities, worksheets and the Internet to strengthen her teaching practices. She wants to learn new math activities for children. These help her understand the interests of children.

Views on/Beliefs about Teaching and Learning

It can be reasonably asserted that – perhaps due to the extensive orientation programme and half-yearly engagement with teachers by the Foundation's Schools Core Team – none of these teachers resorted to simply reading out the text in order to transact some content, even before embarking on action research. While their dependence on the textbook was certainly significant before launching into action research, the importance of doing more than that for facilitating understanding of the content by students had become fairly evident to all of them – well before undertaking Action Research. Interestingly, *none* of the teachers said that they regard these to be the only sources of learning. This could also have been because the question precluded the admission of contrary views. Not a single teacher answered 'Yes' to the question: 'Do you think textbooks are the only source of learning?', probably because, in the present level of awareness that exists amongst many teachers in the country, it is unlikely that anyone would profess agreement, even in theory, with such a proposition. Besides, when we checked for a corroboration of the professed belief with the teachers' *practice* (that is, the manner in which the teacher conducted his class and also in the way in which he carried out one entire cycle of action research) we saw that in all cases, the teacher clearly relied on sources of learning that lay outside the textbook as well.

One of them (Saud) actually admits that he did not use the textbook at all last year (before embarking on action research) as he realised that children could not relate to it at all. Narendra reflects on his own changing beliefs, by stating that his former assumption, that schools and teachers are the only routes to learning, slowly crumbled as he interacted increasingly with students and began to realise that they have many more avenues of learning. He is also careful to point out that this belief did *not* change suddenly. Nor does he claim that this shift happened only due to action research. While Shakuntala and Sahabuddin give the teacher a higher place as a source of learning for the child than do the others, all the teachers admit that learning need *not* happen only through the teacher. Thus, their innate faith in the facilitation that is called for from a teacher is evident even *before* they embark on this research. Apart from Sahabuddin – whose response was neutral – none of the teachers felt that the school was the only place for learning.

Having said this, however, it must be acknowledged that, as they got deeper into action research, several teachers in this school showed (and admitted to) a greater propensity to facilitate their students' learning [rather than 'teach to' their students].

To quote a couple of them:

Sahabuddin: *'I was just a teacher earlier; after doing action research, I have also become a learner.'*

Mohit: *'I used to do all the talking formerly; now I talk less and listen more.'*

Neeraj: *'I find that I am learning a lot from my students.'*

The impetus to explore different pedagogies was clearly felt by the teachers as they sought to address their specific action research problem. Even as they took the first step towards this end, they began to feel the need for resources, became aware of the limitations in their own capacities and were able to articulate several of their own needs, such as engaging with resource persons, reading in depth about the way children learn and for bouncing their ideas off peers, more and more.

Views on Comparing and Ranking Children

Most of these teachers are not in favour of any sort of comparison between students; a few expressed strong abhorrence of this practice. While Shipra is careful to point out that children should not be ranked or compared, ('There should not be any comparison because it can discourage children and create complexes among them') she also employs the practice of giving 'stars' or remarks like 'good' to motivate students. Whether or not such awards will bring about comparisons is something Shipra is still to investigate. Deepak Dixit abhors comparison between individuals (who he regards as unique), and so it is beyond his understanding how any two persons with different sets of capabilities can be compared. Naturally, he feels the same about ranking too. 'When the baseline itself is different for you and me, how, then, can you rank both of us?' he asks, quizzically.

Mohit does not like comparing children and feels that they should not be ranked. 'Children should never be compared as each child has different abilities. While ranking them, some children may be labeled as "slow learners" without taking into account their background. In diverse populations, one can't compare individuals.' With sensitivity and compassion, he admits that the children who were facing difficulty probably felt inferior: 'Somewhere they felt – '*I am not as good as the others.*' Neeraj is not in favour of any kind of comparisons or ranking amongst children. He feels that there is a need to adopt healthy processes that can help children in teaching–learning experiences. In this regard, Shakuntala Chaurasia shares an incident – 'There is one girl in the class who is quite bright in studies and performs well in other things also.' Another girl approached the teacher of her own accord, and said: 'That girl is very good.' When the teacher asked her why, she said that, '*uska dimaag bahut tez hai*'. ('She is very intelligent.') The teacher told her that she too could do better and thus tried to motivate her without comparing the abilities of children. Thus, she exemplifies the belief that there should not be any comparison made by the teacher. The teacher can however try to get all children to do better. Sahabuddin is against ranking or making comparisons between children as he says 'we need to treat them equally'. According to him, comparisons may have the following effects:

- Stop independent thinking
- Cause a drop in confidence
- Cause some students to feel superior and some to feel inferior.

Two teachers bring in a slightly different perspective. Narendra says, 'Some comparison can be healthy. This need not be done directly by identifying and naming these children. It should be done in groups and activities should be such that children themselves will realise which group is doing better. In that way, they also learn how to work in groups and realise that their achievement is because of everyone's contribution. There should not be any ranking of children because it leads to discouragement. Also, then children just focus on that and not on actual learning.' Saud Ahmed Khan draws a subtle distinction between overt and covert comparison by saying: 'Children should not be compared in class, as they are all equal at that time. However, the teacher should make such comparisons in his mind so as to identify those children who need extra help. These children should be asked to stay back after school for extra classes.'

Assumptions about First-Generation Learners

Several children in this school are first-generation learners. The sensitivity of teachers to the reality of children from illiterate families comes through in their responses to this question.

Although Shipra agrees that one should not hold restricting beliefs like 'children from illiterate families cannot learn easily', she honestly admits that 'it becomes difficult not to differentiate thus' when she actually clearly sees manifestations of such hidden connections. Consistent with his other beliefs, Deepak Dixit does not hold that children from illiterate families learn more slowly. Mohit also does not agree with this belief: 'The only reason for this may be the lack of a print-rich or conducive environment at home. But if these are provided they can also learn at the same pace as other children.' Narendra says he agrees with this to some extent, because the involvement of parents and what a child does at home are also important factors that contribute to learning. [This connected to what he previously said about possibilities of learning not only in schools and not just from teachers.] Sahabuddin ranks the home environment at 3 on a scale of 1 to 5, implying that while it has an impact on their learning, it is not the deciding factor for whether or not they can learn. Madan Mohan feels that for their learning, 'the home environment does play an important role. Those who get a positive environment do have an advantage, but teachers should not use this as an excuse.' Shakuntala Chaurasia acknowledges:

'Daily wage parents do not have time and hence cannot support their children.' She has noticed that learning in these children becomes slower. Hence, 'learning is more difficult for children from illiterate families'. In other words, children have the ability to learn but because of circumstances, they could face difficulty in learning. Saud concurs as he feels that children coming from illiterate homes find learning difficult, because 'they are engaged in other work at home and hence cannot practice sums. Also, even if they do get the opportunity, there is no one to help them when they get stuck at some step.'

Assumptions about Gender-based Differences

It is not uncommon in India to find schoolboys engaging more intensely in sports, for instance, and girls preferring needlework. To what extent are such 'preferences' driven by the expectations/beliefs/assumptions of the parents or educators? Located as it is in a semi-rural community, this question was posed to gauge these teachers' stances on traditional mindsets.

It was refreshing to find that all these teachers are unanimous in stating that there is no difference between learning by girls and boys. However, they do concede that there is a difference in opportunities for social reasons.

The Principal, Deepak Dixit does not recognise any gender-based distinctions in abilities, but realises that these are stereotypical, limiting beliefs. The doors of learning are open to all, in Deepak's perception: 'To me, there is nothing that one person can learn and the other can't. I do concede that there may be a difference in each one's level, depending upon interest, practice, relevance of the concerned subject, etc. And yes, there are some things which all of us can learn – and have learnt – like language, life skills, etc.' Narendra points out a caveat: 'The condition is that they should get similar home environment, be brought up similarly and be given similar treatment in school. Then they will show similar results. Here too, even if their home contexts may be different, they have similar achievement in all subjects. In school, they just prefer to mix with children of their own gender because they are more used to that.'

Phrasing the question in a different way, we asked 'Are there any subjects which only *some* people can learn?' While all teachers disagree, Narendra clarifies: 'But we are not talking about any exceptional cases like people with some sort of disabilities.' He also believes that learning can definitely happen at any age. For example, teachers keep on learning. Shakuntala Chaurasia has been told, since childhood, that boys are better at Math but she has never experienced this, either as a student or as a teacher. Saud admits that 'girls are less interested in physical sport.' However, he does not feel that there is any difference between girls and boys in learning any subject. He asserts that even though the speed of learning decreases after the age of 50 years, learning can happen at any age.

Views on Some Children Being Gifted

Most teachers admit to children having different skill sets and abilities. Only two of the teachers (Madan and Mohit) are emphatic in their denial of any child being gifted. However, all teachers stress the importance of opportunities/exposure to draw out the potential of each child.

Neeraj believes that all children are equally talented, albeit in different areas: 'While one child might perform better in one area, another child might be better at doing something else.' He also feels that, given proper exposure, opportunity and a competent teacher, all children have the ability to learn all subjects, irrespective of gender: 'There are several examples like Kalpana Chawla, Indira Gandhi, Sania Mirza who perform as well as boys.' According to him learning 'depends on how the environment is created for a subject and how the teacher introduces that subject to the children'. He declares that there is no age limit for learning. 'Learning is an ongoing process. We learn every moment till the very last moment of our lives.' Shipra acknowledges that while some children are more gifted than others, for various reasons – genes, upbringing, exposure, etc. '*all* children are naturally curious and learn a lot by sharing and group-learning. They should be given opportunities to ask questions, to observe and do things on their own,' Shipra declares. Narendra, Saud and Sahabuddin agree that some children are more gifted than others. Saud adds that he has noticed that some children are able to pick up concepts of mathematics very quickly and then even develop their own techniques for solving questions. He says it could be due to a special gift or it could also be their interest in the subject. Shakuntala attributes her belief that some children are more gifted than others to her experience with the child who had a problem with his vision. She feels though he had this problem, he was very sharp, whereas other children with normal vision were 'really average'.

Mohit strongly disagrees with this belief as he expresses the view that 'everybody can learn anything provided there is interest in it and there are ample opportunities. By putting in efforts, anybody can learn anything but one should try and do only those things that interest one.' Madan emphatically disagrees with the idea that some children are more gifted than others. He feels 'it all depends on the opportunities that children get'.

Views on Curriculum and Textbooks

Posing this question was a deliberate step in understanding the critical thinking of each teacher, for the curriculum – and textbook – is most often taken as given.

To what extent do these teachers view the curriculum and textbook critically? Barring a few teachers, most of them are clearly examining the curriculum and text without mechanical acceptance. Spanning a spectrum, the expressions range from mild discontent to voluble criticism. While some find it vast even as it may be age-appropriate, others would like to see it made more contextual.

Deepak Dixit thinks any curriculum should be evaluated on an ongoing basis, as he finds children of today are learning the same things that he was taught as a child, regardless of their relevance in the present age (e.g. van de Graaff generator). Mohit is very emphatic that textbooks, schools and teachers are not the only sources/places of learning for a child, and does not feel hampered by the curriculum in any way: 'We decide what to teach,' he declares. Both Narendra and Sahabuddin agree that the curriculum is class/age-appropriate, though Narendra says that some chapters in the class VI books are more difficult for children. He declares: 'The textbook is not at all the only source of information for the children. It is important but there are also activity books, other live examples by children themselves, experiments that can be done, models that can be prepared, etc.' Sahabuddin has strong views on textbooks. If there was *one* thing he could change about schools, it would be: 'The textbooks! Because the printing quality is poor, illustrations are poor. It is not attractive; children are attracted to books that look good. I don't see students significantly interested in textbooks. I have some other books where the content level is high but since the printing and layout is attractive, I saw children trying to read those books – but not their textbooks.' Neeraj feels that there is 'little clarity among teachers about curriculum.' He finds the syllabus 'problematic' and asserts that it needs 'proper review.' He emphasises the 'need for lots of work to make the curriculum appropriate.'

Madan Mohan admits that he has not given much thought to the curriculum. However, he has faced difficulty in teaching all the subjects that he now teaches – science, mathematics and language. Shipra has no complaints about the curriculum as she feels that it is fine. Saud declares: 'Nothing can be said about the curriculum – it is how it has been given. However, it is quite vast especially for a subject like mathematics, which is generally perceived as difficult.' Shakuntala says: 'The curriculum is fine, though quite vast. It may be age-appropriate but for children who have not understood things in previous classes, it becomes very difficult.'

Awareness of Different Sources of Learning

Given the firm hold of the textbook (Krishna Kumar 1988) in most mainstream Indian schools, this question was posed to explore what each teacher deemed as 'sources of learning'.

Teachers need not be the only persons from whom a child can learn, asserts Shipra. Deepak Dixit said: 'To me, *everything* seems to be a source of learning. Nature herself is so rich that an entire lifetime is too short to gather the knowledge that She can impart.' One does not have to look far to develop teaching–learning materials: one only has to look around to come up with a lot of possibilities even from scrap. All it takes, he asserts, is visualisation and creativity. He regards learning as a process that cannot be time-bound, and claims he is still learning.

Do children learn only in school or only through teachers? Narendra confesses that he had held this belief but it gradually changed as he began teaching children and seeing how they learn. Having noticed that peer learning is very important, he often uses this in class activities.

Sahabuddin feels teachers and schools play an important role in the teaching–learning process; however, they are not the only sources of it.

Similarly, Neeraj feels children learn from their surroundings whether it is family, society or school. 'Children always learn from their parents. Most of their learning is related to life skills, and this happens through their parents. School can play an important role in this. They can make parents aware so that they assist the students as they learn at home.'

Madan Mohan strongly disagrees with the notion that textbooks or teachers are the only source of teaching and learning. He says, 'Children learn in other places too but school is definitely an important place for it.'

Shakuntala too, disagrees. She considers teachers as important agents of teaching–learning but certainly not the only ones. 'Children also learn from other children and people at home; especially when it comes to learning things that are not merely scholastic.'

Saud also strongly disagrees. Last year, he admits, he did not use the textbook at all because he realised that children could not relate to it. He used his own examples, from things around them (like asking them to count trees in a given area). He experienced that children were not able to connect to the math problems from the textbook whereas if the examples were taken from their experience or when they were creating their own math sums, they were very excited about learning math. 'Children learn a lot from each other and from home.'

Specific Observations by Teachers

When asked what they specifically observe during classroom transaction, all teachers responded similarly: their primary focus was the *degree of engagement of each child in class*. A few go further to say they noticed different learning styles of children as well.

For instance, Mohit observes how children are engaged and what they practise; how they learn; and what topics and activities interest them. He takes note of their work in their notebooks, even as he observes them keenly during school hours. The most significant thing that Narendra observes is whether or not children are participating in class. 'They should understand what is being taught (gauged by seeing whether they can answer questions posed intermittently). It is easier when some activity is assigned. Then the teacher can go around and observe if they are doing what they are required to do. Other than these things, the general behaviour of each child also should be observed, that is, how the child talks to others, etc.' He adds, 'I observe each child while they are working, I also encourage those students who participate less in the class to interact with me.'

Sahabuddin says, 'I observe working patterns, oral communication skills, confidence, types of mistakes, the way in which they learn better, and interest levels.' In addition, Sahabuddin tries to make time to play and chat with his students and also visit their homes in order to find out the mistakes/patterns in errors. Madan Mohan observes whether all children engage in the ongoing discussions. If some work is required to be done in notebooks, or is to be done in groups, he sees to it that everyone is involved in doing it. In order to pay attention to each child in the class, he tries to engage with the individual child, supporting them based on their needs, and pays attention to the distinct learning styles of children. 'I start the class by recapitulating the previous day's work, talk with each student and call them by their name. I also remind them to pay attention to the lesson.'

Shakuntala observes whether or not children are paying attention – she knows that if they do not understand something, they will stop paying attention and get distracted. She therefore tries to ensure that all children are following the lesson; otherwise she stops at that step and retraces previous steps. She moves about the classroom, looks into their notebooks while they are working, and asks them questions and encourages classroom discussion. She prefers not to give direct answers to the children and encourages them to think on their own. This was evident during classroom observation (see box, p 182:) where she prods children to think by asking them questions, encouraging them to ask their own questions and discussing their own thought process about the solutions to the math problems. Saud too checks whether students are paying attention and doing the work that they have been asked to do in their notebooks. To pay attention to each child, he too moves about the classroom, looking into their notebooks. Amongst the strategies that Shipra employs to secure and hold the attention of children are: asking questions to different children, inviting them to use the board to write, getting them to work in groups and using activities and games as important sources of learning.

A close engagement with students by each teacher is clearly coming through in their responses.

Teacher as a Reflective Practitioner

Almost all teachers admitted to the impact of working in the Foundation, with opportunities for attending workshops, meeting resource persons – and almost all of them mentioned the value of learning from their peers. (This was stated even *before* setting out to do action research. However, the degree and nature of peer interaction did increase substantially during the action research.) Questions probing their beliefs and attitudes thus drew responses that indicated some amount of reflection (see below for more) and a freedom from a blind acceptance of some social prejudices – for instance, gendered preferences for learning subjects.

In making the action research optional, the facilitators deliberately allowed for a teacher *not* participating in the study. Thus, by the simple act of opting for action research, a teacher showed her cognizance of a certain problem that she faced. One interpretation of this could be that the novelty created by the context of a research study drew many teachers into it. While this can only be disproved if teachers continue to carry out action research in the absence of a facilitating team (and indeed, as this book is being written, some of the teachers in the school are doing so), there is a less skeptical way of looking at this – the very fact that the teachers are concerned enough about a problem so as to conduct action research on it could arguably be seen as an indication of (a) either their connect with the students or (b) their motivation to improve upon their teaching practice. The team of facilitators from the Foundation believed that teachers who get perturbed by some learning gap in their students are already on their way to becoming reflective. As Pollard (2008) says:

> Reflective teaching implies an active concern with aims and consequences, as well as means and technical efficiency.

Further, the teachers showed other indicators of being reflective:

- by their willingness to examine their teaching–learning practices,
- by being open to learning new things themselves
- by their sustained interest in seeing the problem through from identification to resolution

All of the above point towards their inclination to reflect. In their teacher profiles too (collated at the start of the study), there were some indications of their already being reflective. For instance, while it was found that they all have their personal goals as a teacher, each of them could also *articulate a strategy* to achieve these goals. This link is an indicator of the presence of reflection in their functioning. It is not uncommon, as we know, to find teachers professing lofty goals, but when asked to articulate a route to achieving that goal, many are at a loss. However, that was not the case with this set of teachers.

Another hallmark of a reflective practitioner is the inclination – better still, *eagerness* – to grow. Sahabuddin professes to find ample opportunity to learn new things in this profession and his goal as a teacher is to facilitate the building of a better society by providing better education. Children's happiness motivates him, in his role as a teacher. He puts in a great deal of effort by reading and consulting his colleagues to make his lesson plans interesting.

Deepak's stated goal is to make his students independent thinkers. This was corroborated by the manner in which he conducted his class on '*How we see*' (for details, see pages 95–110). He finds that his students believed that there is a light in the eyes that help us see. He can see that children harbour several myths about physics. He works towards breaking such myths by probing and experimenting with children so that they find for themselves what the reality is. The enthusiasm of his students keeps him motivated.

Narendra wants to ensure that all the children have achieved age-appropriate competencies in the subject that he is teaching. He feels motivated when children show progress. He wishes to understand the factors that inhibit a child and hold her back from realising her capabilities.

Neeraj finds that teachers usually become disinterested if the system does not support them even when they are interested in learning new things. He feels motivated by the self-satisfaction that he draws from working towards improved education of children. He would like to develop his understanding about how children learn, so as to improve their interest in learning. He wants to address social issues like discrimination and making parents aware of the importance of education for their children, through the opportunity that his profession provides.

Madan sincerely wants to see his students succeed. He is energised when his students do well. Having moved from a government school (where he was teaching earlier) to the Foundation's school, he is now trying to gain a new perspective as a teacher. Mohit likes to interact with children/people and his aim is to learn from others and to enhance his students' learning. He finds that as a teacher, he can contribute something meaningful to society and this keeps him motivated. He reads a lot and his interactions with students help him reflect on his practices.

Shipra wants to develop her skills as a facilitator. Observing other teachers perform well keeps her motivated. She is focusing on learning from her peers and also attending workshops to stay up-to-date with new theories and practices.

Both Saud and Shakuntala want to ensure that all children in their class achieve their age-appropriate learning level. When Saud works with children and finds that their understanding and performance has improved, he feels motivated. He works towards his goal by learning new methods of teaching to ensure that the concepts he teaches are understood by children. Shakuntala feels motivated when children become interested in learning. She teaches with great interest and invests significantly in learning for herself. All of these teachers are able to narrate their memorable experiences as teachers, and this too indicates a high level of reflection.

Yet another indication of these teachers being on the road to reflection is the fact that Shakuntala and Saud had identified the problem that they wished to address *long before* the Action Research Study was launched in their school. Seeing that they had to team-teach Math to Class VI, both teachers were perturbed by the fact that a few children in this class had still not grasped place value. This was also the case with Narendra and Sahabuddin, who had undertaken great pains to group children of Classes III, IV and V, to understand their language learning difficulties. [This had been done by them the year before the Action Research Study was launched.]

The concern of these four teachers was evident from their admission that they would have addressed this issue whether or not they did Action Research. 'Action Research gave us two things: the need to document (which we did not do, in such detail, earlier), and an urgency to complete it within a time frame.' And again, 'Now we do routine documentation. And from that, a lot of reflection emerges.' (Their acknowledgement of the importance of documenting this work is described in a later section.)

Further, some of the visible qualities that lay the foundation for the emergence of a reflective practitioner were:

- their practice of engaging in a constant dialogue with each other (which increased as they got deeper into action research),
- examining their teaching–learning processes with their peers on a regular basis,
- learning through different means to find solutions to the problems that they faced and
- supporting each other in solving issues in the classroom

Some of these developed more strongly through this study, while a few of these traits were present in some measure even *before* these teachers began action research. It is with this background that this study is viewed as *enhancing* reflection in teachers through action research, rather than *making* teachers reflective through action research.

Well before embarking on action research, some teachers discussed issues with each other and acknowledged the impact of interacting with resource persons or participating in training programmes. To quote Narendra, who had encountered difficulty in teaching Hindi to a few students last year: '*And then we talked....like we talked to Navneet-ji (Resource Person).... then the training that was conducted in Barsu**...*we talked to our colleagues. And Sahabuddin-ji and Neeraj-ji and I, constantly we would be thinking about how we should work with them.*' Thus, there was already a certain degree of reflection in the teachers' mode of functioning.

All the teachers declare that they are very open to giving and receiving feedback to and from each other. (This is corroborated by a question in the Teacher Profile, where they were asked to list their sources of learning. Almost all of them cited their colleagues as one of the sources.) However, it is well known that it is always difficult to receive critical feedback from anyone, perhaps particularly from one's own colleagues. What, then, could be the reason for this uniformly positive response from these teachers? We surmise that the school's existing practice of sharing difficulties in their classroom practice during Saturday meetings opens up ground for gentle feedback. Teachers who have faced similar issues in the classroom, and perhaps have even found solutions to these issues, find a window here to offer feedback to their colleagues. For example, Madan shared the problems he was facing with Deepak Dixit, the Principal, and found the Principal's suggestions worth acting on. Narendra and Sahabuddin shared the difficulties that they were facing (with the children who were not showing any improvement in their reading) with their colleagues as well as the subject matter experts from the Foundation. The suggestions and feedback that they received helped them zero in on the Whole Language Approach as a possible teaching strategy, which they later found to be helpful in solving their problem.

With this backdrop, it is worth exploring the shifts, if any, that occurred in the teachers' practice, assumptions, attitudes and thinking, as a consequence of Action Research. An attempt has been made to

---

* Hill station in Uttarakhand where summer training was held for the teachers of Azim Premji Schools in 2013.

examine this in Section III. As already mentioned in the Introduction, shifts in teachers' assumptions, understanding and/or theories in action were compiled by drawing from their reflection-in-action (during the video-interview).

While the authors of this work regard the quality of reflection to lie on a continuum, for the purpose of comparison, we refer to frameworks for teacher reflectivity in the literature. Such frameworks are available in plenty, and while we make no attempt to review them all, we refer to that of Stanley (1998) here, in order to gauge the location of the teachers who participated in this study. Stanley (1998) has suggested that there are phases in the development of a teacher's reflectivity; the framework is based on a longitudinal study that she conducted with six experienced teachers:

- Engaging with reflection
- Thinking reflectively
- Using reflection
- Sustaining reflection
- Practising reflection

She emphasises that these phases need not be sequential, and that at any point in time, teachers could find themselves in any phase. If a teacher has personal issues and/or trauma that block her reflection, she may find it difficult to engage with reflection, a concern which Stanley claims has largely been ignored in the literature. 'It takes a healthy degree of ego development to put oneself and one's work under the microscope. Therefore, some teachers may not become reflective for reasons that are beyond the scope of the field of teacher education.'

Stanley stresses that unless basic personal, professional and contextual factors are stable, teachers will not be able to engage with reflection. While some teachers may have previously acquired the skill to think reflectively, Stanley suggests ways of prodding those who have not to think reflectively, by posing pointed questions. Once teachers have understood what reflection is and how to think reflectively, they are now empowered to use it as a tool.
In this phase, 'Teachers begin to sort out the forms and feelings of the process that are most beneficial to their practice.'

> *We are in the problematic situation that we seek to describe and change, and when we act on it, we act on ourselves.*
>
> ***Schon (1983)***

Sustaining reflection may pose difficulties in the form of throwing up difficult emotions and/or hard-to-digest realisations, in which case, Stanley suggests that teachers may resort to external ways of sustaining it, like reading, peer discussions and workshops. Over time, teachers can begin to look at themselves and their students with greater compassion. And thus it is, that reflection can develop into a practice, and become an integral part of the teacher's practice. Stanley then lists out each of these phases of reflective teaching in tabular format, and implies ways in which a teacher educator can respond to teachers who are in any of these phases.

If we use this framework to understand where our teachers are, we will find that the two main 'struggles' that they faced are in

1. The setting of the problem, and
2. Ideas that could lead to the right strategies and resources to address the problem

Some of them needed assistance from the facilitators at these stages, but they were not constrained by the context. Indeed, many of them felt that the atmosphere was conducive to their action research, and consequently, their reflection. All of them could find time for reflection-on-action, as is evident from their own documentation. A few (like Shipra, Sahabuddin and Narendra) attempted specific and precise data collection – both during the action research cycle as well as later. This could well be because the precise collection of data was not rendered possible for some others, in the nature of their identified problem, for example, quantitative data could not be envisaged in a problem like 'development of scientific temper' in students.

Almost all the teachers **made time for reflection-on-action**, even before the start of this study. This was evident in the ease with which they came up with several issues that they felt were worth conducting action research on, thus implying an already prevalent discontent with some of their classroom realities. As elaborated later, some teachers had zeroed in on the problem of deepest concern to them, long before the start of this study. In the **uncovering of systemic issues and classroom realities**, Mohit showed insight: he realised that the prejudice of teachers in assuming that the inarticulate students 'do not know anything' could well have undermined the self-esteem of those students. He went further in reflecting on action, by noting that once their 'minds opened up', they articulated observations which *they could well have been making all along*, and which even students who were regarded as articulate (and therefore, 'above average') missed making. Neeraj too expressed this: even his problem-setting (development of scientific temper in students) was grounded in acute awareness of the way children unquestioningly accept what the teacher and textbooks say.

Madan Mohan Joshi **uncovered pedagogical issues** as he taught Hindi – and noticed that the didactic text did not give room for exploring the extent to which a child can decode as well as understand a word. This revealed to him the need to develop new strategies, which he deftly did and describe in their AR documents. Shipra also invested in a similar effort, as she noted the (in)effectiveness of different pedagogies in getting children to read English words. Shakuntala and Saud also explored (and then discarded) the traditional pedagogy for teaching place value in Math, as they reflected in action and found that it did not work well. Deepak Dixit also struggled with various pedagogies as he taught the process of vision to his students. Sahabuddin confessed that the use of the Whole Language Approach as a pedagogy taught him how remarkable it is that language can be learnt without traversing the letter-to-word-to-sentence route. In his video-interview, he admitted that this was a revelation to him, as he reflected upon how *we*, too, decode and read words – we seldom read every letter in a word or every word in a sentence. Neeraj realised the difference between making students 'do an experiment' and exploring a facilitative process where children *design their own experiments*. The former, he noted, is a process of passive learning where children follow a set of instructions, record observations and often forget about it thereafter, while the latter, he found, is a means to developing scientific temper in children and making them lifelong learners.

Against this framework, therefore, the teachers in this study could be said to be **using reflection**: whether or not they sustain it is to be seen, and the exploration of the extent to which they continue to practice it is of course left for a later study. Some reference has been made in this section to the changes experienced by teachers *as they conducted* action research. A brief account of the blossoming of such efforts *after* these action research cycles were completed is described in the concluding chapter.

Phases of Reflective Teaching					
Characteristic	**Phase**				
	Engaging with Reflection	**Thinking Reflectively**	**Using Reflection**	**Sustaining Reflection**	**Practicing Reflection**
Contextual factors	Requires interest, psychological strength, and contextual support	Struggles to find time to reflect	Can make time for consistent reflection-on-action	Finds ways to sustain reflection from other perspectives	Has systems in place for consistent reflection-on-action
Approaches	Partly or totally lacks skill in reflective thinking	Is unclear as to what reflective thinking is and is not; engages in seemingly random reflective thinking; possibly holds positivist view of education	Engages in clear reflective thinking at will; is mostly engaged with reflection-on-action; has greater awareness of moments of reflection-in-action	Shows greater precision of data	Shows precision of data in the moment or later; easily engages with both reflection-on-action and reflection-in-action
Issues			Can examine larger systemic issues as well as classroom realities	Uncovers problematic pedagogical or political issues	Engages in reflection-on-action that includes analysis of pedagogical and political dimensions of teaching

Phases of Reflective Teaching					
Characteristic	Phase				
	Engaging with Reflection	Thinking Reflectively	Using Reflection	Sustaining Reflection	Practicing Reflection
Responses		Initially has descriptive thinking and feeling responses	Responds creatively and appropriately to situations reflected on; can generate multiple reasons for actions	Experiences painful emotions triggered as a result of investigation	Generates multiple reasons and responses in the moment and later; has strategies in place for dealing with difficult feelings; uses frameworks for analysis that bring broader interpretations
Actions					After reflection, takes action that involves both students and broader educational community

Source: The above table has been reproduced with permission from Stanley (1998).

4. In the Classroom

> *The teacher's isolation in her classroom works against reflection-in-action.*
> ***Schon (1983)***

Classroom observations (CROs) were one of the tools used to understand how teachers engaged with children and the subject, and the relationship that this has with the process of action research and reflective practice. As mentioned in the introductory chapter, the CROs were carried out at any convenient point in time during the four-to-five-month period of action research. Sometimes, but not always, the class pertained to the topic of action research. Since a single classroom observation for each teacher precludes comprehensive analysis, in this section, we present our observations, and also attempt to see the link between the teacher's CRO and his/her belief system (as collated in the teacher profile).

Place of the learner in teaching–learning process: When we examine the classroom observations, it becomes clear that in most of the classes, the learner is not an empty receptacle which needs to be filled with facts and figures. Instead, the student is an integral part of the whole process. This attitude also came through for all the teachers in their Teacher Profiles. Two aspects that stand out with respect to the students is the teachers' connection with the students and the involvement of the students in the classroom processes. Neeraj's efforts to facilitate a discussion on food, Madan's attempts to draw out children's responses on Diwali, and Narendra and Sahabuddin's invitation to children to think if the manner in which they were reading was indeed the way to narrate a story – are all examples of the engagement that these teachers deemed critical for their classroom processes. [CROs described in Section II hold more such examples.]

Connection with students: All the teachers connected well with the students. Shipra, Shakuntala and Saud have ascertained that their students are at different levels of learning. So they plan their activities in a way that challenges all their students. Shakuntala and Saud divide the children into groups based on learning levels, and individually engage with each group. As observed during classroom observations, Shipra provides some picture cards and some word cards. Children make sentences according to their ability and comprehension. Similarly, the connection that teachers have with their students becomes evident in the way Narendra and Sahabuddin conduct their class. Madan's intervention is another example of his connection with children and the situation: when his students are noisy he quietly tells them, 'If you don't listen to others, they too won't listen to you' so as to help them realise the importance of listening.

Involvement of the students: The teachers actively seek the involvement of their students through different strategies. Shipra involves them by giving them an opportunity to think and make sentences using the picture cards and word cards provided to them. Neeraj involves them by creating a learning situation where he encourages students to ask questions and provide answers around the topic under consideration. He also gently prods the quieter students to participate in the discussion when he points out to a student: '........ (*Name*) has not said anything for a long time'. When two children start interacting amongst themselves, he says, 'Don't tell him alone. Tell *everyone.*' Mohit involves them in planning, writing and executing a skit on the subject of *'Pedon ka Mahatv'* (The importance of trees). In Shakuntala and Saud's classes students feel free to challenge the teacher by asking: 'How is this possible? See, *I* can show you this on the number line.' And the child goes on to show his understanding of the issue to all the students. Both Shakuntala and Saud wait for them to complete, before offering further interventions.

Connecting learning to their immediate environment and experiences: The teacher's effort at connecting the student's learning was observed across teachers' classes. For instance, Neeraj, while teaching a topic on food, encourages children to ask questions and answers them based on their experiences. Madan connects the topic of Diwali with children's experiences by asking them to share various aspects of Diwali celebrations in their homes. Mohit very creatively connects the topic to children's experiences by asking them to prepare a skit about it without giving them any inputs; this meant that children primarily relied on their experiences while planning and enacting the play. Shipra staggers the level of words in her word cards, so as to pitch at mixed levels in her class. Shakuntala and Saud use materials like bottle caps to form a number line, and thus make them engage more actively with the classroom.

Flexibility: It can be seen that teachers are quite flexible in their approach and their classroom management. Shipra plans the class in a way which requires the teacher to move around the class and encourages self-monitoring by students. She has prepared and put up charts in the classroom listing students' names group-wise, resulting in students effortlessly dividing themselves into groups and then settling down to work. Neeraj is not in a hurry to deliver information to his students. He first provides them ample time to ask questions and encourages other (quieter) children to respond. Mohit does not show any need to control the outcome of the skit or the discussion that ensues. He gives children an opportunity to express their views and then ties the lesson together at the end, by collating all that students have performed (as a part of their skit). Shakuntala does not appear to feel challenged when a student questions her in class and goes ahead to prove his point of view. Instead, she gives full opportunity to the child to explain before taking charge of the situation.

Creativity: It is clear from the classroom observations that these teachers are creative in the classroom. [For readers who would prefer a tighter definition of 'creativity', we draw their attention to the fact that practically none of these teachers have been taught in a creative way, when *they* were students. Therefore, *any* attempt to think differently is their way of stepping out of the box – or of being 'creative'.] The classroom management in Shipra's class (grouping them and facilitating free movement by putting up charts) is an example of creatively managing the class. Mohit uses a skit very creatively as an assessment tool; this also provides an opportunity for the students' creativity to emerge. Neeraj prods the children to ask questions around the topic that is being discussed, and then allows them to figure out for themselves the answers to the questions that they ask. Shakuntala and Saud use the teaching–learning materials with a lot of creativity, by making children prepare the materials themselves and therefore, gain a sense of ownership. Also, they have the children form the largest three digit number from the digits that they have before them, instead of simply listing out ascending and descending numbers. Narendra writes jumbled words and sentences from a story that the children have already read, and asks them to rearrange the words/sentences in a way that they make sense. Sahabuddin deliberately asks students to correct their mistakes by themselves, when he could well have been the only one to correct their work. Madan connects teaching about a festival (Diwali) to children's own experiences. Shakuntala shows her careful thinking by not giving direct answers to the children regarding the problem at hand. Instead, she explains a different problem to them and encourages them to find connections with the problem.

Patience: None of the above would be possible without the critical element of patience, which every teacher in the study displayed in his/her interactions with children. Shipra gives ample time to organise and re-organise the class as the children shift into different groups. Madan gently corrects children when they become noisy, in a way that enables them to respect the perspective of other students. Neeraj does not feel harried by noisy discussions, so students go on to discuss the topic of food at length, challenge each other, and provide arguments in favour of or against the views presented. Mohit is in no hurry to show them what he knows. He allows the information to emerge from the skit. Narendra and Sahabuddin engage with children patiently. Shakuntala and Saud patiently allow children to figure out the solutions to their sums.

Teacher doesn't 'tell' – teacher learns: In this process, the teacher does not assume the place of a 'know-it-all' authority. The teacher is, instead, constantly engaging with the current reality of his/her students, the understanding of the students about the subject, their interpersonal interactions, their responses to the teacher as well to the subject, etc. The teachers are responding to the situation in the *here-and-now*, taking care of the emerging needs of the students and the subject, modifying their interventions from moment to moment, creating a space for the process to evolve and learning about all that is involved in the process.

For example, Neeraj is constantly learning about children's understanding of the subject and readjusting his plan accordingly. Mohit is learning the same from the skit that his students perform; he then gives his inputs to consolidate their learning. Shakuntala is learning from the children's involvement and the challenges they pose vis-a-vis their level of understanding and engagement, and chooses her next step based on this information. Saud gently nudges the students to recall an activity that they had done earlier, but refrains from being the one to tell them how to solve the problem. Shipra and Mohit have provided for different levels of responses to facilitate learning in the children as they learned from their previous experiences that children need to experience both success and challenge in their learning, in order to stay engaged. Narendra and Sahabuddin sit on the floor with their students, breaking the hierarchy even in their manner of interaction. Madan conducts his entire class in discussion mode, involving the students keenly, without 'telling' them the information. He states his opinions (for example about the pollution caused by firecrackers burst during Diwali) without imposing this view upon the class.

Madan gently ensures that all the children engage with the classroom transaction asking them to listen attentively and respectfully to each other, if they expect others to do so too. Saud's frequent appreciation of the children's efforts is also aligned with his belief that the children's work should be appreciated. Shakuntala emphasises that a teacher must have her finger on the pulse of the room; the way in which she moves about the class and focuses on how much each child has understood will reveal this. Madan believes in aligning transaction with children's innate interests and emphatically disagrees that textbooks are the only source of learning for a child; this comes through in the way in which he engages the children in a discussion on a festival that they enjoy. Mohit wants children to share their feelings without hesitation or fear: this is probably why he revises lessons through role play. The manner in which the class flows shows that children are not aware that their learning is being reinforced or assessed in any way.

Narendra and Sahabuddin confess that they deem it important to observe children keenly to see if they are participating or learning well; this can be seen during their CRO as well. Interestingly, Narendra qualifies his assertion that his own beliefs have been shattered by children after he took up this profession, by elaborating thus: 'That learning could occur only in schools was a belief that changed after teaching. This belief did not change suddenly, but over the years, I realised that students construct and understand concepts on the basis of their prior knowledge that they have built from their environment. I witnessed this more specifically while introducing them to a topic like agriculture, festivals, flora, fauna, society, etc. They learn a lot from surroundings and everything does not require school.' While all of the above observations are taken directly from just one CRO, there are several more such validations from the processes employed by each teacher during their action research. These are described in Section III where shifts in the teachers' thinking and/or practice are also analysed. The *Overview* at the end of Section III presents a summary of each teacher's overall experience.

As detailed in Chapter 3, 'Teacher Snapshots', most of these teachers were reflecting on their practice even before undertaking action research. Yet, just providing a structure for each teacher's approach to an identified problem proved to be very impactful and actually led to many new insights for the teachers. Every teacher admitted to having gained significant benefit from the practice of action research.

The authors of this work see this as an encouraging sign; we hope that principals who wish to infuse their schools with a reflective ambience will adopt action research to help nurture the thinking and intensify the reflection of teachers. It may help free them from predictable patterns of thought and behaviour and set them on the road to reflective teaching.

SECTION II

NARRATIVES

Edited by
Neeraja Raghavan, Vineeta Sood and Sneha Titus

1. Introduction

This section comprises the work that was conducted during this study. It contains teachers' action research documents, self-analysis and facilitators' notes.

The research was conducted and documented by the teachers who have been named herein, facilitated by the team of facilitators from Azim Premji Foundation. Teachers documented their action research in a detailed and unstructured manner (which is not included in this book) as well as in the structured template provided (which finds a place at the end of each teacher's chapter). Each teacher has been named (with their permission) and described in detail in the case studies that follow. Nine teachers conducted seven action research studies, as four teachers chose to form two pairs. Facilitators conducted detailed interviews with teachers to collate the Teacher's Profile and also observed a single classroom process for each teacher/pair of teachers. We list below the names and brief backgrounds of the **facilitators** who worked with each teacher.

Aanchal Chomal is a Postgraduate in Geography. She has been working in the development sector for nine years in the area of social science pedagogy, large scale assessments, teacher based classroom assessments and research. Her role in this project was to co-develop the framework and tools for documenting the teacher profile and action research template. She co-facilitated a workshop with all the teachers of Azim Premji School to introduce the concept of action research. She worked with Deepak Dixit and Rakesh (who is still completing his action research) in the initial phases of the project and was later supported by other members of the AR team. Aanchal has been working with Azim Premji Foundation since 2006.

Ambika Mohan is a Postgraduate in Life Sciences, in which she carried out research work for three years. Being also interested in the field of Education, she joined Azim Premji Foundation in 2011, as a resource person for research. As a member of the team in the action research project, she participated in further evolving the proposed idea of the study, inducting school teachers into action research, facilitating the work of some, and profiling, documenting and observing the classroom processes for other teachers.

Neeraja Raghavan holds a PhD in Chemistry from Princeton University and has been a school teacher, Principal and teacher educator for nearly two decades. She worked in Azim Premji Foundation from 2007 till November 2014, when she was Professor, Azim Premji University. Her role in this project has been that of Principal Investigator: she conceptualised the study and facilitated its co-evolution with the team. She anchored it through the five-month duration, conducted the initial and wrap-up workshops with teachers, interviewed each teacher at the end of the study (so as to allow for reflection on reflection-in-action), video-shot the interviews, coordinated their conversion into eight short films and compiled the overall study in the form of this book. She founded her own consultancy service for teacher development, Thinking Teacher (www.thinkingteacher.in), in December 2014 and now works with different schools to develop reflective teachers.

Tapasya Saha holds a PhD in Geography, and has been a high school Geography Teacher for almost two decades. Her role in this project was to facilitate the teacher researcher, using her subject expertise in EVS and Social Science. She facilitated two teachers in their action research: Mohit (who worked in the field of EVS) and Rakesh (who is presently working in History). She also co-facilitated a workshop on reflective writing, so as to help teachers understand the significance of documentation. She is presently taking the study forward so as to further the development of the teachers who have successfully completed one action research cycle. She has been working in Azim Premji Foundation since 2009.

Vartul Dhaundiyal is a Resource Person of Educational Research at Azim Premji Foundation's Dehradun State Institute since 2012. A Postgraduate in Mass Communication, he has been working for the last seven years in the area of academics and pedagogy across organisations like Pratham, Room to Read, etc. His main role in the action research project was to co-evolve the proposed idea of the work, induction of the school teachers into action research, facilitating the work of some of the teachers, profiling, documenting and observing the classroom processes for some teachers. Along with Ambika, Vartul made regular visits to the school for four months.

Vipin Chauhan is a Resource Person of Educational Research at Azim Premji State Institute, Dehradun, since 2009. He holds a PhD degree in Psychology. He has been engaged in the area of social research since the last one and a half decades. His main role in the action research project was to co-evolve the framework of action research in the Indian context, induct participant teachers into action research, develop tools for reflections and documentation and implement the study. He continues to be engaged with the teachers who participated in the study.

The case studies here are intended to give the reader an insight into the teacher's mind. Each case study has a teacher profile, a classroom observation and the documentation of the action research project in the teacher's own words.

In an attempt to do the same for facilitators, these case studies are interspersed with pages from the respective facilitator's diary, written by the facilitator before, during and after a visit to the school. Since they follow a structure, and are arranged chronologically as the study panned out, they sometimes refer to the work of the teacher in the previous/next case study, but more often than not, they are unconnected to the adjoining case studies.

From a Facilitator's Diary...

Vipin Chauhan, August 2013

Before Going to the School

The great concern for me was whether teachers will be willing to participate in the study and accept it and comply with its requirements. At the same time, as it was decided to conduct the study in Uddhamsingh Nagar (UDSN) after a long struggle with government school teachers, I was also worried as to what will happen to the study if these teachers too do not accept the idea.

The purpose of the visit was to discuss the AR problem with teachers and decide on a topic for each teacher, based on the interaction. It was also our intent to assess their enthusiasm for the study.

At the UDSN School

Teachers welcomed us wholeheartedly. I was able to interact with most of the teachers (Neeraj, Mohit, Shipra, Prachie, Narendra, Sahabuddin, Madan and Shakuntala). The interaction with all of them was quite motivating. However, in one or two cases, they were somewhat doubtful whether they would be able to do the AR properly as it demands systematic work and documentation of all the processes related to study. One teacher also questioned the purpose of the study as s/he was apprehensive about the intent. S/he asked why the study is being done in the school and whether this study will be carried out to measure the performance of teachers?

Teachers are, by and large, motivated. I observed Narendra, Sahabuddin, Neeraj and Mohit highly willing to undertake the study. They shared their thoughts through several rounds of discussions. They were also looking quite motivated as they were happy to hear that their work may be published in a book.

The question raised by one of the teachers on the purpose of the study (whether it is to understand the classroom process or to study the performance of teachers) indicated some hesitation in their minds. The intent of the study was made clear on the spot. After that, they all felt freer.

I enjoyed the interaction with the teachers and Deepak (the Principal). Deepak's interest in the study is remarkable.

I was sure that as part of the design of the study we will be able to assist all teachers adequately. But, so far as academic issues are concerned, there were some doubts as to whether or not we will be able to resolve all issues, as many of us are not from an academic background, especially where teachers are quite reflective and experienced.

After Visit

I felt quite motivated that we are on the right track after struggling with the study. There was great hope that we will be able to do something significant for the study.

2. Enhancing English Vocabulary and Reading Abilities

Name of Teacher: Shipra Agarwal

Qualifications: MCom, PGDCA and BEd

Name of Facilitator associated with Teacher: Ambika Mohan

Action Research Problem: To increase the English vocabulary of children of Class 4 so that they recognise and understand the meanings of words in stories, by factoring in individual needs

Identification of Problem: Reading was felt to be the most important competency because further learning also depends on it.

Analysis of Problem: Four children were facing this problem – these were the same children who were facing problems with speaking and writing. Unfamiliarity with words (insufficient vocabulary) was the main cause.

Identification of Alternative Approaches: Drilling (traditional rote method), peer-learning and word-with-picture cards were possible approaches. Picture cards were selected as the best approach.

Implementation of Identified Approach: The activity was repeated in several classes over a month. Then, the teacher wrote ten sentences on the board using the same words as those in the cards and asked children to read them aloud.

Review and Reflection: The process was quite effective even though learning of children was not 100%.

With seventeen years of teaching experience, Shipra Agarwal is comfortable teaching English, Computers and Social Sciences to any class. In her early years of teaching, her lifeline was the textbook and her definition of student achievement was their mastery of prescribed answers to predictable questions. Shipra tracks her progression curve from there to being a teacher in whose class 'the children definitely become better at the subject. They start understanding *how* they should learn.'

Shipra believes one can learn at any age, and deems such lifelong learning to be especially important for teachers. Even today, Shipra is motivated by observing other teachers teach and by peer interaction.

She likes to discuss – and read about – teaching strategies with her colleagues, and enjoys meeting resource persons too.

She draws fulfilment from watching children enhance their own learning abilities, improving their performance and sometimes, doing even better than expected. She deems the inclusion of *all* children and paying equal attention *to each student in the class* as one of the biggest challenges for a teacher.

Shipra seems to be a sensitive and committed teacher who is eager to improve her teaching practice.

Though she has often sourced stories from outside the textbook, she also ensures that she covers the stories given in the textbook 'because they are required to be done'.

As a teacher, Shipra found it a challenge to cater to the needs of all the children in class. She struggled as she tried to take them forward together while making the class engaging and challenging for all. When she had questions and wanted to do things differently, finding help was not always easy. During the course of teaching children, she has found that children feel motivated when:

- They feel confident that they will be able to do what they have started.
- The teacher appreciates their work.
- They see other children doing well.
- They are given responsibility.

Shipra asserts that she found action research result-oriented and no extra time was required, except some for documenting. Further, it enabled her to think about and involve the children who were not performing well. Equally, she could provide enough of a challenge to the students performing well, by creating multilevel learning material which was challenging for all. Shipra asserts that given support, she would definitely like to continue to conduct action research in the future.

Teacher's Learning after Action Research

- Use different teaching methods to address the problems children face.
- Work with children according to their abilities and interests.
- Ask questions and find solutions on one's own with increased confidence and empowerment.
- 'It is not important to simply finish the chapter. What is more important is to examine if every child is learning.'

As for the four children she did her action research project with, even though they have more or less reached the level of the average child in the class, Shipra thinks they still need a little more attention than the rest.

The Outcome (in Shipra's words): 'Children have definitely become better at English. They have also started understanding how they should learn.

Children were able to read a lot more words as compared to what they could read earlier.'

Q: While conducting AR – or after conducting it – did you see any change in your teaching-learning? If yes, what was the change?

Ans: While performing AR, there were several concerns revolving around the selected problem, like adopting different pedagogies to solve the issue, according to the capacity of each child, the amount of time to be allotted to cover a particular topic, etc. Earlier, before AR, my focus was more on covering a particular topic in a fixed time, and I would assume that children would more or less 'get it' in that fixed time. But while doing AR, I perceived that it is not as important to cover a certain topic as it is to ensure that every child has learnt, and to see how much each child has learnt.

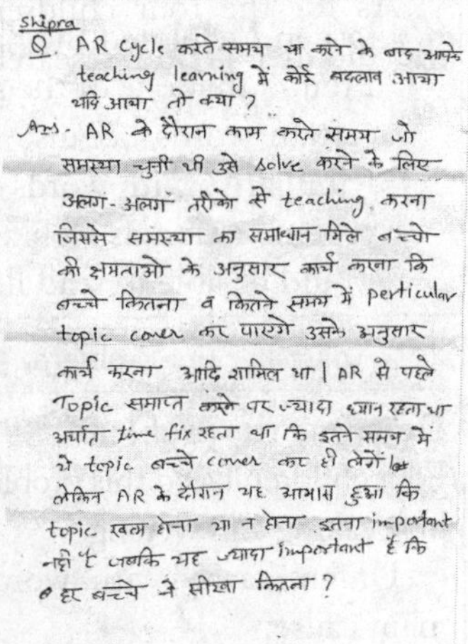
Shipra

Q. AR cycle करते समय या करने के बाद आपके teaching learning में कोई बदलाव आया यदि आया तो क्या ?

Ans- AR के दौरान काम करते समय जो समस्या चुनी थी उसे solve करने के लिए अलग-अलग तरीको से teaching करना जिससे समस्या का समाधान मिले बच्चो की क्षमताओ के अनुसार कार्य करना कि बच्चे कितना व कितने समय में perticular topic cover कर पाएगे उसके अनुसार कार्य करना आदि शामिल था। AR से पहले Topic समाप्त करने पर ज्यादा ध्यान रहता था अर्थात time fix रहता था कि इतने समय में ये topic बच्चे cover कर ही लेगें लेकिन AR के दौरान यह आभास हुआ कि topic खत्म होना या न होना इतना important नही है जबकि यह ज्यादा important है कि हर बच्चे ने सीखा कितना ?

Action Research (AR) Document – Shipra Agarwal

AR Topic: To increase the English vocabulary of children of Class 4 so that they

i. recognise words and
ii. understand their meaning

1. Identifying the Problem

Listing out problems faced

- I carried out assessments of children after teaching a couple of chapters to see if they had understood. Written as well as oral assessments were done to assess different competencies. I realised that children had problems in all of the following:
    - Speaking
    - Reading
    - Writing

Identifying one problem (the most important)

- I chose Reading as the problem to be dealt with first. I felt Reading was the most important competency because a lot of further learning also depends on it. Children will be able to learn better if they are able to read books on their own. Also, in higher classes, children have to take the board examination and they have to read and understand the paper.

- When I explored the problem of reading further (see 2. below), I found that one of the specifics was that children got stuck with certain words because they were not part of their vocabulary. Familiarity with words needed to be increased, both in terms of pronunciation as well as meaning of the word, so that children would be able to read fluently and also understand.

2. Analysing the Problem

Detailing the problem

Four children faced this problem. They were also the ones with problems in speaking and writing.

Unfamiliarity with words (hence limited vocabulary) was the main cause.

I made different efforts, including teaching through the traditional method which involved making children memorise word-meanings. To assess reading ability, the story 'My Home' was written on a chart and children were asked to read it. The four identified children did not show any improvement. (That is, they continued to read only a few words and could not understand the meaning of what they were reading).

3. Identifying Alternative Approaches

Efforts made by the teacher to tackle the challenge

Suggestions were made by my colleagues during the Saturday (sharing) meeting. They suggested that peer-learning could be an effective way and suggested an activity for it. I tried this in the class. I divided Class 4 into four groups and ensured that the identified four children were distributed such that there was one child per group. From among the rest of the children, I appointed one child per group as group-leader. The group-leader had to ensure that all children in their group were trying to read the story sheet given to them. The group-leader also had to see whether they were able to read and understand or not, and prompt them where required. I could see some improvement in the four children, as they were able to identify 4–5 new words. A challenge that was faced in this peer-learning method was that though the group-leaders were trying to teach by making other children repeat the story several times, they were not able to learn and often did not pay attention to their leader.

To make it more interesting, I tried teaching through activity or games.

Passing the parcel game – I made a ball by rolling up several sheets of paper. Each layer of paper had one word written on it. Children sat in a circle and passed it around with music. They stopped passing when the music stopped and the child with the ball had to unwrap the topmost layer, read out (hence identify) and enact (hence know the meaning of) the word written. If a child could not do it, other children could help. This game, although it proved useful, could not be played often because of lack of proper music system. I was often playing music through my mobile phone.

- ***Key observations*** – Peer-learning and *passing the parcel* game were useful to some extent because the four children identified some new words. As I have described above, each method had some challenge.

Identifying and listing out alternative approaches to deal with the situation

- By drilling method – Traditional method of memorising (rote-learning) words and stories
- By peer learning – Children working in groups with children working as mentors of other children, as described above
- By word with picture – Children were given cards with pictures instead of only words so that they will be able to use them in sentences (described in detail below).

Identifying best possible approach

- By word with picture – This approach as well as a peer-learning approach were suggested by my colleagues. I discarded the drill method because it is now understood that it is not an effective method for teaching–learning. I felt that peer-learning could also be a good approach and so I tried that too. I encountered challenges of ability of group-leaders to manage other children and to help them understand. Hence, I found 'Word with Picture' to be the best possible approach. Another advantage of this approach was that it would deal with the competency of not just identifying and understanding a word, but also that of using it meaningfully in a sentence. Also, children would try to learn on their own without help and those facing problems with reading and writing would be able to use pictures to relate to words.

4. Developing Strategy to Implement Identified Approach

Developing a plan to implement the strategy

- I would first select some words that children should understand and use. I would prepare cards with one word per card. Also, I would prepare another set of cards which will not have the written word but will have a picture of the thing that the word depicts. I would also prepare cards with words like *this, that, a, an, the, is, they* etc.
- I decided to focus on some words that depict objects like *bat, tree, bag, frock, cat* etc. and focus on *colours*. Also, singular and plural forms will be used.
- I decided to see if children are using the word cards or picture cards and allowed them to use picture cards at first, but later encouraged the use of word cards.
- I expected this activity to take about two weeks.
- As possible outcomes, I hoped that children would begin to recognise some specific new words. They would also know the meanings of those words and be able to use them in sentences. Familiarity with these words (which occur in stories in the textbook) would help children read and understand those stories more easily.

5. Implementing the Identified Approach

Implementing the approach as per plan

I made the cards, and in class, randomly assigned the cards to pre-decided groups of children. I asked the groups to form sentences using the words and pictures on cards. Then each child had to write the sentence in his/her notebook.

I found that children tried to use as many pictures as possible and formed several sentences with the cards. While writing these sentences in their notebooks, different children used different styles – at first, most children drew pictures of objects instead of using their written words. For example – Those are 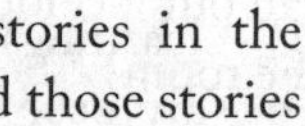 (For – Those are *three trees*). This is a (For – This is a *purse*). Then, I told them that they should also start writing the words. After that, I could clearly see three different formats emerging, with different children following different formats – For example, for the sentence – 'This is a bat', a picture-card for bat was available but not a word-card.

While writing in their notebooks, some children wrote 'this is a' and drew the picture of bat, some wrote the complete sentence 'this is a bat' and did not draw the picture, while some wrote the complete sentence and also drew the picture.

After writing the sentences, I asked some children from each group to read out the sentences. I observed that, while reading, all children were reading out the complete sentence properly i.e. *These are three trees, this is a purse,* etc.

I repeated the activity in several classes over a month (only a few English classes were scheduled per week). The four children took longer than others to start using words instead of pictures, or along with pictures. They often had to be prompted by me.

After that, another set of words were added. These were colours. First, I carried out an assessment (through a reading exercise) where I found that children could read the names of 2–3 colours which were introduced in the previous story. I chose some basic colours and used 'Ring toy' and 'Tippy Tippy Top' games to familiarise children with names of these colours. (In 'Tippy Tippy Top', one child has to call out a colour and others have to touch an object of that colour in the room). Then, moving to the written word for each colour, I wrote out the names on the board. Children had to copy that in their notebooks and make a circle next to each name and fill it with the corresponding colour. The next day, the 'Sentence Formation' activity with word-cards was repeated, where children had to also use names of colours. For example – One __ bat 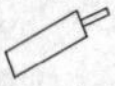. Two __ trees .

To take the reading competency further, I wrote ten sentences on the board using the same words as those given in the cards, and asked children to read these aloud. Out of the four children in action research, one had 50% correct answers and one had 20%. Since one was absent during the activity, that child could not answer correctly and the remaining one did not get a chance to answer. (When this activity was repeated later, I noted that this child also answered about 50% correctly).

6. Reflections of Teacher on the Processes

I found that all children were more excited about using cards which had pictures on them, even if they also had a word-card with the same word. Hence, pictures attracted children more, as it was new, and hence more interesting – to work with.

The children also found the activity of filling the right colour next to the name of colour very interesting. Hence, I learnt that if children take interest in activities, they will pay more attention to learning and will be able to learn.

The process was quite effective even though learning was not 100%. I think the process was effective because children took a lot of interest in doing it and hence remained engaged. Also, I can see that learning is taking place in this way and only more practice and repetition is required to make them learn better.

Though the process took longer than expected, I do not feel it was a loss or a time-consuming activity because at least the children were able to learn something that they had not been able to learn earlier. Also, the activity took longer because of lack of regular English classes with the children.

Classroom Observation

Shipra started the class by asking the children about something that she had asked them to bring. After that, she asked them to sing a particular poem. She sang along with them for a while and then let them complete it and repeat once more. While they were singing, the teacher prepared for the day's activity, taking out some sheets of paper from the cupboard and sorting them. Then she asked them to sing another poem. This time, she led and the children repeated after her. She also performed actions to suit the poem.

After this, the teacher asked them to sit in their groups. The children knew which group they belonged to. The class had previously been divided into four groups and a chart with names of children of each group was glued to the wall of the classroom. The children also knew that they had to rearrange their desks and sit in their own groups. Once all the children had settled down, she started the activity for 'Sentence Formation'. She distributed several cards to each group. Some of these cards had words written on them – *he, they, thirsty, is, two, many, hungry*, etc. Other cards had pictures – two cats, a bat, purse, trees, etc. Children had to use these cards to form sentences.

They could use any number of words or pictures or both, to form sentences, and then write them down in their notebooks.

While the groups were working, the teacher moved around the class, listening to each group. Occasionally she would ask a specific child to add a word to half a sentence, or check whether or not a child was writing in his notebook. Children would ask her the meaning of some word, or whether the sentence they had formed was correct or not. A child asked the meaning of 'Those'. Another confirmed that the word he was pronouncing as 'hoongry' was actually 'hungry'. Another child could not read the word 'thirsty' and asked the teacher to say what the word was. The teacher was also trying to focus on discipline. She pointed out to specific children and asked them to pay attention. She also said that children had to settle down and become quiet within the count of three.

It could be seen that children were writing the sentences in their notebooks in different ways. Three variants could be seen. For example, for the sentence – '***This is a bat***', the picture card for bat was available and not a word card. While writing in their notebooks, some children wrote 'this is a' and drew the picture of bat, some wrote the complete sentence 'this is a bat' and did not draw the picture, while some wrote the complete sentence and also drew the picture. While moving around in the class and looking at their notebooks, the teacher repeated a couple of times that the children should also make sure that they write down the word and not just draw the picture.

At the end of the activity, two children from each group had to say out aloud one sentence formed by the group. The teacher pointed to specific children from each group to come up and present. One child shared the sentence – 'This is green trees'. The teacher corrected the group by saying that it should be '***These are*** green trees', because there is more than one tree in the picture card. Other examples of phrases and sentences made by the children are

- This is blue bat.
- They are cats.
- I am hungry.
- One red colour bat.
- Two blue colour cups.
- They are rich.
- This is black brush.

From a Facilitator's Diary...

Vartul Dhaundiyal and Ambika Mohan, September 2013

Before Going to the School

The main worry was whether we would be able to effectively answer queries and provide the support needed by the teachers. Also, how satisfactory would the discussions be for both the teachers and our team? Though we knew that we could call the other team members for their suggestions or discuss things with them later, it is always a good practice to respond at the time itself, so that further discussion may take place.

Another apprehension was whether we had been able to ensure that teachers were really interested in this work and were not doing it under pressure, and to make sure this continued.

Also, we wondered whether teachers would have been able to carry on successfully with their action research.

Since teachers had seemed enthusiastic in the previous visit and had already identified topics that they wanted to work on, we were looking forward to discussing what further work they had done and what thoughts they had.

At the School

We were able to discuss in detail specific points of action research with all the teachers. They had done quite a bit of work and importantly, had also documented it. This was quite useful.

Some teachers had been able to do quite a bit of work – implementing a planned strategy and even collecting pieces of evidence. They seem to be nearing the completion of one cycle of action research.

When we started discussions with individual teachers, a couple of teachers said that they were eagerly waiting for us and looking forward to discussing their work. This was very encouraging. Also, some of them proactively asked for our phone numbers. They said that they would like to be able to call us if they were stuck at some point.

We were unable to have any discussion with the teacher whose problem related to History, due to lack of time. We found this challenging because he was excitedly waiting to have a discussion and start some work.

Memorable Images

Seeing one of the teachers working with a child very devotedly, after other children had left, was quite memorable. This interaction was important for two reasons. One was that we got to know this child a little more. Two or three teachers had talked about this child when discussing their problems. Hence, we ourselves wanted to understand it better. The second was the way the teacher worked with the child. He had planned what he wanted to do and patiently worked with her, trying to coax her to say at least something by asking simple questions related to her family, her likes and dislikes.

One of the teachers told us that she will not be continuing her action research. She said that she was not really facing any problem. She added that she anyway writes her weekly reflections and discusses it at team meetings. This is adequate for now. We did not try to persuade her to continue or to use her weekly diary for discussing reflections with us, and just reassured her that she need not continue if she has not identified an area for action research now. This too was a significant event during this visit.

The problem of explaining the concept of vision to children, and the discussion we had on it was very interesting. Although a good strategy to deal with it could not be identified, the way in which the problem had emerged and its documentation were interesting. We also learnt about how children think, and make connections with what they hear.

Overall Updates on Teachers

All participating teachers have identified their problems, except one (on History, though it seems that he has some ideas in mind but needs help to articulate it as an action research problem). Some of the topics were further refined to make them clearer or specific. They have also identified one strategy each that they want to implement. (Hence the 'Plan' stage seems to be covered. When discussing steps of action research, it was highlighted that they could all also identify other possible strategies and then justify why they had chosen the one that they did). Most teachers are now at the 'Act' stage and in the process of implementing their strategy. (Again, while discussing 'Act' and 'Observe' components of the steps, teachers were encouraged to list the indicators that they want to work on. This will be useful to collect evidence). Most teachers are documenting their work simultaneously. Some of them sought guidance on how to go about this. This was discussed individually and also with the group.

Documentation

Teachers were encouraged to share their documents with each other so that everyone could get ideas for their own documents. We also suggested that they could discuss their documentation with each other at their Saturday meetings. There was also a discussion about video documentation, its advantages and disadvantages as compared to written documents.

Steps of Action Research

A 15-minute recap on action research steps was done. The teachers were able to tally the steps with what they had covered and what was left to do to complete one cycle.

Telecon (telephone conference): We suggested that we could also be in touch with the teachers on the phone. Deepak said that the AR team needs to initiate it and on their side there is no problem in attending a telecon but it must be after school hours. We also said that the teachers may attend these if they are interested.

3. Teaching Children 'How We See'

Name of Teacher: Deepak Dixit

Educational Qualifications: MSc, MBA and BEd

Name of Facilitator associated with Teacher: Aanchal Chomal

Action Research Problem: To enable children of Class VI to understand the process of vision, through scientific enquiry and verification

Identification of Problem: Students had a host of unexamined ideas about the process of vision that they had acquired from films, elders in the family, etc. They had simply accepted these ideas.

Analysis of Problem: Except for two children, all the others in class had strongly held misconceptions about the process of vision.

Identification of Alternative Approaches: Reading, discussion, showing video clips, explaining the anatomy of the eye and debating were identified as likely strategies to address this issue.

Implementation of Identified Approach: The best possible approach which I identified was to have students engage in small group discussions, where students with an opinion would convince others holding an opposing view. This discussion was to be based ONLY on verifiable scientific facts and experiences.

Review and Reflection: The process was quite effective even though learning of children was not 100%.

Thirty-nine year-old Deepak Dixit is the Principal of Azim Premji School, Dineshpur. He has sixteen years of teaching experience.

Spurred to becoming a teacher because of the ineffectiveness of his own school teachers, he nevertheless succumbed to family pressure to do an MBA. However, he returned to teaching after trying a corporate job for a while.

As the Principal of the school, he does not take on a full teaching load, but usually teaches for about three periods in a day – either Physics or Math, in both of which he occasionally co-teaches. He spends the rest of his time in administrative work, planning with the teachers, chairing and attending meetings, responding to e-mail, etc.

He notes with pride that there is a noticeable change in the children of his school as compared to when they first joined. 'I don't know of many schools where a student of class 5 or 6 would dare tell the Principal that he is wrong. Here they do it with ease!'

He believes that nature has not created a single useless thing, and wonders how 'the best creation – a human being – NOT be gifted?' He holds that an educator's role is to help each person open the 'gift box' which he/she is carrying and enable them to see how this set of skills can help him/her! He himself had a flair for patterns as a student but he feels that nobody helped him develop this and he did not want his students to suffer the same fate.

The best part of being a teacher, according to Deepak, is the enormous amount of satisfaction that this work can give: 'When I have transacted a topic effectively – that is the most rewarding thing. To this day, when I get an e-mail from any of my ex-students expressing their satisfaction – it gives me a feeling of achievement.'

When asked to recount any lesson that he taught well to his students, he retorts that he would rather recall something that *they taught him*! 'The first thing is that I really don't believe that anyone can teach, but I do hold that everyone can learn. Starting the class with the words *I am not going to teach you anything – because I am still learning. I am here just to help you learn and that, too, because I may have a bit more experience than you have (but that is also doubtful)* proved fruitful. After every class, I would – without exaggeration – come out with some new learning.' He regards two qualities as being critical for a good teacher: 'Patience and trust: teachers don't trust the capability of students and therefore, seldom permit them to explore different possibilities. They don't have the patience to wait for the students' inputs.'

His response to a question about when children perform best

is interesting as it is thought-provoking: '*Perform better* means…? Everyone always gives his 100%. To the teacher it may not be so, but from a child's point of view he always gives his best. No one ever wants to underperform.' Deepak is of the view that children learn best when their interest is provoked and they are able to relate the content that is being taught to their own daily life. Surprisingly, they do NOT learn when they are bound by a fixed time constraint, or they are under pressure or when the topic is below/above their level.

He recalls with wonder how the manner in which children, on their own, pointed out to him that 2 × 6 and 6 × 2 are the same. 'The understanding of present-day school children is definitely useful to all of us as it helps us to create a new syllabus, pedagogy, value system, and we realise that there are so many things which we still continue to use that are outdated in the present context.'

Classroom Interaction

Deepak undertook action research when he was asked by a teacher to join him in explaining transparent, translucent and opaque objects to students of Class VI. In his own documentation about this class, he describes how he found rich ground for an action research problem. He records with honesty the dilemmas he faced and the dead end he saw himself in. The rest of the story is described in his structured documentation in the action research document.

Deepak took pains to talk individually to several children and find out exactly what caused them to change their initial beliefs about the process of vision (that light flowed out of one's eyes). 'Did you feel you had an incorrect understanding earlier? Or do you now feel that what you had believed all along was actually correct?' he asked. Upon receiving the answer from a girl that she is now convinced that her earlier belief was wrong, he probed further to find out exactly how she had reached this state of conviction.

'Did you do an experiment? What convinced you to change your mind? How do you now claim that light does *not* flow out of our eyes?'

'There is no machine which we can use to detect whether or not light is flowing out of our eyes,' admitted the girl, after some thought.

'Then is there anything you can suggest that we can do to *actually verify* whether or not light is coming out of our eyes?' persisted Deepak. Seeing the silence of the girl, he changed track, and asked: 'Suppose you had to convince your younger sister that light does NOT flow out of our eyes so as to enable us to see things. What could you do to convince her?' After a pause, during which she seemed to be thinking hard, the girl replied: 'I would first tell her about the various sources of light. Then, I would tell her that light from these sources falls on objects and that is how we see them. And if we could see due to light flowing out of our own eyes, then even in a pitch dark room, we should be able to see things, as the light from our eyes should fall on objects enabling us to see them. But this doesn't happen – so obviously, light does not flow out of our eyes.'

Persisting, Deepak asked: 'But have *you* ever tried this? Have you ever turned off all the lights in a room at night, and tried seeing objects?'

'Yes, I have tried to do this,' replied the girl, 'but I could not see a thing.'

Note: In place of a Classroom Observation for Deepak Dixit, his own documentation of his classes follows.

HOW DO WE SEE?' THROUGH THE EYES OF CHILDREN BY **DEEPAK DIXIT**

Day 1

Monday, 29 July 2013

Today, I had the third period with class VI and the topic was to introduce transparent, translucent and opaque objects. I was a co-teacher with Mrs. Shakuntala. The class started with our assumption that the students had some exposure to these terms as they had already been discussed by the chemistry teacher, Mr. Mohit Sharma, and he had told us that the students were familiar with these three terms. So we were quite relaxed. The class began with our asking for examples, prior to which they were asked to state the definitions – as they have understood from their previous classes. The students came up with the definition of transparent as 'the objects through which we can see clearly.' Examples were air, glass, filter (net), mirror, sari, etc... The next one was opaque and its definition was given as 'the objects through which we can't see'. Examples were house, stone, brick, paper, book, mirror, iron, metal, etc. and for the translucent category the definition was 'the objects through which we can see partially'. Examples were 'butter paper, oil paper, dirty water and fog/cloud.'

Listening to the above discussion, I was a bit disturbed, as the baseline of their definitions was clearly shaky, being based totally on vision and not on the property of transmission of light. So I thought, if this is how they have understood the optical property of the substance, they need to be checked on their understanding of vision. I wanted to know what the students thought about vision. To formulate it simply, I asked them to explain how they see things. Everyone was ready to state his/her own understanding of how (s)he was able to see anything. I sensed that they were certain they knew this because it is something which seems so obvious, that hardly anyone ever thinks about the depth of the process that is involved in the transfer of an external body to our own field of perception (vision). Many interesting points with examples came up, and as the question was asked, I invited the students to answer one at a time.

First, J (names withheld for confidentiality) said: 'I know, light from our eyes moves out to the object, falls on it and this is how we are able to see that particular thing.' So this was considered as one point with which others could either agree or disagree.

V said that she disagrees with J, as in her opinion, 'some light from our eyes travels towards the surface and then it returns to our eyes, which enables us to see the object.'

Further, there were some students in the class who didn't agree with either of these viewpoints, but said that these two theories are incorrect. Instead, they proposed that 'Nothing goes out, only the outer light enters into the eyes.' This was P's point of view.

So I called for a vote after counterchecking that there was no other point of view in the class. Now the condition was that each student had to either support one of the three groups or state their own theory (if they had any). They were also free to say that they don't have any idea. So leaving all three choices open, I asked them, one after the other, what their stand was. Of 27 students who were present (out of a total of 29), 6 were in support of J, 18 students were in favour of V, and the remaining 3 supported P.

Next I asked them how they knew that there is light in the eyes. I asked this of the group who said that the eyes emit light and also of those who said that there is a two-way process for vision. Here, the entire class had the same idea despite differences in the approaches to the process of vision. In this respect, the unifying idea was that they believed there was a *mani* (मणि) or gem in the human eyes.

Here I feel that the mistake is not theirs, as it was very clearly pointed out by many of the students that they have heard their elders say, when a person has lost his vision, 'उसकी आंखों की रोशनी चली गई है।' This very clearly meant that there is some light in the eyes which has been lost. They had picked up this idea from proverbs and phrases in Hindi. When I thought about this, I too found that many idioms in Hindi such as 'आंखों का तारा' and 'आंखों का नूर' clearly indicate that the eyes have some inbuilt source of light. It's a myth that is repeated all the time!

Now my basic problem is how I help the students arrive at the correct conclusion. Right now, I have no idea how I am going to take it forward; I know that one day (sooner or later) they will explore it on their own. But as Newton said 'Nothing moves on its own', so I think I will need to push them.

How? That is what I have to think about now.

Day Two

Tuesday, 30 July 2013

I was finishing the monthly report for the month of July as it was to be dispatched by this evening and was a bit busy collecting the data and photographs, and typing them. At this time, Mrs. Shakuntala stepped in and told me that the entire class was asking for me (as I am the co-teacher with her). This came to me as a surprise, because they had never done so before. I was also excited as now it had become my responsibility to take their interest forward (since I knew why they were calling *me*). I was also excited because last night, I planned my next set of actions, and was eager to implement it. The intent was to inquire about the *mani* factor, by conducting interviews. I was also aware that because of this, the class should not lose sight of the main topic, transparent, translucent and opaque substances. Keeping a balance was important. To my delight, I found that everyone was painted by a brush stroke in the hue of PHYSICS – this *colour* is impossible to define in terms of frequency, wavelength and other characteristics, but it resembles something like excitement, enthusiasm and everyone chattering in class *only about vision*, 'How, what, who told you, and how does he know it?' such questions were heard.

I knew it was time to strike while the iron was hot. But before I could have asked them anything, they started asking, 'Who was right?' I told them that everyone was correct, because they told me what they knew or felt, and since it was their observation, I was not the one to judge it. 'No, what we mean is, which group was correct?' While this was being asked, I noticed V (who earlier had given the theory that light goes out from the eyes and in turn, some light from outside enters into the eyes) was quiet. So I left their question unanswered and asked her what happened. 'Why are you so quiet?' She said '*I know that I was wrong*' and as she admitted this, I could clearly see a lack of conviction in her admission.

'How? How do you know it?' I asked her.

'My father told me.' (Her father is a doctor.)

'OK, that may be so, but how do *you* see it? That's what really matters!' I countered.

She said that she still believed that what she had said was correct, but since she trusts her father and he is educated, what he has told her may be the only truth.

I let that rest. Now all the other students started asking the same question, 'Which group was correct?'

I said, 'I don't know.'

'But how you can say this?'

I tried to explain, but before I could, they came up with the logic that I must have learned it during my own schooldays. I told them that what I had learned should not become a barrier for *them* to think, and not everything is written in the books; there are certain things which we have to think about and develop our own understanding about. Had it not been so, I pointed out, no new invention or discoveries would have been possible, because then everyone would have looked into books for the final verdict.

Then I pointed to V and said: 'Science is always changing, and that's the nature of the subject. If something doesn't change its not Science, it's History (in my understanding), because history won't ever change – what has happened has happened. If Gandhiji was born on 2nd of October, that will never change to 31st of December. But what was correct a couple of years ago in Science may not be the same for the generations to come. These changes may or may not be visible in our lifespan, but they can always be challenged. So whatever your father said, it's you who need to analyse and check, and build your own understanding. I don't want to say we should not trust our elders, but, you must adopt a scientific approach to keep your understanding alive. Otherwise it is others' understanding that is running through you.'

I don't know how far they understood this, but they were mesmerised. So I came back to my point to ask about the *mani*. I anticipated that there would at least be a couple of answers and was ready to note them down. But to my surprise, all the answers were the same. The entire class had a common understanding of the term *mani* – 'It's something which is very shiny; it's at the center of the eye.'

'But can we see it or have you seen it or just heard about it from someone?' I asked.

'We have seen it.'

'Can you help me to see it?'

'Yes!' the class said. 'If you stand in front of a mirror and look very carefully at the center of your eye (inside the black circle) you will still see a smaller shinier object, it looks like glass, it is black in colour. It looks different from the outer black circle…' and thus, they went on explaining.

Now V was also looking relaxed and was discussing the topic with others. I said 'Ah, I have also seen it, so that's the *mani*!'

'Yes!' they all replied.

'OK…it may be so, but we need to check it in the class, and think about something which can prove the point that you made yesterday – or the point to which you agreed yesterday. We will share our findings, experiences and demonstrations in the class on Friday. Will this time be enough?'

'Yes!' the class said.

'OK,' I said, and so we resumed our topic of transparent, translucent and opaque objects. I gave them a task: think about the behaviour of light that falls on a surface. What all could possibly happen to light? The class was divided into five groups (red, green, orange, blue); every group member was asked to present his/her idea. The entire class came up with three basic scenarios:

1. when light can pass through the substance.
2. when light can't pass through the substance.
3. when some of the light could pass through the substance.

We didn't have any names for these categories. I suggested that we play a game wherein I will write on the board names of some objects; they need to analyse them, based on their statements, as 1, 2 or 3.

'You will get one point if you guessed it right; if others could counter your arguments and if it's acceptable to the rest of the class they will get +2. If it's not agreed to, by the rest of the class, they will get –1. Simple rule: none of us will be winner or loser. It's just for fun.'

Amidst much excitement, the game started, and I first wrote *air* and the red group said 1. None of the groups came forward to counter this, 'So it means that we all agree with this?' I checked.

'Yes!' came the resounding answer.

'OK, so we move to the next one: *water*.'

Again, the red group said 1, but this time, the blue group came up with a point that it's not always 1; it could be 2 or even 3. This was a surprise for the rest of the groups because during their chemistry classes, they have seen it as a clear, transparent object and I think they were also told this by the teacher (I need to check with the teacher). Interestingly, the supporting argument that the blue group gave was based on their daily observation from their surroundings. They asked, 'How about the pond water these days (in the monsoon)?' Additionally, Shakuntala asked: 'Where will you slot *ditch water*? Will you not accept it as water?' The others agreed to this, and they got +2. By now, other groups also realised that transparency depends on the level of purity, so they said that in the case of air too this should be valid.

I was confused not just because I couldn't decide whom to give points to, but because the speed at which they learned this concept was in sharp contrast to the many years that it had taken me to grasp these ideas. Now there was a race for judging *everything* based on this parameter!

The next object was *paper* for which one group (green) said it is 2 whereas the orange group said it was No. 3. Several supporting arguments were advanced but no one was ready to give up their stand.

So I stepped in and said 'OK, we will see this in the class.'

I then brought an A4 sheet of paper and kept it against the light and kept my fingers behind the sheet. Then I asked the class, 'Can you see my fingers? How many are they?' They were able to count and answered correctly. The next thing I did was to add 20–25 sheets of paper and repeat the same exercise to which they replied 'No we can't see through these'. They still didn't say that light can't pass through it, but that's OK.

Discussion immediately erupted across the class. This was the end of the period.

Day 3

Monday, 5 August 2013

The class was unable to find the answer to the question and was also held up. Today the topic of transparent, translucent and opaque continued as there was a basic shift in the level of understanding of the class from the previous definition where they had said that the 'transparent objects are the objects through which we can see', to 'transparent objects are the objects which allow the light to pass through them' (Here the direction of the light is still under question). 'Allow the light to pass through them partially' or 'do not allow any light to pass through them' were the corresponding shifts for translucent and opaque objects.

I am happy with this transformation. I don't recall, in my own experience, making a distinction between these two definitions at any time. What I can recall is that I just memorised the definition and kept on reciting it as and when asked. I feel that now I understand the difference between the two, although to many people they may still seem the same. Still, I am unable to bring the whole thing onto a platform so that the students may see the entire process clearly.

What should be done? Since last week, I have a feeling that I need to interview the students separately, so that the idea of one student may not influence the other. Though in the class they all have discussed this issue many times, I still have a feeling that it may suggest to me the direction to work in. So I said 'I would like to talk to all of you but individually, and not in class.'

This was quite a difficult task as it took a lot of time, but there were many things that I got from the children. A, who was a supporter of J (the child who had said that the light moves out from the eye, falls on the object and that is how we are able to see the objects) said 'I know for sure that light is in our eyes because my uncle who is blind now told me, and even my mother confirmed it.'

I was surprised, so I asked: 'What did they tell you? and how do they know it?'

He told me the story that a couple of years ago, they had had a land dispute in his family. His uncle who was involved in it and till that time was OK lost his sight during a fight when he got hit with a stick over his head.'

'सिर पर चोट लगने की वजह से उनकी आंखो की रोशनी चली गई। मम्मी और मामा दोनों यही बोलते है।'

(Translation: Because he got hit on the head, 'the light went out of his eyes'. That is what both my mother and uncle say.)

It seems very clear that his belief is based upon the sound rationale, that only if something is present can it be lost. Otherwise, they would have said something inside the eyes was damaged.

One of the students, PB, who supported V, said during the interview that there is sufficient amount of light in our eyes and she had seen it too. 'During a dark night you can also see the eyes of the cat; they shine like fire.'

I asked her: 'But what about our eyes? Why don't they shine?'

She had a very strange theory behind this, she said: 'In meat there are certain things (whose names she didn't know) which gives light to the eyes. So all the carnivorous (this term is mine; she said *meat eaters*) animals have shiny eyes. Cows and other (herbivorous) animals don't have these, because they eat grass.'

Some of the others who had said that nothing goes out from the eyes (like P) had no clue as to why they had said so. I was more interested in talking to the students who had come up with the idea of light as an external factor and who suggested that it enters into the eyes. I discovered that they too had no clue as to why they had said so. Now I too was at a loss as to what to do to enable them to get the right idea on their own.

I have to think. But the thought that I had needs to be discussed with someone. Will it be advisable to tell them about the anatomy of the human eye? This is not included in their syllabus. My personal feeling is that the human mind is quite capable of understanding much more then we expect it to. Maybe the problem is from our side – we don't give knowledge freely or hesitate to give it. On the other hand, my idea is not to impart the knowledge: I am working on the creation of knowledge.

How do I push them in the right direction? Here too, I have a doubt that what we believe is correct now may not be the absolute truth, so who knows? This may just be one of the most commonly believed facts, based on the tiny amount of knowledge that the human race currently has.

I feel totally stuck and at a dead end because without the proper understanding of prior concepts, how can they reach a final conclusion? And even if they do so, it will be just an assumption. It's not as easy as I had initially thought it would be…

Conclusion

After a long struggle and discussion with many people, I decided on the path that I would take. I understood that there is no point in describing everything to the class, as it may be beyond their understanding. The better option is to enable them to create knowledge on their own. So I decided to ask the class to form groups and ask them to discuss the issue and help others in the group to understand the concept. So each group consisted of students with differing thoughts. Now the task was for each to convince the others in the group of their idea, based on everyday experiences. There was no place for statements like: 'I know it!' Or 'My father told me …' etc.

This worked, as most of the students had similar experiences in their day-to-day life. They discussed the following points:

- Can you see anything if it's absolutely dark?
- How about standing in front of a mirror in the dark? Can we see the mirror itself?
- If there is no light and you say that the light comes out from the eyes, how can it be dark at any place?
- Can we see light?
- Do we see the light or the *objects* because of the light?

These were some of the questions I heard as I monitored the groups' discussions.

Now I realised that students do have the potential to observe and explain their findings to their friends in simple language. Our duty is just to give them the chance and opportunity to engage in the discussion.

That's all. The rest of the things will be sorted out on their own. Mostly.

Action Research (AR) Document – By Deepak Dixit

AR Topic: To enable learners of Class VI in the creation of knowledge using a scientific approach to understand the process of vision.

1. Identifying the Problem
Listing out problems faced • Students of Class VI had vague ideas about vision – they were confused as to whether light travelled from outside into the eyes or from the eyes to the outside. Some beliefs which they held,

such as losing one's vision is like losing light from one's eyes, led children to believe that light is inside the eyes. Some had also internalised what they had seen in movies – they recounted that sometimes, when people turn blind in movies, two flames travel from the universe and reach/enter the person's eyes, which means that light travels from an outside source and enters the eyes.

2. Analysing the Problem

Detailing the problem
Except for two students, the rest of the class had such misconceptions.
Key observations – Most of the students had their own views regarding vision (like light comes out of the eyes and falls on the objects, which enables us to see these objects) – and were not willing to give up their stand, though they looked confused when they entered into a debate with others. There were gaps in their arguments, and topics like physical bodies and theories about light were missing. The students were able to identify the objects from their surroundings but couldn't name the three things (source of light, object, and eyes focused on the object) needed for vision. The understanding of the fact that if any of the three is missing we cannot see things was absent.

Efforts made by the teacher to tackle the challenge –
I held formal as well as informal discussions with the children. A platform for discussion was provided to children by raising questions in a logical manner. The discussion revolved around their current beliefs and some scientific facts. Questions asked were –

- How do we see objects?
- What could possibly be happening to light as it falls on an object?

3. Identifying Alternative Approaches

Possible alternative approaches were:

- Get the children to read from library books where the topic of vision has been discussed in detail
- Provide them with other suitable reading material
- Explain the anatomy of the human eye
- Show suitable video clips
- Hold small group discussions

Identifying the best possible approach

- The best possible approach that I identified was to engage in discussion in small groups, where students with a certain opinion would convince others who held an opposing view. This discussion was to be based **only** on scientific facts and experiences.
- Other approaches like reading, or explaining the anatomy of the human eye or showing them a video clip etc. were discarded as they would end up as yet another piece of information to the child.
- Small group discussions, on the contrary, would allow them to express their views and argue their point. I was convinced of the value of this approach, as students could validate their ideas or seek validations of their ideas through active participation.

4. Developing Strategy to Implement Identified Approach

Developing a plan to implement the strategy

- I would ask the questions in a systematic manner
  - Can we see the objects in a dark room?
  - Do we see the light coming out from anyone's eyes in the dark?
- The students would discuss the above based on their experience and then would try to convince others in their group.
- They would experiment at home during the night.
- They would benefit from peer-learning and sharing of experiences.
- Approximately 2–3 weeks would be ideal to analyse problem.
- *Hypothesis: The students will discover that there is no light coming out from the eyes; they may also end up understanding other connected things.*

5. Implementing the Identified Approach

Implementation of the approach as per plan

- The class was split into small groups, each consisting of people with different views. Each child was asked to convince others, using experiences that they share. This discussion was closely monitored and in the next class, the students were asked if any one of them was convinced by the explanations given by their group members. The discussion was monitored by me. It was ensured that students stick to their arguments and do not digress from the topic. Scaffolding was provided to guide them towards the topic. Questions were asked as and when required, or were even reframed, as they were asked by the others in the group.

- Secondly, they were asked to perform some of the demonstrations at home, such as to observe in a dark room what was visible: could they see anything in a pitch dark room, standing in front of a mirror?

  It was observed that about 60% of the students began to understand what really causes one to see. Though the others came up with the same results, they still wanted to hold onto their earlier thoughts.
- On many occasions, I felt I was stuck, because students always came up with different answers which were based on some myths. e.g. *There is a mani in the eye. During the solar eclipse, a devil eats the sun* and many more.
- I could easily make out that there is a visible difference in the behaviour of the children, for instance, now they have started asking questions like: 'Why is light not visible?' and have started creating 'problems' in the History class. While dealing with the students in the History class, the teacher ran out of time and had to deviate from the schedule/plan, because the students have begun asking questions like: 'Why didn't King Ashok's son become King? Because you told us that the son of a king becomes King.' Indeed, they have started seeking the authenticity of evidence ... Many students ask 'Why should we study History? It is in the past, so there is no need for it.' Some of the students also questioned the teacher 'Why is the study of these kings needed? After all, they didn't do anything for us.'

6. Reflection of Teacher on the Processes

- The process was very effective as it helped me to understand how scientific temper could be developed in the students along with age-appropriate learning.
- The key learning from this action research was 'Children do have a lot of information, although this may be incorrect. This entire contribution is from the society where we all talk without thinking about the meaning that could be absorbed by the younger ones. On many occasions, we use some commonly used phrases like आंखों की रोशनी चली गई / आंखों का तारा (the light went out of the eyes, or star of my eye [the equivalent of 'apple of my eye']) but one must be careful to explain the correct meaning to the students.

- I will continue the work on the lines of creation of knowledge by the children. I will help them to explore all the dimensions of each thing. I will motivate the students to countercheck the details available to them.

7. Reflections of Facilitator on the Processes

a. *On the topic of the study:* It was evident from the choice of topic that the teacher was connected to the children of his school, despite being the Principal of that school and particularly wanted to work on a daily life concept as critical as 'What causes vision?'

b. *On the process and methodology adopted:* The teacher seemed to rationalise each and every approach and then select the best approach, again revealing his understanding of both the children and the problem at hand. Secondly, the process of dialogues and discussions with children, giving them complete freedom to discuss and share their experiences, was a meaningful strategy. Its impact was evident not only in the class on vision but on other classes as well.

c. *On the effects of the study:* While it is still too early to observe the effects of the study, the examples from the teacher regarding the history class clearly suggest three shifts in the classroom processes, which could be read as possible impact/effect of the study –
   - Children began to ask more questions of other subject teachers too.
   - They began to question the validity and authenticity of facts, which was particularly visible in the history class.
   - Other teachers in the school, in this case, the History teacher, began to reflect on their teaching methodology.

The teacher could continue with the same research objectives and try doing this process with another concept in science.

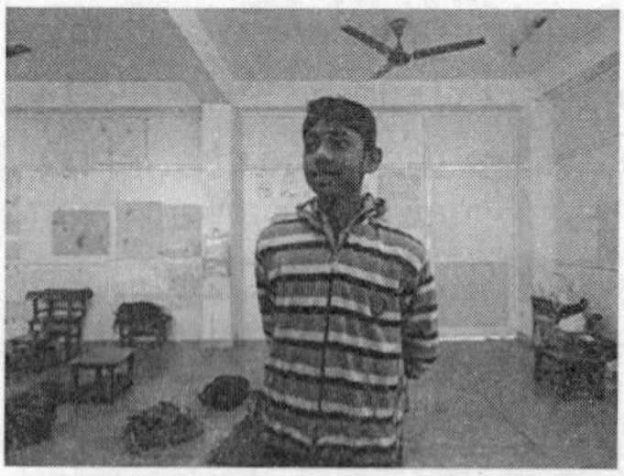

From a Facilitator's Diary

Tapasya Saha, September 2013

Before Going to the School

I am already acquainted with the background of the teachers and share a warm relationship with them since I had worked with them on two occasions, on account of Teacher Development workshops of Azim Premji School.

I am apprehensive in a different way; now, I would get a chance to know if the various training programmes that the teachers have participated in, during their stint in Azim Premji School in the past one and half years, have made any difference to their understanding of the teaching–learning process in the classroom, planning for teaching or even about how children learn.

Ambika's and Vartul's joint report mentions that the teachers are completing their first AR cycle. I am eager to know about the teacher's learning about their teaching, what they thought, why, which criteria they kept in mind while planning for the next cycle, etc. What about their energy and patience levels?

I am waiting to meet and talk to them to see:

1. how they are working towards their problems in the first AR cycle.
2. what their learning from their experience has been.
3. how their experience is informing their next step.

At the School

The teachers interacted well. They were eager to talk about their work. I felt Shipra has some kind of confusion about the objective and her planning; we will need to help her with these. Rakesh has a good AR topic but has not yet finalised his plans. Almost all the teachers were highly enthusiastic and many have completed the first cycle. I found them all eager to talk to me and had long discussions with all of them. The things that I enjoyed are:

1. Teachers waited to talk about their research.
2. Teachers themselves were changing their strategy and planning for their next cycle.

3. The school was hosting their first-ever exhibition, where all activities and arrangements were being done by the children.
4. Classroom observation was interesting. I noticed good planning by Saud and time was very well managed. I was struck by how he gave level-appropriate work to children. All students were visibly involved in their written work.

I had a long discussion with Shipra, at the end of which she understood that she had completed one cycle. Some teachers are confused about the process of documentation.

Memorable Images

- The energy of the children was very palpable in whatever they did. I learnt new things from them.
- Children can be guided to think logically: a nine-year-old boy of Class 4, could find the similarity of shape between a bird, fish, airplane and the boat he made; he could also guess why all these have such a shape.
- Shakuntala is such a delight to talk to when it's about her teaching Math. She would not rest till she has done some work even with the least interested ones. She has been successful to some extent with a girl of class IV.
- All teachers are beginning to write reflections in their lesson plan. (I think we must go through these reflections, to see if their concept of 'reflective writing' is correct).

4. Teaching Environmental Studies to Children Who Cannot Read and Write the Language

Name of Teacher: Mohit Sharma

Educational Qualifications: MSc, BEd

Name of Facilitator associated with teacher: Tapasya Saha

Action Research Problem: How to teach EVS (Environmental Studies) to children who are not able to read and write the language (Hindi)

Identification of Problem: These children did not have a major issue in understanding or speaking Hindi. Their problem was mainly in reading and writing Hindi.

Analysis of Problem: Five students of my class formed the sample of my AR study. These were the children who could not read or write in Hindi.

Identification of Alternative Approaches: I could either work with these children outside class hours or do something meaningful within the class that would allow them to learn easily.

Implementation of Identified Approach: I designed an activity to teach Animal Habitat, by incorporating it into my lesson plan, instead of doing this separately with the five children.

Review and Reflection: I found this activity had quite an impact, because all students got equal opportunity to learn. I involved every child, and this made them all feel united.

Twenty-five-year-old Mohit Sharma has been teaching for four years. He is comfortable teaching Chemistry till Class XII, Science till Class X and Sports to any class. He honestly admits that biotechnology was his career choice, yet he opted to become a teacher 'because I knew that I can't do much in the field of biotechnology. I wanted to get a job and picked teaching – later, I realised that I have a flair for teaching and I can do it well.' He now feels that he is doing some good, meaningful work that reinforces

his family traditions of patriotism, culture and social service. If he is now given an opportunity to switch careers, he doubts he would do anything else but teach. Yet, he does feel undervalued every now and then and that tends to disappoint him.

He likes interacting with people – and especially with children. When he sees children share their feelings and views with him without any hesitation or fear, it warms his heart. The biggest challenge for a teacher is that 'a teacher can't take her/his job lightly; (s)he has to provide equal opportunity to *all* students to learn.'

He thinks a friendly relationship with the teacher motivates them to learn and perform better, and he takes time to watch cartoons and play with his students. Mohit is gratified to see a shift in his class of learners: 'At the beginning of the year, many students were not able to write or express themselves but they are confident now. They can stand up and speak – express themselves.'

He has attended several workshops, undergone training in science pedagogy, and can recall a gene-cloning seminar that he attended.

He acknowledges several benefits from action research. Primarily, he recalls how 'earlier we would not do so many activities. There was

Changes observed by Mohit in children after conducting action research

- One of these four children answered a question that another asked: 'Where do we get butter from?'
- One of the AR sample study children said he had seen his mother extract butter from milk.
- And those I considered 'above average' children…they became quiet and these 'below average' children began speaking!
- What I liked best was that at least these children began observing and saying something…they can't write or read…but to observe and say something…this itself, for me, is a very good thing.
- I feel that it is something to do with observation. This child's brain opened up…he could be seeing other things, too….without doubt, but he never got the opportunity to express.

greater emphasis on writing or reading. Even if we did, the activity would be pitched at a higher level than was comfortable for these children.' Sometimes, he admits that he would even do something *separately* for them, suited to their level. 'I used to make a separate Lesson Plan for them.' This was because he used to think that these children may not understand the lesson of the day…' so I would teach them about trees and plants, even if I was teaching the rest of the class about sunlight and sound...I would lower my expectations from these children and say if they learnt about how food was made….it was more than enough for me.'

But when he embarked on action research, things changed. Now he wondered, why not do something which is *right for all of them*?

'Can't I do something through action research, such that *everyone gets an equal opportunity*?' Had he followed the 'old' ways, he would perhaps have said to them: *'You write and show me, okay*?'

Not surprisingly, this took a lot of planning and effort. Before embarking on a new classroom strategy, for instance, he admits to investing a lot of time and effort in winning the trust and increasing the confidence levels of the five children who were facing difficulties in the classroom. While implementing the selected strategy, he took special care to see that the five children did not feel different in any way from the rest of the class. He also ensured that every child got an equal opportunity to learn. 'In this, what I liked most was that they all *felt they were equal*.'

'So this is how I benefitted from action research,' he says, with a smile. 'I felt we were doing something different.'

Learnings after action research

- If a child does not participate verbally in class, it may not necessarily mean that (s)he does not know anything. It may just mean that (s)he lacks confidence.
- Somewhere, this could be our fault because we think that just because he can't write or read in the class, he doesn't know anything.
- When he felt confident and we asked that child, 'Did you see anything?' he raised his hand to respond. His raising the hand was a great thing for me because earlier he would never do so.
- The effect of this could be seen in other subjects also … like in Math. The report I have is that he has improved in every subject.
- So I felt that…yes…*because of confidence, something has truly changed.*

Action Research (AR) Document – By Mohit Sharma

Identified AR Problem: How to teach EVS to children who are not able to read and write the language (Hindi), by depending on the minimal number of competencies

1. Identifying the Problem
Listing out problems faced 1. The first problem was how to teach Hindi to children who were not Hindi-speaking, because language is fundamental to all learning. 2. The second problem was to explore the right assessment tools to evaluate the level of these children. 3. The third issue was to investigate how to bring children to more or less the same level, knowing that some children are not even able to understand the language. **Identification of one problem, which is most important** – Some children learn (EVS) quickly, while others take a long time to learn the same things, and these are found to be the very children who have difficulty in the language.
2. Analysing the Problem
Detailing the problem: Five students of my class formed the sample of AR study. These children could not read or write in Hindi. In class, I talked with these children at length about this. Further, my language teaching colleagues were doing substantial work with the same children to enhance their comprehension of the language. It turned out that these children did not have an issue in comprehending spoken Hindi as well as in speaking it. So the problem was mainly in reading and writing.
3. Identifying Alternative Approaches
I first thought that I could work with these children outside class hours, when I would address those issues while I was teaching in class. But the doubt in adopting this approach was that it could well lead to the children suspecting that they were in some way deficient compared to the others, and that was why they were being detained after class hours. I wanted to retain their newly built self-confidence, because I deemed this to be critical. Another approach could have been

that I do something meaningful within the class which would allow these children to learn easily. Then I began to work on an approach which would incorporate activities so as to teach these children.

4. Developing a Strategy to Implement Identified Approach

Keeping the lesson plan in mind, I began to devise activities. For this, I sought ideas from my colleagues as well as the Principal. I had to teach **Animal Habitat** to my class. After considerable thought, I designed an activity to teach this topic. I incorporated this into my lesson plan. I had designed this activity mainly for my sample of five children for AR study, but instead of doing this separately with them only, I felt it would be better to conduct it with the entire class. This would prevent the five children from feeling excluded or separate in any way from the rest.

Also, I had designed the activity in such a way that the assessment of the children happened simultaneously. Only through assessment of the children would I be able to gauge the effectiveness of this approach.

5. Implementing the Identified Approach

I had to transact the lesson plan, in which I had incorporated the activity. To make this activity interactive, I had asked the children to prepare the requisite materials, so as to bring in a sense of ownership amongst them. For this, I asked each child to bring five chits, each with a picture of an animal. At the beginning of this lesson, we spent two days discussing about the habitat of animals. Further, they were all asked to put forward their own observations. I ensured that those five children got a chance to

speak as well as to ask questions. All the students had not yet understood the concept, as indicated by their inadequate participation in the discussion. On the third day, all the children shared their observations. On the fourth day, I began to use the planned activity. As decided earlier, the entire class had to participate so I chose the school hall for transaction. I placed the chits prepared by the children in the centre of the hall. The entire class sat around the chits in a circle. I wrote the numbers 1, 2, 3, 4 on the walls of the hall, at a certain distance from each other. On the white board, I made an index for the children to consult during the activity (as given below).

 land	1	 water	2
 clouds (sky)	3	 land and water	4

After this, the students were instructed to come one at a time, and pick up a chit. By noting the animal on that chit, they were told to silently go and sit near the white board, at the number indicating the habitat of that animal, e.g. if they got the chit with the picture of a lion, they had to first think about the habitat of a lion, and accordingly sit near that number (1). In this manner, we began and one after another, the turn of the action research students came and four out of the five children sat in the right place. The student who did not sit in the right spot as per the indicated number, orally told us the right habitat. We did this activity twice more. All the action research children managed to identify the habitat of their animals correctly, and sit at the right spot. Two days after this activity, I assessed the children orally. They also had to draw pictures of two aquatic, two land animals, two which could fly in the air, and two amphibians. This was done satisfactorily by all.

6. Reflection of Teacher on the Process

I found this activity quite impactful, because all the students got an opportunity to learn. I involved every child, which made them all feel united. If we had done our work with the action research group separately, perhaps their self-confidence would not have reached this level. If some students cannot read and write some concept, that does not imply that they have not understood anything about that concept. They can observe and listen, so as to talk about and form an understanding of that concept. All that is needed is to give them a chance, because a child's mind is very sensitive. It has unbounded capability to learn. We only have to awaken their self-confidence and listen to their problems.

Classroom Observation

Mohit told the facilitator that today he is going to ask students to prepare a skit and ask questions on a chapter that he had recently taught.

Mohit greeted the class and said 'Today, we will revise the chapter ***Pedon ka Mahatv*** (***The Importance of Trees***).'

'You have to choose one of two options for the revision; you can choose to do a skit on the chapter or you may prepare questions on the chapter.'

All the students unanimously voted in favour of a skit. He divided the class into three groups such that there was a mix of boys and girls in every group. Mohit then instructed students that as they are all familiar with the chapter, they have to prepare the dialogues and characters themselves.

Children went out into the open space for preparation.

After 20 minutes, the class resumed and Mohit asked each group to present their skits, one by one. He added that while a group is presenting, other children should quietly watch the presentation and at the end of it, they can comment on the skit.

Presentations

The storyline of the skit revolved around a tree and the importance of trees for the ecosystem was the central theme. After every presentation, other students as well as the teacher gave their feedback on the play. After this, the teacher listed out all the benefits of trees as they had emerged in these three presentations. He then asked them to make drawings of the products that we get from trees, as homework.

From a Facilitator's Diary

Neeraja Raghavan, November 2013

Before Going to the School

I was apprehensive whether the teachers and Deepak would feel we had visited them too often or too little. I was also apprehensive about the state of their action research as I could only recall discussing the language problem over telephone, but had no idea about the others.

I was looking forward to meeting and video interviewing all of the teachers as well as Deepak. I was also looking forward to seeing the school in session, as the school was not in session during my previous visit.

At the School

I thoroughly enjoyed every minute of the visit. The teachers' response, their account of their work, the children…everything!

The communication gaps between facilitators and teachers is a challenge. While facilitators are of the view that they are maintaining fairly regular contact with teachers (which, of course, could be higher), teachers' expectations are not in alignment. I wish to understand this as we can improve upon our process when we upscale this study to other AP Schools. I also wish to ascertain that the Dehradun team, Aanchal, Tapasya and I, do not leave this study with any sense of incompleteness. I want to ensure free and open discussion among all the members. I hope that this will be possible.

Memorable Images

The animated faces of teachers talking about their AR work and how it helped them to think better, learn, and structure their thoughts, flash before me.

Some Other Points

I expect that we can make a film and write a book out of this work, and this will inspire others to undertake similar work. [Eight films were indeed produced based on this work, and are available with the Azim Premji Foundation.]

5. Enhancing Competency in Reading and Writing the Hindi Alphabet and Words

Names of Teachers: Narendra Joshi and Sahabuddin Ansari

Educational Qualifications:
Narendra Joshi: MA (Hindi, Sanskrit), BEd
Sahabuddin Ansari: MA (Political Science, Sociology and Education), BEd

Name of the Facilitator associated with the Teachers: Vartul Dhaundiyal

Action Research Problem: Some of the problems identified were inability to read the Hindi alphabet and words, lack of interest in learning and lack of self-confidence.

Identification of the Problem: The problem identified for research was to deal with lower than expected competency in reading and writing Hindi alphabet and words.

Analysis of the Problem: The children had varied abilities in reading and writing. Ten students each from Class V and VI were identified as those who were not able to recognise the alphabet and words. Extra classes were held for them after school.

Identification of Alternative Approaches: A combination of whole language and phonetic approach was used. But it did not deliver desired results. Therefore, only the whole language approach was adopted.

Implementation of the Identified Approach: Stories that were contextual for the children were used. The children were first introduced to the written story, then to reading sentences, and finally to identifying words. The Hindi alphabet was not introduced to them.

Reflections of the Teachers on the Process of Action Research: Children participate when meaningful content is transacted, and then learn. During the initial phase of learning, the teacher has to accept the mistakes that children make during reading and writing as this motivates them to do better.

Narendra Joshi and Sahabuddin Ansari are co-teaching Hindi to classes V and VI.

Narendra Joshi has an interesting story about how he came to be a teacher. He was not a studious sort (especially in Mathematics) and had no particular career in mind. Since his father was a *pandit* (priest), he too was sent for training in that field. But he felt that this work did not have dignity. He practised it for a while to earn money but left it in a short while. On a friend's suggestion, he completed his BEd and then started teaching in a private school in Dehradun, where he taught primary classes for some time. Later, he was given the responsibility of teaching classes IX and X. Ever since he joined Azim Premji School, he has been teaching Hindi to classes V and VI.

As a teacher, he aims to ensure that all children achieve the competencies required for that age group. One of the obstacles that he experiences while striving to achieve this goal is when he feels a need to think of several possible ways to bring those who lag behind others at par.

When a child shows progress and learns something after he makes special efforts, it boosts Narendra's confidence and keeps him motivated. To achieve his goal as a teacher, he says, 'I am trying to understand what is inhibiting a child from achieving his/her full capabilities. If extra time is required, I give that time to the child.'

He now likes the job because it is a noble profession and has a specific time schedule. But the most rewarding thing in the teaching profession for him is that this profession involves a lot of learning – both for children as well as the teacher. '*Apne* beliefs *bhi dhwast ho jaate hain*' (Our own beliefs get shattered).

He was earlier of the view that children will learn only when they are taught but he has now discovered that they can learn on their own too. He recalls an incident that has stayed with him. In a Hindi class, there were 4–5 children who were lagging behind and not participating at all. One day, the teacher was doing an activity with a song '*gaadi aayi*' (the train came) where one word changed each time and something just clicked. Somehow, by listening to the others, these children also caught on and started participating. They were able to insert new words and also read what was written. 'That day it felt like an achievement. I remember it because those children showed a lot of involvement and confidence.'

As a teacher, he finds social concerns a big challenge. 'You are dealing with society and at times it is difficult to satisfy everybody because they may have different expectations from a teacher. Students from all the communities come to us. We have to confront their different habits regarding hygiene and cleanliness, different levels of learning, etc.'

Narendra is of the view that children need appreciation of their work in order to stay motivated as learners. 'It is important for a teacher to identify areas of interest of the students. By doing this, the teacher may keep their interest in mind while designing his lesson plans or activities for them,' he adds. He has also found that laughing at children or dismissing questions that they raise can be the biggest obstacle in their learning. It will discourage them. In addition, he claims that giving direct answers to their questions is not useful. 'That way, children will not be able to explore things and will just get a correct answer which they will have to memorise.' He has experienced that children learn best when they are given opportunities to observe and also to create – when, even if they face any hurdles, they learn from those too. He asserts that group-work is also important. 'Children also learn by imitation' is his claim.

The change that Narendra has observed in children after one year of teaching is, 'Now children share their thoughts with me very easily and openly criticise or appreciate my thoughts.'

Sahabuddin Ansari was a General Manager in a company before joining this school. He says, 'Right from the beginning I felt I must do something ... I have left a very good post to come here .... There, my salary was very good. Even today I have such offers, but I am not going only because of the enjoyment ... because what I get to learn here, as a Manager over there I was not learning. That is an industry where I have worked for 15 years ... and I gained a lot of experience. But still, I have decided to stay here in education. How do I build myself? How do I grow? These are the things that I found missing there. Teaching is a challenging job and provides a lot of scope for learning. It provides an opportunity to be exposed to new thoughts and ideas as compared to other professions.' He joined the Azim Premji Foundation in 2006 and worked in the Foundation's Learning Guarantee Program before joining school. He adds: 'Initially I was not very aware of the perspectives of education but in the last seven years, I have understood the value of education in society and I also enjoy my job. If I get an opportunity to choose a career, I don't think I will opt for a change. I can think of becoming a teacher educator or researcher but will not move out of the education domain.'

During his teaching experience of five years, he has had a one month long in-service teacher training and a seven-day

training on assessment with Digantar. He has also attended in-service training programmes for primary school and upper primary school. He has also attended several training programmes in language, mathematics and assessment. He is comfortable teaching Hindi, English and Math to Class II. He is also interested in teaching Geography and Civics.

His goal as a teacher is 'to facilitate the development of a better society by providing better education'. In order to achieve his goal, he says: 'Whenever I make my plan, I consult many references, I discuss with my colleagues and read lots of books, I try to use all possible sources to make my lesson plan effective.' He declares that he has not experienced any obstacles in teaching till date 'because the culture of the school is good, our work is appreciated.' When asked what keeps him motivated as a teacher, he says: 'When I am delivering my plan and students are enjoying it, this brings a conviction that I am doing the right thing. The happiness of the students keeps me motivated.' For him, the most rewarding aspect of being a teacher is also 'the happiness of the students. They share their feelings and views with me without any hesitation and fear.' He finds it challenging to work with children who are slow to learn.

He recounts with enjoyment a story that he worked on with children, 'I worked with a story "*Where is my mother*". There was no student in my class who didn't know this story well. I also helped students to role-play it. We played around the theme. Students liked this story a lot.'

Sahabuddin is of the view that children do NOT learn when the topic being taught is not connected to their lives and the facilitator is unable to bridge this. Again, if students are under any sort of pressure, learning cannot happen. Thus, Sahabuddin feels that children learn best in an environment where they feel free to think for themselves. Further, by appreciating their work and providing an opportunity for doing work by themselves, the teacher can get them to learn better. In addition, the teacher's good relationship with students, the teachers'

Improvement in children according to both teachers:

- They started reading whole words without breaking them into sounds and they also relate to the meanings of these words also.
- Children started making connections between similar-sounding words or similar sounds in different words.
- Significant improvements were seen in their spoken language as well as in reading.
- They showed increased levels of self-confidence. Children also started telling me if they didn't enjoy the class and began giving suggestions as to what they would like to do.
- Children became interested in learning.
- Though their self-expression is still not fully developed, they do try to express themselves in verbal communication and through writing.
- Children themselves are ready to make presentations in the morning assembly.

efforts to welcome the ideas of students, the teacher's efforts at listening and involving them to make TLMs (teaching–learning materials) can motivate students to perform better. 'This will bestow ownership of the work and they will feel free to talk.'

He is open to multiple perspectives from students and is ready to listen to them. This is corroborated by his admission that children share things openly with him, without any fear.

'I have seen a lot of change in the students – such as acquiring good behaviour, improved communication skills, confidence level, learning level, subject knowledge. Their interest in the subject and books, and willingness to come to school has increased.'

One of the challenges faced while teaching Hindi was that the children were from Bengali-speaking families. They could not understand Hindi well enough, so teaching them how to read and write Hindi was a challenge. Many of these children joined school in Class III or IV. The admission was given based on their age but their skills of reading and writing at that age had not been taken into consideration.

Various activities that were done with children to introduce skills of reading and writing:

- Finding rhyming words
- Finding words starting with first and/or last letter of their own name in the story
- Helping children listen to the entire word, identify different sounds and associate them with different letters of the words; for example,

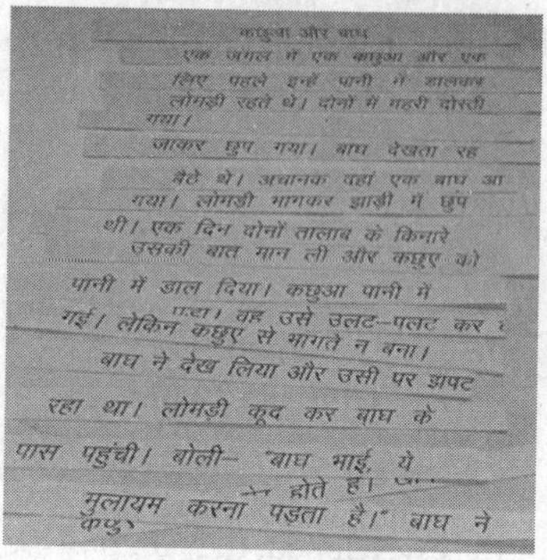

they were asked to listen carefully to 'KOEE' ... with 'KA' there is the sound letter of 'O' ... so it would become 'KO' and there is 'EE'.

- Children were excited about building new rhyming words. They made meaningful words as well as words which rhymed but didn't have any meaning, such as 'papa', 'kapa', 'lapa'.
- When children find it difficult to read words, instead of reading the word for them, teachers would give them hints like 'it is a fruit/animal/bird etc.', 'it has two horns', 'it has a skin', 'it is yellow and it can be eaten,' etc. and thus help them guess the word.
- If children would get stuck with a word that was similar to a word they had already read, teachers would tell the children, 'You have read a similar word in the story earlier!' and encourage them to find that word. This would help children recognise the older word and read the new word too.
- Whole language approach was used where children first become familiar with the whole story, then start associating words with memory and then start reading words, before they can associate sounds with alphabets.
- The alphabet was never taught to the children. It took them about five months to start reading with this whole language approach.
- Using sentence strips to put together and create a complete story, and then match it with the story chart
- Using word strips to join and make sentences from the story
- Over time, they started mixing word and sentence strips which were not present in the story, but which had deliberately been inserted by us. Then children used to wonder where to put these strips. They would come asking what was written on the strip. This helped to draw their attention to the written word.
- Displaying frequently used words in the classroom which children could refer to while reading or writing

- Starting a story, leaving it incomplete and asking the children to complete it using their imagination. For example, 'There was a rabbit and there was a fox; they were friends.... Now complete this story.' Children would use their own thinking to complete it, and see that by applying their own logic they could complete it and bring it to class.
- The class would start with a light-hearted discussion and fun activities like making rhyming words, *antaakshari* (a group game, where one child says a word and the next child starts the next word with the sound the previous word ended with) and then something new would be introduced. Over time all these words would become a part of their listening and speaking in the process of learning a language.
- Using a set of stories prepared by Digantar, which were set in Rajasthan. These stories were found to be very contextual for these children as well.

Further, some practices deliberately adopted by both teachers to facilitate learning were:

- Appreciating children's work
- Avoiding criticising them
- Avoiding putting a cross mark on their work
- Giving them feedback and showing them the correct way of doing things.
- Avoiding interrupting children in the middle of their reading.
- If there were gaps, after the children finished reading, the teacher would tell them, 'Now *I* will read and *you* listen.' After that, the children would again read and during this process, the gaps would be filled.

Challenges faced by both teachers during action research

- Teachers felt that if they had more support from the parents, it would have made the process of teaching–learning much faster.
- They would have appreciated some support in resolving individual personal problems of children.
- If they needed any documents [like sample worksheets, story cards, etc.] from the facilitators, it took time for the documents to become available. By then, their research was completed.
- They needed adequate time for action research because reflection on any process is very important to make it effective and it takes time to reflect and make meaning of one's own experience.
- Sometimes, they experienced a lack of resource materials.

Benefits of Documentation and Action Research: Documenting the process of action research was a challenge because it was difficult to find time to document. Sahabuddin says, 'Documenting is not just about writing something. When it comes to documenting all this, identifying each and every thing...that is a very big process and I won't say it is easy. Because we are working with each individual child, when we see with what kind of pattern he works...to note down these patterns we need to always have paper and pen with us. And then, we note down those patterns...after all, how much can we remember?'

Teachers used to write reflections before they started action research. However, the quality of reflections has improved, says Sahabuddin, with the process of documentation of action research. Documentation has helped them adopt a more systematic approach towards reflective writing of their practices. Now they focus on the evidence of the impact of their work and are also cognizant of what they are communicating. Earlier, the focus was on *what the teacher is teaching*. Now the focus has shifted to the evidence of *what the children are learning* e.g. what a child is able to do or which way a child is able to do his work. The teachers realised that sometimes 'children cannot even understand what we are doing, so just perceiving this gave us some clues, some ideas, how to work.'

Documentation and action research gave teachers an opportunity to test their ideas and see the effectiveness of those ideas in action. Before embarking on action research, the focus was on how to teach children reading and writing to bring children at par so that they could move to the next level. During action research, the objective changed to how to help children understand *whatever they are learning*. For action research, no readymade ideas were available. The teachers had to generate their own ideas. So, the teachers were also learning in the process.

During action research, co-operation between colleagues and the principal blossomed. Everybody put their heads together to find solutions to the problems at hand. Earlier, in the groups, children were of mixed abilities. During action research, they created a group of children with similar needs which brought in a focus on the approach of teaching. Action research helped teachers become learners themselves,

Key Learnings from action research:

- Providing chances to children for reading and writing; guessing also plays a role in reading.
- The process of learning reading and writing became clearer. When we are working on a poem or a story, and read it for students, then the students remember the story. When they are asked to read, they can guess what word will come next. This is how they try to read. So associating the written word with memory plays a role in the process of reading.
- Children participate in meaningful content and then learn.
- During the initial phase of learning, the teacher has to accept the mistakes that children make during reading and writing – this motivates children to do better.
- Content that is concrete and related to life strengthen the understanding of children more than content that is abstract.
- Once children start enjoying the process of learning, they become interested in learning and start taking initiatives.
- When children start writing, they will sometimes write wrong spellings but read them right. For example, they will write '*amurad*' but read '*amrud*' *(guava)*. Write '*koshi*' but read '*khushi*' (happy). (This is also one of the stages of learning reading and writing.)

and cater to the needs of children at different levels of learning. It also helped in CCE (continuous comprehensive evaluation). The teachers were able to observe a range of things 'from the behaviour, to the learning speed or learning patterns, that I can see. And in the same way, we try to create an atmosphere so that it benefits all the children.'

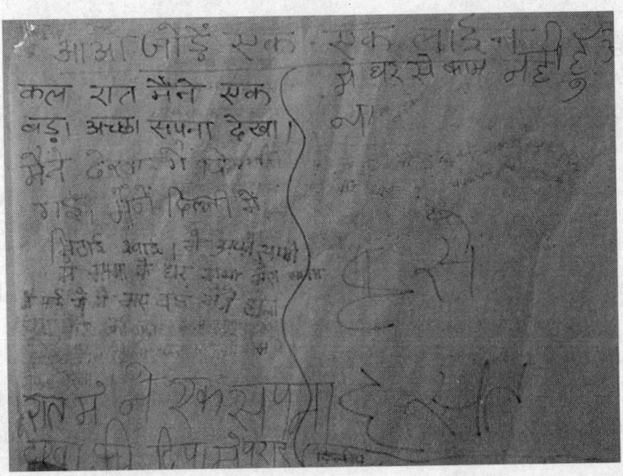

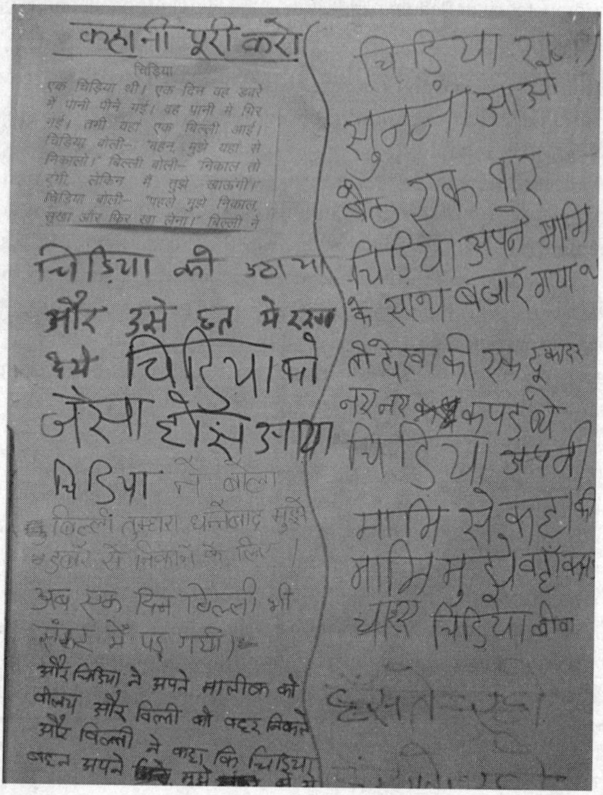

Action Research Document – Narendra and Sahabuddin

1. Identifying the Problem
Listing out problems faced by teacher • We found that some students of Class V and VI were facing problems related to reading and writing the Hindi text of their class level. The details are: ○ Some were unable to recognise letters. ○ Some were able to recognise letters but could not read or write words. ○ Some were not able to write down their thoughts and make sense of the sentences that they had read. • Different learning levels in a class • Lack of interest and confidence in reading: it was observed that during teaching, some students do not participate in class

discussions and activities. Even efforts put in by the teacher to motivate them did not improve participation. It was also observed that these children seemed to be lost in their own world, and when asked to read or write, they would become silent. Such students were less communicative and did not interact with other students or teachers. They often disturbed the class and bullied other students.

Identification of one problem which they feel is most important – Ten students each of Class V and VI were facing problems related to reading and writing the Hindi text of their level.

2. Analysing the Problem

Detailing the problem

The details of the identified problem are:

- 6 students of Class V were able to recognise some letters and read out some words.
- 4 students of Class V could read words with some difficulty; they were also not able to recognise all letters and *maatras.*
- Five students of Class VI were able to recognise some letters and read out some words.
- 5 students of Class VI could read words with some difficulty; they were also not able to recognise all letters and *maatras.*

Efforts made by the teacher to tackle the challenge

We started interacting with these students about their interests, their families, games they liked to play, etc., to establish a rapport with them. When they began to talk freely with us, we began working on their known vocabulary, e.g. making words with given letters, writing words from their language, rhyming words, using word cards, taking sentences from familiar stories and using words from the sentences to make new sentences, etc.

Key Observation

We noted how many children learnt it well, what method of teaching – learning was useful to some extent, etc.

Children began participating in the activities and most of them also started learning. The activity we thought was useful helped children move from known words to making words, sentences and stories. Children were not only able to understand the meaning of these but they also began to take interest in learning, in general.

3. Identifying Alternative Approaches
As an alternative, we began using a mix of whole language and phonetic approach. It was helpful but we were not getting sustainable results. **Identifying the best possible approach** Then we discussed it with our colleagues and subject experts; we felt more inclined toward using the whole language approach because we could see more logic and opportunity in using this approach. We were told in training sessions at Jaipur and Barsu that the whole language approach can be used with children who have been in school for at least three years and who know at least 40–50 per cent of the alphabet. We can use this approach to enhance the child's pace of reading and writing. We discussed with colleagues and the resource person about how to work with such children. The resource person provided us with a set of 12 short stories which had been developed in an education programme at Bara district, Rajasthan. We started using these stories to work with children.

4. Developing a Strategy to Implement Identified Approach
What will the teacher do? We worked with our colleagues to plan, and started working on the identified stories. **How will it be done?** The plan was modified on the basis of prior planning and felt need. The sequence of work is: a. Writing a short and interesting story on chart paper and pasting it on the wall 3–4 days before actually starting work on it b. Then reading the story aloud to students with gestures and action c. A copy of the story is given to each student and it is then read out to them. d. Asking students to read the story on their own e. Asking students to arrange the sentence strips from the story in a sequence, and then doing the same with word strips f. Making a new story by changing the characters of the story, making sentences, playing word games (rhyming words, identification of words, writing the identified words from the story, etc.)

What resources would be required to implement the approach?
Set of stories, chart papers, sketch pen, copies of the stories, sentence and word strips
What duration would be enough to deal with the problem?
4–5 months
Possible outcomes: Students will be able to read and write independently; all the students will achieve the expected learning levels; students will gain confidence

5. Implementing the Identified Approach

Reflect upon processes at regular intervals
We openly discussed the process of learning with students and frequently reflected upon the processes, to check if our efforts were leading us in the right direction. We had to make some modifications in the process.
On-site change in efforts, when needed
We had to change our strategies many times, for example, we omitted the step of joining different words of the story, introducing word games from time to time, listening to the stories made by students, making new stories, asking students what they were interested in and including these topics.
Challenges faced by the teacher during teaching–learning
The students who were not regular were not able to participate freely and were lagging behind. They were facing problems in reading and retaining words, and were not able to cope with the new strategies. We need to check if anything could be done about this.
Change in learning
In the beginning, students were trying to recognise words by using their pre-existing knowledge and guessing, but they were unable to recognise the words that appeared frequently in the text. They were also trying to recognise similar sounding words. It was also observed that their confidence level was also rising concomitantly with an increase in their vocabulary (students were able to read the words at first sight without thinking, students were helping each other in reading; they were also seeking help freely from the teacher. They were also trying to read independently and were able to read if some hints were provided by the teacher). The assessment showed that now the children were able to read similar words and familiar text in different contexts.

6. Reflection of the Teacher on the Processes

How effective was the process?
An important aspect was that the text was one that children could relate to, and was also interesting to them. The entire process was systematic and graded in the sequence of language competencies. This was ensured so children could participate and understand.

What insights did you gain from this plan?
We think that if the environment is conducive for learning, a child learns more. S/he will be able to guess only when s/he has some prior knowledge about the topic.

What was your key learning from this action research?
Providing opportunities for reading and writing; guessing also plays a role in reading. When we are working on a poem or a story and read it to students, they remember the story, and when they are asked to read, they can guess what word will come next. This is how they try to read.

Children participate and learn when meaningful content is used. During the initial phase of learning, the teacher has to accept mistakes that children make during reading and writing, as this motivates children to do better. Content that is concrete and related to life strengthens the understanding of children, as compared to content that is abstract.

What are the things that you will continue to practise?
We feel understanding the interest and reading habits of students is very helpful for a teacher. We will also try to understand this and put in efforts to infuse variety into our lesson plans.

Quantitative Data Collected During Action Research

Given below is the baseline, midline and endline data showing the number of words that children could read across this action research cycle.

It is evident from the data that when Narendra and Sahabuddin started working with children in July, the reading abilities of many (represented by baseline data) were very low. Within a month and a half, they showed considerable improvement, and the number of words (both familiar and unfamiliar) that they could read was considerably higher. This trend of improvement in their abilities continued, and is represented as endline data. A sample of children's work (randomly selected) is also shared below in the form of a story written by one child.

S. No.	Class	Baseline (out of 100 words) July 2013	Midline (out of 100 words) August 2013		Final (out of 100 words) December 2013	
			From familiar text	From unfamiliar text	From familiar text	From unfamiliar text
1	V	07	60	28	87	83
2	V	25	86	78	96	–
3	V	03	22	16	53	70
4	V	11	67	44	86	90
5	V	57	93	71	97	95
6	V	04	35	16	48	40
7	V	15	68	42	51	62
8	V	20	48	25	79	73
9	V	08	30	16	98	95
10	V	20	78	59	95	83
11	VI	20	64	45	84	83
12	VI	55	92	66	92	83
13	VI	47	91	71	99	93
14	VI	00	21	11	32	44
15	VI	20	76	62	93	89
16	VI	28	95	97	96	97
17	VI	80	99	98	100	100
18	VI	64	95	93	100	100
19	VI	60	95	85	98	98
20	VI	42	92	74	100	97

13

अज़ीम प्रेमजी स्कूल दिनेशपुर
नाम– नमिता राय दिनांक – 3 Dec 2013
कक्षा – 6

शेर और गिलहरी

एक शेर जंगल मे रहता था। वह रोज शिकार
करने जाता था। शेर ने शिकार करते समय
एक गिलहरी को देखा। गिलहरी शेर को
देखकर भाग गई। शेर भी उसके पीछे
भागने लगा। गिलहरी एक पेड़ पर चढ़
गई। गिलहरी पेड पर से बोली शेर भाई
मुझे मत खाओ।" तभी वहा एक लोमड़ी
आ गई। शेर ने लोमड़ी को झपट कर
पकड़ लिया। लोमड़ी ने कहा "शेर भाई
छोड़ दो मुझे क्यो खा रहे हो ?. मै तो
दुबली– पतली हू उधर देखो एक
मोटा हिरन आ रहा है। इतने मे
लोमड़ी भागकर झाडी मे छुप गई। यह सब
देखकर गिलहरी जोर–जोर से हंसने
लगी। शेर के देकर गोस आया शेर
अपने जंगल में चला गया जंगल में एक बिल्ली
आया

Classroom Observation

Narendra and Sahabuddin

In a discussion prior to the class, teachers told us that they take extra classes for students who are lagging behind, and today they will work upon the syntax of the language. They will use a known story taught in the class recently. Narendra wrote a phrase in which the words were shuffled. He told children that he has made some mistakes while writing the story; they have to read it and make corrections in their respective notebooks. He then pointed to the word '*Nikaalo*' and asked students to read it one by one. The students read it as '*Nikaala*', '*Nikla*' and finally '*Nikaalo*'.

He then asked them to read the story once silently and start correcting their notebooks. The students began working on the task.

Some students came to the board to read the story (that had been written on the board) and then went back to correct the sentences in their notebooks. Three teachers – Neeraj, Narendra and Sahabuddin – were present in the class and they sat on the floor among the students. Students were showing their work to them for assurance that they were doing their work correctly. Teachers were asking students to read the story and think if this is how we narrate a story. Students corrected their sentences again and showed it to teachers. While correcting the work done by students, teachers were appreciating them and were asking the students to correct their mistakes themselves. Narendra also wrote down some words on the blackboard and asked students to make sentences using these words, as homework. Students left the class after showing their work to the teachers.

From a Facilitator's Diary

Ambika Mohan and Vartul Dhaundiyal, December 2013

Before Going to the School

We were wondering how teachers would perceive us – this was the main worry before this visit. We were apprehensive that teachers feel that action research and our visits are a burden. We were thinking of ways in which to address such issues if they were raised by teachers.

On the other hand, since most teachers have finished work on their first cycles and have also completed most of the documentation, we were looking forward to interacting with the teachers, to fill in the gaps in their documents.

We were also looking forward to finding out what each teacher wanted to do next – whether they wanted to proceed with another cycle of action research; and if yes, then what mechanism could be adopted.

At the School

We met Deepak first. He told us that he sees a distinct difference in the teachers before and after action research, and could even see a difference in Prachie's reflections, even though she had chosen not to participate in the study. He speculated that her participation in the first workshop and some of the initial interactions had also had an effect. Earlier in her reflections, she would just write 'completed' or 'done'. Now she writes a whole page of reflections about the work. We appreciated her effort and also Deepak's observations. We added that another factor affecting her reflection could be formal and informal interaction with her colleagues and listening to their discussions about their action research.

We interacted with some of the teachers (Shipra, Madan, Saud and Shakuntala) regarding their documents and got answers to some of our questions. They all willingly spent time with us and discussed their documents. Hence, some of our apprehensions were reduced.

We discussed what to do next. Both Deepak and Vipin had suggested that we should have this discussion. We interacted with all the teachers together. We first asked how many would like to take up further action research. We clarified the following:

- Deciding not to take it up again would not mean that a teacher is 'dropping out' (even though there is no problem if someone wanted to drop out). This is because they have completed the work that we had set out to do together. Further work would be need-based and interest-based – as another component, separate from the current study.
- If some teachers wanted to take it further, it could be either a second cycle of the same topic; or new action research with a new topic or even a totally new context; or any other kind of interaction that they wanted for reflection.

Most teachers showed some interest in taking up action research again. A couple of teachers said they were not sure about it and if and when they faced any problem, they would take it up as action research. The others, who agreed, said that most probably they would take it up only in the next session because now they will not be able to do much work because of winter vacation, examinations and report writing. Sahabuddin said that he may continue to do a little bit of work now too.

Then we discussed how they would like to proceed with the next action research or the next cycle. The following options came up:

- Doing it on their own and asking for support from us when they felt the need
- Continuing in the same way as in the first action research cycle
- Doing it entirely on their own, without any support from us and taking support instead from their own colleagues

All the teachers who wanted to continue, wanted to do it using the first option. (We feel that it is important to work according to how teachers want. Wanting to do it on their own could mean that they are feeling confident that they will be able to do it, now that they have understood the steps).

During the interaction with Deepak, he raised a question about collecting evidence and validity of observations made by teachers. He wanted to know if it is essential to have photos, videos and some other written documents (like actual work done by children) or if it was enough to have reflections and observations written by teachers. We thought it better to have a discussion among our research team before sharing our thoughts with him, so that there is no contradiction in what each one conveys to the school.

Memorable Images

- The interaction with Deepak where he openly shared his confusions with us; our interaction with him about Prachie's efforts
- The interaction with all the teachers where they openly shared whether or not they wanted to work like this further and that they would not be able to do it now

6. Developing Scientific Temper in Students

Name of the Teacher: Neeraj Kothari

Qualifications: MSc (Zoology), BEd

Name of the Facilitator Associated with the Teacher: Vipin Chauhan

Action Research Problem: To develop scientific temper amongst children of Classes V and VI

Identification of the Problem: Though some children are able to talk about theories and laws of science, they are not able to relate these to lived experiences, discuss and give their rationale. They are not in the habit of making observations and maintaining records.

Analysis of Problem: Children don't ask questions, and blindly accept whatever is taught to them. A few of the children are less interested in science and do not connect it to their local environment. They don't find support for learning at home.

Identification of Alternative Approaches: Some of the alternative approaches identified were: revision of every activity after demonstration so as to arrive at the principles through experiments. Also, to make children engage with their environment and connect to examples from day-to-day life.

Implementation of Identified Approach: Learning by doing and understanding theory so as to draw conclusions was the identified approach. Experiments were designed to establish a connection between the subject and local environment. Opportunities were created for children to learn by doing through peer group interactions and interactions with families so that children find support at home too. Opportunities for peer learning were created and students were encouraged to record their observations.

Review and Reflection: Children's curiosity and motivation was developed and they started asking questions and participated in the process of teaching and learning. They could connect their understanding from their daily experiences with the subject.

Neeraj Kothari attributes his passion to be a good teacher to 'a conducive academic environment in the family, father as faculty at DIET (District Institute of Educational Training), self-confidence that I can do something significant and self-satisfaction for doing something for children for their better education'. He attributes much of his learning to the role his father played in his life, along with that of his colleagues. He remembers how attending some of the training workshops conducted by DIET has helped him develop as a teacher. He also feels it is important to learn from self-observation and one's own experience. He finds the Internet to be a good source of resource material.

Neeraj taught Science and Zoology upto class XII in a public school for three years before he joined Azim Premji School Dineshpur, where he has been teaching Science and EVS (Environmental Studies) for about two years now. Sports and History are the other subjects that interest him. He has had some experience in managerial work in schools that he worked in earlier and likes to participate in work related to school management.

He feels that the most rewarding part of work is that it helps him develop an understanding about how children learn and how their learning can improve in the classroom. The latter also happens to be his goal. It gives him an opportunity to work with parents to increase their awareness about the education of their children. He also uses this opportunity to address social issues like discrimination. His commitment as a teacher and his resolve for self-improvement are revealed by the frequency with which he makes home visits to establish contact with the students' families, and by the considerable time that he spends in reviewing and planning his work.

He knows all the children of his class, as he engages with them on a day-to-day basis. He always plans his classroom processes based on his understanding of each child. He often reflects on his own pedagogical approach. He also keeps in mind the capacity of every child. Some of the parameters that indicate to Neeraj the children's interest (and that they are learning) are the participation of children in dialogue, questioning and the discussions that they get involved in even outside the class.

'It should be aligned with our context. Especially for early primary classes, we should focus on the local context of the concerned state'. He asserts, 'Books are not important if we are clear about the sort of learning that we want to

ensure in children. If a teacher is clear what he needs to teach, he will hardly use the textbook. His understanding of the local context will add more value in the learning of children.' He noticed that children were not completing their homework, because of which there was a gap in their learning.

'There is definitely something lacking in the kind of science education that makes children passively accept whatever the teacher says,' he declares. He attributes this sort of blind acceptance to the fact that children are not exposed to the kind of science learning which makes them curious and ask questions. He thinks that learning becomes difficult when children are not given an appropriate learning environment or are not given adequate learning opportunities.

As is evident from the observation of his class (see Classroom Observation), he involves his students in the teaching–learning process in very creative ways. He invites them to ask questions, express their opinions and take charge of their learning by creating a space for their participation in the classroom, while he facilitates the whole process skillfully. He has also created opportunities to involve parents in the learning of children. He recounts an experience of attempting to generate electricity by using dynamo attached to a bicycle wheel with children which helped him see that children are actually learning and gave him insights into how children build upon their scientific temper. He remembers that on one of his house visits, a family said that their daughter asked them to not use polythene bags as these were harmful. He narrates, 'She was insisting that her mother stop using it as her father was not accepting her dictum. Based on that learning, we organised a camp at school for making paper bags that can be used while shopping.'

While exploring the process of germination (as described in the action research document), Neeraj used an approach that circumvented 'direct teaching' – his phrase for telling children the facts, rather than having them arrive at it themselves. He prompted them to find things out from their own explorations, questions, experiments – so that they drew inferences from their own observations. It is interesting to see how children proceeded step by step, asking relevant questions, figuring out what could be tested, making observations and drawing inferences. Some of the questions asked, solutions found and inferences drawn by children during this exploration are presented in the following table.

S. No.	Questions raised/ Hypotheses proposed	Experiments designed to test the hypotheses proposed	Inference drawn after testing their own hypotheses
1.	*What are the various things required for a seed to sprout?* Soil, Water	Use of wet cotton to provide moisture Not using any soil	Without soil, too, sprouting will occur.
2.	*How can a seed sprout without soil?* Soil gives warmth. Cotton wool gave it warmth and performed the function of soil.	Remove the cotton wool too (So they put seeds in a bowl with only water and no soil or cotton wool.)	Germination requires water
3.	*The seeds were kept near the window, so could light also be one of the things needed?*	Let us keep the seed for sprouting away from the sunlight, behind a cupboard.	Germination does not require sunlight.
4.	*Could soil be from dust, water etc.?*	Instead of an experiment, they discussed this in detail.	Ruled out the possibility of soil coming from any other source

One of his concerns as a teacher was that children forget what they read and they do not document their learnings/observations in their notebooks. So he initiated a system of recording children's daily observations of germination of seeds on the chart and encouraged them

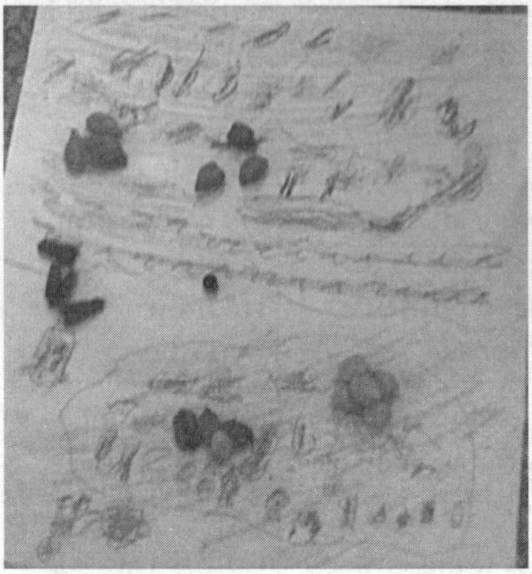 

to prepare their own system of recording the data in their notebooks, too, since these are an integral part of children's exploration of various topics, in his view.

Neeraj believes that children learn by themselves – no one can teach them. A facilitator can only provide a suitable environment, which helps them in learning. He also maintains that the teacher-student relationship is an important determinant in the learning process. The examples used during teaching–learning must be related to the local context. He has found that giving responsibility to children also promotes better learning – something that he learnt through action research.

Neeraj was introduced to the idea of action research when he attended a training programme conducted by the Azim Premji Foundation. He enjoyed the experience of learning and refining his own understanding and practice. It made him curious about how this will work in the classroom in future. When he started examining the possibility of applying action research in the classroom, he got really excited as he realised that by doing so, he could find solutions to the problems that he was facing in classroom situations. As he saw the possibility of awakening curiosity

Shift in students after he conducted action research:

- Children are more open and ask questions without hesitation.
- Children are more interested in learning now and they don't want to go back home.
- Their self-confidence has increased in a surprisingly short while.

amongst children through action research, he felt this approach could make children more independent in their learning and reduce their dependence on the teacher. He also saw the possibility of encouraging children to observe and ask questions and not accept everything the teacher said, without examining or understanding it. He felt that through this process, he could encourage children to develop scientific temper.

Observations of Vipin Chauhan

In the initial interaction with Neeraj, while the team was in the process of identifying AR topics, he confessed that he was struggling with issues like creating interest in every child in the teaching-learning processes, connecting science/EVS with the children's context. In the action research study, he could not only connect content with the environment of children, he even found that he was able to ensure learning of every child (Nyquist and Wulff 1996). Neeraj now realises the role of teacher as facilitator, where he considers himself as environment builder who could improve the learning processes. As a reflective practitioner (Biggs 1994) he always reflects on how he could improve his own practices to empower students' learnings and never blames their guardians or other external factors.

Observations of Tapasya Saha

After peer review of the AR Template one of the questions put to Neeraj was: 'What do you do with the children in your class who do not attend classes regularly? How do you ensure that they too are learning?'

I was observing Neeraj. The question, I thought would confuse him; but that was not the case. He looked very relaxed and confidently said, 'Every experiment is recorded in a tabular format, which is created by children and hangs in the class. This is updated by them every day. Moreover, every day class starts with recapitulating the previous lesson. This keeps the absentees on the same page as the others.'

Definitely Neeraj was a partner with the children in the teaching–learning process.

Neeraj's learning from action research:

- Before action research, he used to tell children about the principle/law etc. first and then explore it further. He now realises that telling them about the principle/laws etc. first was not such a good idea. He could see the possibility of exploring a method of teaching where children can investigate and reach the principle through their own experience and their own thinking.
- He found a way of using children's immediate surroundings and their direct experience as a context for their learning.
- He found a way to involve the parents of children in the learning of their children, and this addressed one of the challenges that he had been facing as a teacher.
- He realised the difference between making them do experiments and exploring a process through an experiment. In the latter, children design and explore the experiment to ask questions and find out what is happening through their observations and experiences. In the former, children stay disinterested in the subject and accept what is taught to them without asking any questions to explore further and develop their own understanding.
- He feels the environment created in the school by the Foundation helps him develop scientific temper in the children and build upon their skills.
- He has the freedom to decide what he wants to teach and how he wishes to go about it.

Action research helped him identify the problems he was facing in the classroom and find solutions to these problems in a systematic way.

NEERAJ KOTHARI, DINESHPUR
USN (UTTARAKHAND)
SCIENCE/EVS TEACHER

मैंने AR के Process में बच्चों का प्रतिभाग ज्यादा से ज्यादा रखने की कोशिश की। मैंने इसको result में पाया बच्चों को खुद ही सीखने के लिए मात्र प्रेरित करना चाहिए एवं उनकी जिज्ञासाओं को, प्रश्नों को आने देना चाहिए वो एक जिज्ञासा भी बच्चों के अन्दर रुकी न रही चाहिए जो उनके मन में है चाहे वो उस Topic से पूरी तरह जुड़ी न भी हो क्योंकि बच्चा अपने अनुभव से विषय को अपने अनुसार जोड़ता है और उसके प्रश्न उसके मन में कभी भी कक्षा उपरान्त या कई दिनों में भी आ सकते हैं जो अध्यापक के लिए महत्वपूर्ण होते हैं अतः इसके लिए मैंने कक्षा में <u>मेरे सवाल</u> पर बच्चों के लिए चार्ट लगाया जिसमें बच्चे कभी-भी कक्षा के बाद और पहले पढ़े गये पाठों में उठ रही जिज्ञासा को भी लिख सकते थे फिर इन प्रश्नों पर चर्चा कर उनमें सीखने का मौका होता था साथ ही बच्चे उन प्रश्नों को पढ़कर खोजबीन करते थे। अतः मैंने पाया बच्चे प्रयोगों को भी करने के बारे में स्वयं सोच पाये एवं Concept तक पहुँचे।

In the process of AR, I tried to keep children's participation to the maximum. As a result, I learnt that we should only motivate children to learn by themselves and let their curiosity and questions emerge. We should not snub their curiosity, even if it is not entirely related to the topic, because the child relates to the subject from his/her own experience. And related questions can come to him/her any time after the class or after many days – all of which are important for the teacher. So, to bring out all their questions, I put up a chart titled 'Our Questions'. Children could record the questions arising out of their curiosity related to topics studied earlier or later. This provided an opportunity to learn by discussing these questions. Along with that, children would do some research on these questions. Thus I experienced that children could think about performing the experiments and arrived at the concept by themselves.

Action Research Document – By Neeraj Kothari

1. Identifying the Problem

Listing out the problems

- Poor self-study habit in children for Science subject
- Inadequate connect between Science and the local environment
- Problem of non-completion of homework in the case of some children
- Children's low level of interest in Science

Identification of one important problem

Inadequate scientific aptitude among children

2. Analysing the Problem

Detailing the Problem

I have realised several times in class that children often are able to recite the definitions/theories but they are not able to discuss the rationale behind the theory. They hardly entertain any 'why' and 'how' questions. Very rarely are they able to provide examples from their experience.

The children neither make observations in detail nor do they maintain their records. There is no practice of noting down observations or to use these observations whenever needed.

Number of Children who were Part of the Study

55 children of Class V and Class VI.

Efforts made by the Teacher to tackle the Problem

I made efforts to ensure that children develop their understanding of the subject.

Activities like group-work, demonstration, play and quiz were organised to encourage children's participation as well as to elicit their enthusiasm in classroom processes. For example, when the topic 'Germination' was discussed with the children, they were requested to sit in small groups to discuss and document the processes. They were encouraged to note down all their observations and experiences on chart paper or in their own notebooks. There were also some suggestions that they can try to write down all the observations or they can draw diagrams if they are comfortable drawing.

Key Observation

While implementing these activities as part of the teaching–learning process, I found that most children started participating in the activities of their own accord, with increased interest, attention and enthusiasm. Timely accomplishment of homework was still an unaddressed issue, however. While discussing this issue with children, I realised that the children have very little support (if at all) from their parents. They do not chat with their children about what they did in school. Children also do not find themselves connecting with the subject.

3. Identifying Alternative Approaches

- Revision of every activity after demonstration
- Come to conclusion only after experiencing

Identifying the Best Possible Approach

Learning by doing and understanding conclusions as well as theory

As I have described earlier children do not display a scientific temper in class. They do not have the habit of self-study and hardly complete their homework on their own. There does not seem to be any connect between Science and their local environment. Children do not show interest in Science. All these issues have impelled me to choose self-study as the main topic among all the highlighted problems. I assumed that if this issue is addressed, all other issues will themselves get resolved.

4. Developing a Strategy to Implement Identified Approach

What will the teacher do?

- Prepare a plan to establish connect of subject with local environment through a variety of experiments
- Provide better opportunities to children through learning by doing
- Develop process for peer group learning
- Connect with family to create possibilities for family support to children

How will this be done?

Children will go through practical exercise, collect data and record the same. The experiments will be carried out using locally and easily available resources.

What resources would be required to implement the approach?

- Locally available seeds like pulses and gram; cotton wool, bowl, a piece of cloth, white chart paper, worksheet etc.

What duration would be enough to deal with the problem?

- 2 months

Possible Outcomes

- Children will understand the causes/reasons behind theory/concept.
- Children will be able to maintain their records and share the rationale of their understanding. They will also be able to connect the subject with their environment.
- Development of scientific temper among children

5. Implementing one Identified Approach

I implemented some activities in the classroom using the material brought by children from their homes. All the children participated in the experiments conducted, so as to understand the process of germination. They also sat together in groups and recorded their own observations. They updated everything on the chart and in their notebooks as well. This was done by the children on a day-to-day basis. It was quite encouraging to see the curiosity with which the children discussed this with others. It was also interesting to see that they had tried to document everything that they found useful for the topic. There were heated discussions among the children, where some were putting forward arguments and counterarguments to prove that they were right. Children also started actively participating in classroom processes and there was evidence that now they have also started completing their daily homework.

6. Reflections of the Teacher and the Facilitator on the Processes

- It was observed that children were quite motivated and started participating in the discussion.
- Children started framing questions on their own, using their surroundings.
- Some children quoted very relevant examples during discussion with the peer group and with the teacher.

- They were now using their prior understanding to connect with the subject.
- Their presentations in class were now more focused.
- The enthusiasm increased – as indicated both by the quality of discussion as well as frequency of participation

Challenges faced by the teacher during teaching–learning

- Irregular attendance of children in the classroom
- Poor reading–writing competencies of children

Change in the Learning of Children

- Children were enthusiastic during their presentation and discussion in the classroom
- On some occasions, children were found discussing their topics of study after class, even during lunch.
- Now, many of the children were not satisfied with simply mouthing the answers. They started raising meaningful questions and could be convinced only if the responses were based on evidence: for example, children of Class VI debated whether the plant gets water from the roots or from the leaves and then designed experiments to see for themselves where the water is absorbed from.
- They also started giving their own rationale for the opinions that they expressed. When they were talking about how cotton wool would have helped in the process of germination, they came up with the logic that cotton wool (like soil) could have provided heat to the seed for sprouting and then went on to test it through the experiment.
- There was evidence to show that children started participating in the Science class with interest. Their questions and discussions covered many more aspects of the topic at hand. In Class V, while exploring the topic of germination, they asked questions about whether soil, light, water, etc. are essential for germination and found out by designing experiments themselves. The discussions led them to the conclusion that soil is not required for sprouting but it is required for the plant to grow. They were also seen discussing their topics outside the class.

How effective was the process?

Personally, I found the action research process quite useful in developing scientific temper among children, as seen by their increased participation in the classroom processes. The children started asking questions like Why? How? and What?. They kept their records safe and also shared these with other children. Unhesitatingly, they presented the rationale of their responses every time, and more often than not, this rationale was based on their own experience.

What were the key learnings from the action research?

I learnt that it is very important for children to learn science by conducting experiments. So it is necessary to organise activities by respecting their experience. Children should be given the opportunity to address their curiosity by doing things. We should understand children and should also give them the opportunity to take decisions for their own learning. We can help children by supporting them so that they can find responses to their questions on their own. We should also provide positive reinforcement to children. For me, this was only a belief that children learn better if the teaching–learning processes are activity-based. Conducting activity with children on 'Germination' verified this belief satisfactorily. I also saw how the children could arrive at a concept. Children experienced how they could observe processes and document their learnings.

Classroom Observation of Neeraj Kothari

The topic was 'Food'. The teacher wrote 'Bhojan' (Food) in the middle of the board and asked children to frame questions around it. (A discussion with the teacher revealed that he was using this as a strategy to teach them. He would discuss a topic from the textbook and on the next day, he would ask children to frame questions based on the topic, which other children would have to answer and the child asking the question would have to say whether the given answer was correct or not).

A child asked, – 'Hamein shakti kis se milti hai?' ('From where do we get strength?') The teacher repeated the question and encouraged other children to answer. One child answered, 'bhojan se' ('from food'). Another child asked him to name what kind of food gives energy. The same boy replied again, naming things like milk, roti and fruits. Another child said, 'phal to phal hote hain, woh bhojan nahin hai. Bhojan to paka hua khana hota hai'. (Fruits are fruits. They are not food. Food is cooked food.'). Some children agreed with him while others began to disagree. The child who had been answering, thought about this and said 'Carrot is eaten both raw and cooked, but it is also part of bhojan (food) and hence, fruits are also bhojan (food).'

While this discussion was going on, the teacher was mainly trying to moderate the discussion, ensuring that only one child spoke at a time and others listened. He was also encouraging different children to state their opinions and tried to get quieter children to speak too. For example, he said, 'Sakshi ne bahut der se kuch nahin kaha hai'. ('Sakshi has not said anything since a long time'.) At a point when two children were discussing something with each other, the teacher said, 'Sirf usko nahin, sabko bataao'. ('Don't tell him alone, tell everybody.') Throughout the discussion, the teacher did not state his opinion and just let the children state whatever they thought. The teacher wrote the key words on the board, like milk, fruits, energy, carbohydrates etc.

The discussion then moved to what bhojan (food) is and then to carbohydrates. A child's question was, 'hamein carbohydrates kin cheezon se milte hain?'('From what sources do we get carbohydrates?') From the answers that came, one child said that sweet things have carbohydrates. Another child said that grains (like manduwa [a local crop of Uttarakhand which is cultivated mostly in the hilly regions]) and aata (flour) also have carbohydrates but they are not sweet. This was discussed for a while and the teacher encouraged the children to talk about the specific things they eat at home.

When the class ended, he asked the children to copy down what he had written on the board.

From a Facilitator's Diary

Vartul Dhaundiyal and Vipin Chauhan, March 2014

Before Going to the School

Though the AR study project is complete, there were a few requests from school team to assist them with their new research studies. It was an opportunity to observe their enthusiasm after the completion of the first cycle of action research. There were several questions in our minds: will the participating teachers continue to be enthusiastic? What are the experiences of AR teachers after the first cycle? Do they feel strengthened by the action research; if yes, what and how do they feel? How do they view the action research project in their professional lives?

The idea was that we will have a meeting with three interested teachers and will discuss the possibility of presentation of their papers in seminars/conference or publishing them in research journals.

We were confident that we will certainly have good interaction with all the teachers as we have very good relations with the school team. We were also well aware that there are three very interested teachers in the school apart from Deepak.

At the School

At the time that we entered the campus, all the teachers were busy in a meeting. Once the meeting was over we sat together for discussion; the teachers welcomed us wholeheartedly and discussed their ideas about publishing their work freely with us. We discussed this matter for two hours approximately. We had been told that only three teachers will be interested in the discussion but we were amazed to see that all the teachers showed their interest and actively participated in the discussion.

They were all very excited about the dissemination of their work. The discussion was focused mainly on how and where to publish their articles/studies etc. We had individual discussions with five teachers – where the reflection of their past AR experience was very evident. Their arguments were more logical and systematic, the documents were organised, and their evidence was presented using multiple sources. Both individual as well as team interaction were specially enjoyable – when they discussed the progress of their new research work, this was truly remarkable.

Memorable Images

The images that keep flashing through our minds, as we think of the UDSN visit are: teachers inquisitively asking questions related to their practices and research, and their plans for new research projects.

7. Enabling Children to Recognise Letters and Read

Name of the Teacher: Madan Mohan Joshi

Qualifications: BSc (Biology), BEd

Name of the Facilitator Associated with the Teacher: Vipin Chauhan

Action Research Problem: Finding a way to deal with the difficulty in recognising letters and reading in Hindi

Identification of Problem: Letter recognition and reading words

Analysis of Problem: The problem was encountered in five children whose parents were at work the whole day and could not help them.

Identification of Alternative Approaches: Three alternative approaches were identified: traditional method, whole language approach, traditional and whole language approach combined.

Implementation of Identified Approach: A combination of traditional and whole language approach was identified as the best possible approach to tackle the problem. Story charts were prepared and children were introduced to the familiar words in the story.

Review and Reflection: If children are able to connect the word to their context and environment then the word becomes meaningful to them. Apart from this, children are also exposed to different letters in the word.

Madan Mohan Joshi consciously opted for teaching as a profession. After teaching in a Government School for five years and in Kendriya Vidyalaya for one year, he joined Azim Premji School, Dineshpur as he wanted to widen his perspective through this new experience. Though he is most comfortable teaching Science to higher classes, he was called upon to teach Mathematics also in his previous school, due to a shortage of teachers. This year, in Azim Premji School, he is facing a similar challenge and, to accommodate the needs arising out of lack of staff, he is teaching Hindi to children of Class IV. But he feels that since he does not face any systemic challenges in this school, it gives him a space to deal with the diversity of children. And he fondly remembers that when he took up the challenge of teaching

Mathematics, all the students appreciated his efforts on the day the results were declared. This is something which has remained in his memory because of the confidence that it gave him.

As a teacher, he wants to see his students succeed. [By 'success', he means that children should have understood what the teacher set out to teach.] He is concerned about his efficacy and wants to ensure that he is able to deliver what is expected of him, in terms of developing requisite competencies in children. He asserts that what really motivates him as a teacher is the performance of children. 'When they do well, it gives energy to a teacher to continue. When a teacher invests efforts and sees their positive effects, it gives him a lot of satisfaction.' Madan believes that children perform best when they receive appreciation and their interest is aroused – according to him, these are the most important factors. Children like to explore things that interest them and hence, they can perform better in those areas. Also, appreciation from the teacher (and other children) when they do something, helps – 'because everyone likes to be appreciated'. Further, they learn best when they are in an environment that is friendly and can provide lots of experiences. They should be provided guidance from the teachers and their peers. Contrarily, children do NOT learn when the teacher is strict with them, because they are then afraid to tell the teacher they do not understand or to ask any questions. The teacher, therefore, has to be patient.

His sincerity in wanting to become an effective teacher shines through some of his efforts, such as involving the parents of children in the process of teaching–learning. He made home visits to understand the causes of the difficulties experienced by some Bengali-speaking children in learning Hindi. He also noticed interference between the sounds of the two languages. To overcome issues like these, he invested extra effort to learn some Bengali words so that these children could relate to Hindi. He is very observant and tries to get to the root of the difficulties that his students might be facing.

He created his own content by writing stories on the chart and improvising to draw children's attention to reading and writing of Hindi; he tried to draw the content from the children's daily life.

Madan Mohan recalls that he was introduced to the action research study in a meeting with representatives from Azim Premji Foundation. There he understood that when the teachers face a problem in the classroom, the solution can be found through the action research approach. It was then that he realised that he could use action research to teach Hindi in Class IV. So he tried to learn more about this.

In the case of one of his students, he feels that even the whole language approach that he used during action research has not worked, and so he is planning to go back to using the traditional approach with her. The child comes from a Bengali-speaking family, where the language has very different sounds for the same symbols in Hindi – and that is why the child finds it difficult to learn the new sounds. He says, 'I learnt some *Bangla* words from them, like 'tree' is '*kaaj*' .... if she didn't understand 'tree' in Hindi or if she didn't understand something else ... I tried teaching her using words and sounds from her own language ... but even then, she didn't understand.'

He finds it disappointing that even after repeatedly talking to the parents about the importance of spending some time with the children, there is no parental involvement.

Another problem that he faced was in documenting action research: recording action research work was not challenging but it certainly added to his work. He could not find the time to document in the school, so he needed to do it at home.

He also found that when he started doing action research, since children were at different academic levels, he had to deal with two groups with different needs. He tried to deal with the five children who were slow in learning as a separate group and continued teaching the rest of the class based on textbooks and lesson plans, '... the greatest problem I had ... in my class, was that there were two groups ... and I had to teach the two groups separately. I did more activities with the larger group where I could follow

How action research helped:

- Action research helped him analyse the problem and find solutions to it.
- The action research approach gave him an opportunity to think about children and their problems in a different way.
- The approach that he adopted helped capture the interest of the children.
- It gave him an opportunity to connect the learning of children to their immediate environment – for example, when he was teaching them about trees, he drew their attention towards the jackfruit trees that children could see growing around them and asked them many questions about it. He shares these questions: 'What do you do with jackfruit? When does it ripen? When do you eat it? How do you eat it?' He realised that children knew a lot about their surroundings.
- When he connected their learning to the immediate surroundings, it helped him learn a lot of things from the children.

my lesson plans … so that they were kept engaged while I worked with other children.'

He expresses satisfaction that four out of these five children are showing progress.

In terms of the outcome of his action research, he states, 'The main thing is that the learning of children improves. They face a lower degree of challenge in the same things that they were struggling with earlier.' He states that children now do not need him to sit with them while reading. Their enthusiasm for reading has increased and now, they all want to read.

Best of all, they have started doing a little work at home too.

Here is an example of a picture story that he prepared to introduce the reading of certain words to children.

Teacher's Own Documentation (Translated from Hindi)

To work with a class where children are at different levels of learning is quite challenging. I came face to face with this problem while teaching Hindi to Class IV, at the beginning of the session. Most of the children in the class could read only by joining letters. But five children of Class IV were clueless about the alphabet in Hindi. Initially, I was teaching all the children using the same method. But these five children were neither taking an interest in these methods nor were they making any progress. I was looking at different pedagogies to solve this problem.

At this stage, I met the action research team. From them, I came to know that action research can be used to figure out the possible reasons of the problem at hand, analyse them and then solve it in a systematic way within a given time frame. So I decided to do action research on the problem that I was facing.

Before starting action research, I was turning over in my mind the following question: 'What does it take to read a word?' If I see a word and I am not able to connect this word to something concrete, then this word has no value for me and does not provide any meaning. To provide meaning to words is called reading [sic]. We use symbols to provide hints for words. These symbols are an integral part of language. So I decided to teach these children, keeping this understanding as the base.

In this teaching method, I chose to use a small picture story titled, 'The sparrow who found a pearl'. In this story, each sentence was shown and read out to the children by linking it with its illustration. After this, the children narrated the story in their own words by referring to the illustrations. In the next stage, I picked up four words from the story. The words were: *kauva* (crow), *chiriya* (sparrow), *ek* (one), *daanaa* (grain). I talked to the children about these words. Once they became familiar with these words, I introduced the first letter of the words to the children. A new story was created on the basis of these four words in which some words were slightly changed for example, instead of *daanaa* (grain), I used the word *daadaa* (grandfather). Children were able to read that. Using some previously used words along with some new words, a new story was prepared, in which a similar process was followed.

Action Research Document – By Madan Mohan Joshi

1. Identifying the Problem

Listing out problems that the teacher is facing

- The children were able to recognise letters in a word but were finding it difficult to form words using the recognised letters.
- Children were not taking interest in activities performed in the classroom.
- Children were making grammatical mistakes in the language of communication/interaction. The mistakes were commonly related to gender and number.
- Children were unable to read and recognise letters.
- Children were making mistakes in *maatras* while writing.

Identification of one problem, which s/he feels, is most important

I had to choose one problem for my action research out of the many problems stated above. I chose 'recognition of letters and problem in reading words' which I felt was the most critical problem.

2. Analysing the Problem

Detailing the Problem

Profile of parents of the identified children

I made efforts to understand the reasons for the problem. These children were not first-generation learners. When I went to the community to meet the parents of these children, I could not find them, since they are either daily wage labourers or work in a factory. The parents leave the house early in the morning and return from work late in the evening. The children take care of their younger siblings. There is no one in the family to support them in their studies at home; this could be a reason for the identified problem.

Identification of problem with letter recognition and difficulty in reading words

A poem was read out to the students to identify the problem:

'झबबर झबबर बालोंवाले, गुबबरों से गालोंवाले
लगें दोड़ने आसमान में, झूम-झूमकर काले बादल

After this, I discussed the poem: what, according to you, do these clouds resemble; what are the different colours of the clouds? All the students participated in the discussion. Then I asked them to do a simple writing exercise on the poem. All students except five were able to do that.

I then asked all the students to write the answers to questions from the poem. Some students were able to answer the questions orally but not in writing.

- These children were asked to read out the poem written on the chart but they were unable to read it.
- One word was taken out from the known poem and was split into the letters. Children were asked to read the letters but I found that they were unable to do this, too.

How many children have this problem?

- This problem is mainly observed among students whose parents are working or where there is no one at home to teach them. These children often don't complete their homework either. There are 5 students in the class who have such a problem.

Description of the problem

- These children were able to read out words for which pictures were given in the text but were unable to link the sounds to the letters in the words.

Why do children have this problem?

- Most of the students in our school are from the Bengali community. Hindi is like a third language for them. I think the difference in sound system of these two languages and the fact that the children were not able to understand the words of Hindi and relate these to their environment were the main problems.

Effort made by the teacher to tackle the challenge

I was working on the problem using the Whole Language Approach. One reason for choosing this approach was that it provides an opportunity for children to express their feelings and thoughts freely. They can relate the words that they read to different objects in their environment. The words provide them meaning and finally, children even find reading interesting.

Key Observation

- In this teaching method, I found that children were able to read a story in a sequence but if they were asked to read any random word from the story, they were not able to read that word out. One reason for this could be that the children memorise the story and its sequence.

3. Identifying Alternative Approaches

- Traditional method
- Whole language approach
- Traditional and whole language approach combined

Identify best possible approach

Traditional + Whole language approach

4. Developing a Strategy to Implement the Identified Approach

In this approach a short story with illustrations was taught "कौए को मोती मिला" (The Crow found a Pearl). Every sentence of the story was connected to the respective illustration when teaching it in class. After this, children told the story in their own words by referring to the illustrations.

In the next step, four words were taken from the story, these were: कौआ (Crow), चिड़िया (Sparrow), एक (One), दाना (Grain)

I facilitated discussion around these words, for example, 'What colour was the crow? What sound does a crow make?' etc.

Once the students became familiar with these words, they were introduced to the first letters of these words. For example:

चिड़िया → चि
कौआ → कौ
दाना → दा
एक → ए

Develop a plan to implement the strategy

Take a short story in which each sentence is linked with the related illustration and read it out/show it to the children. Later, children will look at the illustration and retell the story in their own words.

Taking four words from the story, initiate discussions around those words.

Introduce children to the first letter of these words after all the children learn to recognize these words.

What resources would be required to implement the approach?

Stories with illustrations

What duration would be appropriate to deal with the problem?

3 to 4 months

Possible outcome

In this process, the students should be able to identify letters along with reading out the words.

Implementation of Identified Approach

All the work done with children was well planned and the plan could be deemed successful to an extent. Many activities based on letters were used in class.

Challenges faced by the teacher during teaching–learning to address the problem

After observing the illustrations and when retelling the stories, the children were using Bengali words. As a result they could not be introduced to the letters of the words. To take care of this, I learnt some Bengali words so that I could use words they could relate to.

Change in learning of children

In this process, children take an interest in reading and try to read stories and poems by themselves.

5. Reflections of the Teacher on the Process

If children are able to connect the read word to their own context and environment, then the word becomes meaningful for them. Apart from this, children are also exposed to the letters that constitute the word.

What things will you continue doing in your journey?
I will use action research as a tool to understand the reasons behind various problems that I will encounter during teaching, and probe their solutions.

Classroom Observation of Madan Mohan Joshi

In a discussion prior to the class, the teacher told students that he will work on the topic 'Diwali' which had been introduced in the class a few days earlier. After greeting the class the teacher asked 'What do we do at home on the occasion of Diwali?' One student said that *'ghar mein diya jalate hain' (we light lamps at home)*, another said Kali worship, other students said Lakshmi worship, and so on. The teacher summarised their points by adding that people from the Bengali community do Kali puja as their Lakshmi puja falls 20 days before *Diwali* and is called *Lokhhi Pujo*; however some others perform Lakshmi puja on *Diwali* eve.

He further questioned *'Kya aap gharki safai bhi karte ho?'* (Do you clean your house too?) Students said that their parents clean the house and paint it too. The teacher then asked 'Why do you clean your house?' Different students listed different reasons for cleaning the house. One student said that because on *Diwali* day, guests visit our house and also Ram-Ji comes, so we clean our house to welcome them. Other students said that *'Kali maa ghar aati hai'* (Mother Kali comes home) or because in the monsoon, insects lay eggs in the house, so we clean and paint our houses, to keep them away.

The teacher then asked them what they cook for *Diwali*. Children replied – *Halwa, poori, Kheer,* etc. One student said that those people who work in factories get a *dibba* (gift in a box); there could be a pressure cooker or glass bowl inside the *dibba*. Other students mentioned other possible gifts and they started arguing amongst themselves and making noise. The teacher interrupted them by saying that if they do not listen to others, then others too are not bound to listen to them; the students then stopped making noise.

After this, the teacher asked: 'What else do you do on *Diwali*?' Some of the students replied that they burst crackers. The teacher asked the class if we should burst crackers. Some students said that it is fun to burst crackers and they enjoy it while others thought that we should avoid crackers as they cause sound and air pollution. He asked students to write down their views in their notebooks. As they were writing, the teacher prepared a worksheet for the students who had a problem with writing. Teacher checked the notebooks of every child and summarized by saying: 'We now have your opinions and most of the students are of the opinion that we should enjoy crackers while a few feel that we should avoid them. My opinion is that if we want to enjoy crackers then we should burst very few of them since they cause sound and air pollution.' He then gave them an assignment. As homework, he asked them to ask their parents the name of the month in which Diwali is celebrated.

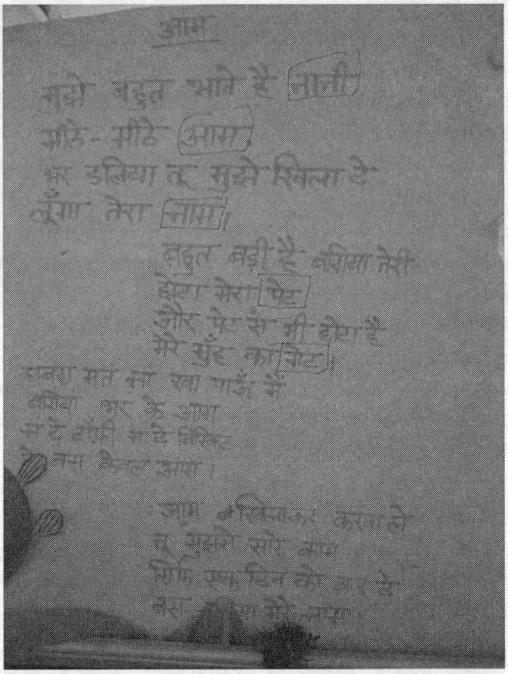
आम
मुझे बहुत भाते हैं नानी
मीठे-मीठे आम,
भर डलिया तू मुझे खिला दे
लूँगा तेरा नाम।
बहुत बड़ी है बगिया तेरी
छोटा मेरा पेट
और पेट से भी छोटा है
मेरे मुँह का गेट।

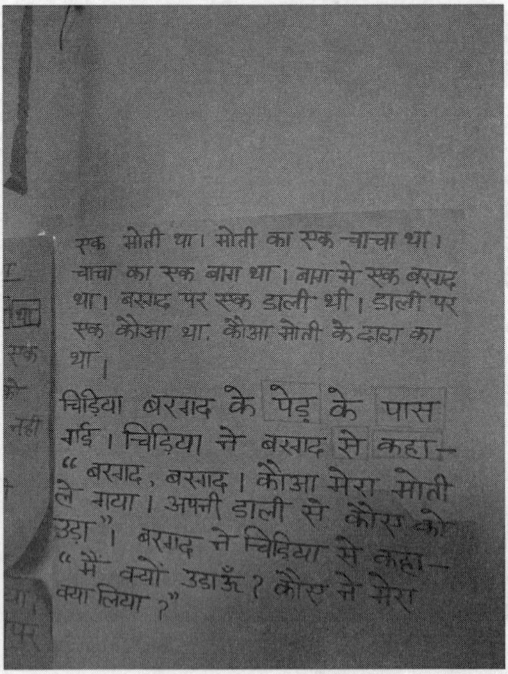
एक मोती था। मोती का एक चाचा था।
चाचा का एक बाग था। बाग में एक बरगद
था। बरगद पर एक डाली थी। डाली पर
एक कौआ था. कौआ मोती के दादा का
था।
चिड़िया बरगद के पेड़ के पास
गई। चिड़िया ने बरगद से कहा –
“बरगद, बरगद। कौआ मेरा मोती
ले गया। अपनी डाली से कौए को
उड़ा”। बरगद ने चिड़िया से कहा –
“मैं क्यों उड़ाऊँ? कौए ने मेरा
क्या लिया?”

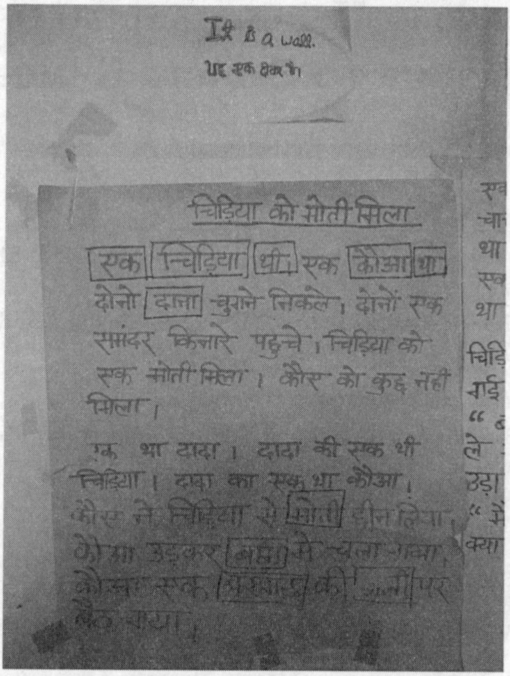
It is a wall.
चिड़िया को मोती मिला
एक चिड़िया थी। एक कौआ था।
दोनो दाना चुराने निकले। दोनों एक
समंदर किनारे पहुचे। चिड़िया को
एक मोती मिला। कौए को कुछ नहीं
मिला।
एक था दादा। दादा की एक थी
चिड़िया। दादा का एक था कौआ।

8. Ensuring Understanding of Place Value up to 3-digit Numbers

Names of the Teachers: Shakuntala Chaurasia and Saud Ahmed Khan

Educational Qualifications:

Shakuntala: BSc (Physics, Chemistry, Math), MA (English), BEd

Saud: BSc (Physics, Chemistry Math), BEd

Name of the Facilitator associated with them: Ambika Mohan

Action Research Problem: A range of problems were identified, like different levels of learning, some children not being able to identify numerals and a general lack of self-confidence amongst the children.

Identification of the Problem: Teachers decided to bring about an understanding of place value in some children, while engaging the rest who had already grasped this.

Analysis of the Problem: The concept is abstract for them and they are unable to connect numbers with their daily lives and therefore unable to appreciate their importance. So activities were needed where children are given real-life problems and can be actively engaged in making efforts themselves.

Identification of Alternative Approaches: Some of the approaches identified were drilling method, using number line, and using activities that took children from the concrete to the abstract. Teachers zeroed in on the method of using activities.

Implementation of the Identified Approach: The children with difficulties were grouped together to focus on developing their abilities (however there were further subgroups based on abilities). Activities with concrete objects were used. Children were encouraged to make their own TLMs, create mathematical problems and solve them.

Reflections of the Teachers on the Process of Action Research: Children making their own TLMs motivated the teachers. It was realised that action research is not something different from what they had been doing. Learning about action research helped them to do the same work more systematically.

Shankutala Chaurasia and **Saud Ahmed Khan** co-teach Mathematics to Class V and VI where they decided to conduct action research.

Shakuntala always wanted to be a teacher and hence chose this as her profession. She has taught for five years in a private school, where she was teaching at the secondary level. Though her postgraduate degree is in English, she prefers teaching Math, and is comfortable teaching across age groups. She has not attended any training programmes.

Her goal as a teacher is to ensure that children learn and understand things well. She describes the biggest challenge that she experiences as a teacher: 'The whole educational environment in our country makes children hate studies. They do not get help from home either.' She feels motivated when she sees good results from children, and when they show interest.

To achieve her goal as a teacher, she is currently 'teaching with all the interest possible and learning and trying to improve all the time, so that – from the teacher's side – there is no shortcoming.' She recalls an incident when she was a student of Class V. There was some unpleasant comparison between children and partiality by the Math teacher, accompanied by the teacher's use of foul language and even corporal punishment. That made Shakuntala decide to become a Math teacher and ensure that she would never behave like this teacher, whom she detested.

She declares that she would not have chosen any other profession even if given an opportunity to do so. She feels the most rewarding part of being a teacher is 'when a teacher realises that students are able to grasp what she is teaching, and solve further questions independently – especially in Mathematics.' Her biggest challenges as a teacher have been to teach children from different backgrounds and abilities, and to complete a given curriculum.

She remembers that one of the children she worked with (classified as a 'challenging child') had a problem with his vision. Though he was interested in Mathematics, he was very weak at it (even at addition and subtraction) and his parents told her that she will have to teach him Math right from class I to class X. She took it up as a challenge and taught him both at school, and after school hours. Soon she realised: 'He had a problem with vision but *not with his mind*.' She ignored geometry (as he could not do constructions) and focused on algebra. He was very bright and hard-working and scored very good marks. She recalls this incident because it was inspiring for her as well as for the other students. They noted that this student was able to do even better than them, despite his challenge.

Shakuntala believes that children learn best when they have a healthy and friendly environment, where they are able to fearlessly tell the teacher that they have not understood something and are facing

problems, even if the teacher has explained it several times. Shakuntala claims that she is quite open to multiple perspectives that children bring in. Especially because she faced discrimination as a child, she is very sensitive about this. She encourages children to bring in their own examples and also encourages their questions.

Saud studied Physics, Chemistry and Mathematics in college and teaches Math in this school. He taught in private schools for eleven years before joining this school. Though he can teach all classes from I to X, he is more comfortable teaching Classes IX and X. He has attended computer training conducted by IGNOU.

His goal as a teacher is 'to ensure that all children of a class achieve the learning levels that they should, for that class.' Some of the obstacles experienced by him are that 'the cognitive levels of most children are much lower than required. A lot of extra effort needs to be invested in them, especially when they do not get support at home to practice.' To achieve his goal, he took extra classes to raise the learning levels of children, especially girls, to the required level of the class. 'It was motivating to see them achieve something.' In alignment with his goal, he is engaged in finding new methods of teaching all topics, to ensure that the concept gets through to the children.

He chose teaching as a profession because of his own experiences. A girl in Class X failed in Mathematics. Being a secondary school-leaving Board Examination, this was a significant failure. He told her father that he would help her by teaching her. He started tuitions for that girl and from that experience, he realised that he really enjoyed teaching. He pursued computer science for better professional prospects, but returned to teaching. Given a chance to choose a profession of his choice, however, he asserts that he would like to be an engineer.

According to him, the most rewarding part of being a teacher is 'when children understand concepts well and, when even those children who had been lagging behind catch up with others' since it gives him 'a sense of achievement.' The experience that has stayed

with him goes back to the time when he himself was a student of Class XII. At that time, he was given some numbers to add. He made a mistake in place value and felt insulted by the subsequent reaction of the teacher. Since then, he tries to ensure that he doesn't make such mistakes.

The challenges that he has faced as a teacher have shown him how important it is for a teacher to have a sound understanding of the subject to be able to teach it well and answer all questions. He adds: 'A teacher needs to have skills to transfer that knowledge to children. This is challenging even if one knows the subject. Regarding social things like values, a teacher needs to set a good example.' He believes children learn best when the teacher has sound basic knowledge of the subject, and if the teacher finds out what the children already know and builds on that. He draws support from his colleagues through discussions, exchanging suggestions about activities and also their thoughts about the (same) children. His wife, too, is a teacher in a college so they often share their experiences.

He considers Azim Premji Foundation training programmes (and workshops for child-centered education) as factors that have contributed to his growth as a teacher and provided him support. He gets ideas from these and takes them forward by adding his own ideas to them. He takes extra classes with some of the children, if he feels they need it. Some of the things he would like to learn in Math teaching are:

- How to teach the four operations (addition, subtraction, multiplication, division)
- How to get children to work without learning multiplication tables

Currently, he is trying to find more activities to conduct in class. When children bring their own examples, he notes that it helps him understand the kind of environment that they come from.

According to Shakuntala, the relationship between the teacher and students is crucial for their learning. She recalls that her students told her 'Madam, earlier we were scared of you. Now, after learning from you, we don't feel scared anymore.' She believes that in the absence

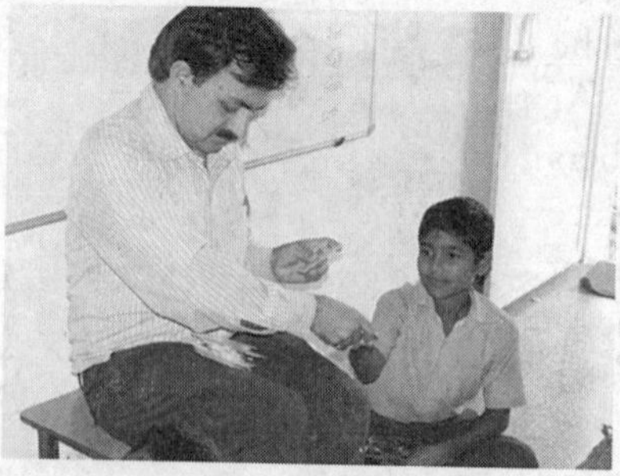

of a friendly and accepting environment, children don't learn. The teacher must become a friend of the students.

In one of her earlier classes, when a challenging student did not pay attention in class, she asked him whether he wanted to study or not. He said he wanted to become an engineer. She pointed out the necessity of learning Math for it. Since then 'a great interest for Math was created in him' and he is always asking her to give him more sums to work on. She believes that children become motivated to learn when a teacher establishes a personal connection with children. Also, when children become interested in learning for some reason, and when they see that they are able to perform to some extent, they are motivated to do more.

Saud echoes her sentiments by adding that when children see that they are able to do something that they had thought they could not, they are motivated to learn. In addition, when they see that teachers are making special efforts to help and are encouraging them, this spurs them keep learning. According to him, children do not learn when they do not get time to study and practice at home. He is open to multiple perspectives that children bring in as this ensures that he connects to each child, uses their knowledge and examples that are relevant to them.

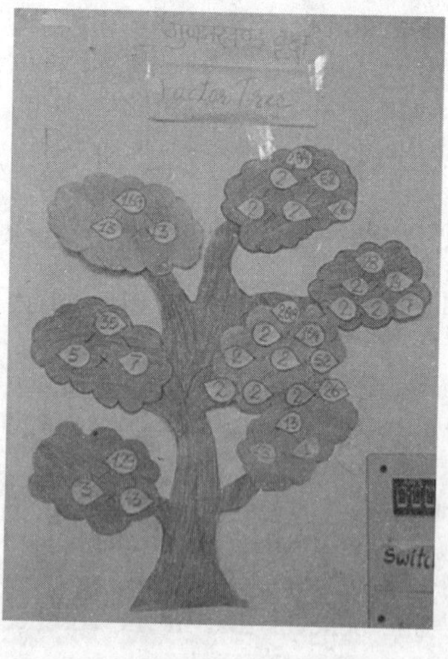

After teaching these students for a year, Shakuntala has seen a visible change in them. Their concepts have become clearer. This is because she ensures that they understand all the previous steps and do not just memorise a method/repeat by rote.

'Children are now also familiar with whole numbers, natural numbers and three-digit numbers. The twenty children from Class five and six are still slow as compared to the rest of the class. However, these children are supported by the other children in the class and the teachers also support them. Some more work needs to be done to bring them at par with the rest of the class.'

Saud has been working with these children for the past year. One change that he has observed is in terms of improved cognitive levels, on which he focused throughout the year. In addition, he says that some improvement could be due to age itself – as they grow during the course of the year, some concepts are clarified on their own.

He has also noticed that the behaviour of a children changes – they become more disciplined – over the course of a year. He focuses on that, too, because he has worked in private schools where discipline was emphasised.

Improvement noticed in children:

- Increased self-confidence
- They were able to understand the concept of place value till hundreds (three digit numbers)
- They had developed an understanding of expanding numbers. When asked how much three times ten and four times one is, they were able to answer '34'.
- They had started to question statements and write as equations simple addition and/or subtraction problems (e.g. 5 – 3 = 2).
- They started making their own problem sums and solving them systematically.
- The interest level of children had increased. The children started asking for more work.

Both teachers were sensitive to children's ability to learn. When they introduced a concept and found that children are struggling with the level of difficulty, they simplified the problem sums, for example, children were comfortable with reading and writing numbers in thousands. But when Shakuntala increased the complexity of the sums by introducing numbers like 5,503, she found it was difficult and so she dropped it.

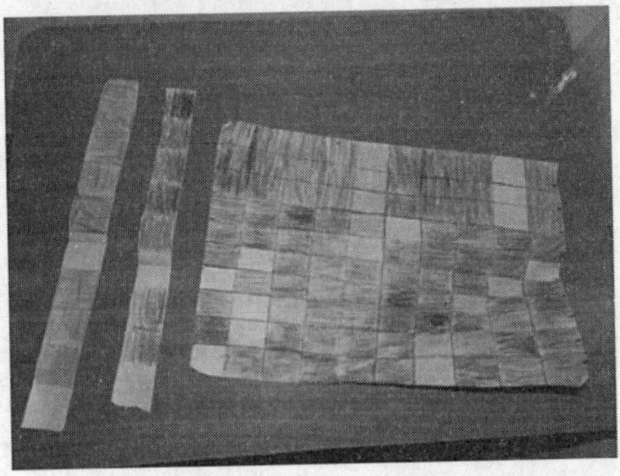

Initially, Shakuntala and Saud were not interested in using action research for their classroom teaching. Burdened by the vast syllabus that they needed to cover, Shankutala and Saud had decided to use the traditional method in class. They soon realised that

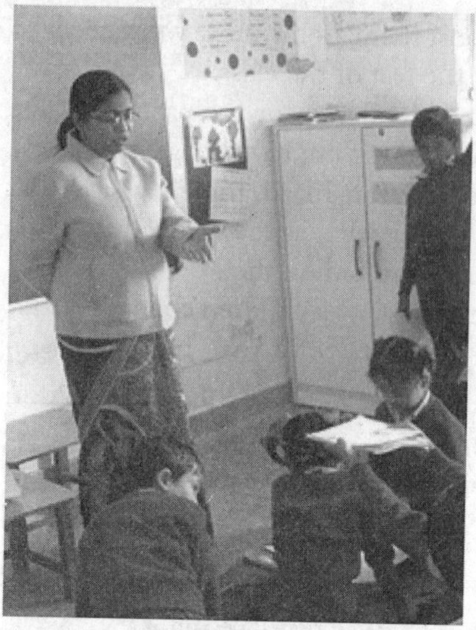

there were nine children in the class who could not understand basic concepts like place value. Some of the children could count till hundred but when asked to write eighty-nine, they didn't know whether it is written as '89' or '98'. They also could not figure out which of these numbers was bigger/smaller. So the two teachers used a different method to teach them the basic concepts, adapted to the needs of these children. They also continued to teach the concepts from the book at their level, so that they are not left behind the rest of the class.

The teachers paid attention to the fact that though they were working in separate groups, the children should not feel a sense of being separate from the rest of the group. So, they made them participate in whole class activities together. During this process, children also made their own Teaching Learning Materials like number strips, number cards, bundles of tens and hundreds with matchsticks and abacus etc.

During the process of action research, Saud said that the presence of two teachers in the class helped them to manage the diverse needs of the children.

Shakuntala and Saud said they were already mindful of the children's needs and were using different methods based on these needs, well before action research was introduced to them. Now they gave the process a name, 'Action Research'. For documentation, Shakuntala and Saud had divided their responsibilities, with Shakuntala deciding to write by hand and Saud taking on the task of entering her handwritten documentation into the computer. They also jointly decided that they would not document every day. Instead, they would complete the documentation over the weekend, and only if something extraordinary happened on a particular day, then they would record it immediately.

Both teachers paid attention to the child's prior knowledge and gauged where the child was experiencing difficulty before designing exercises for the child. Regarding action research, Saud admitted that it would have helped them if the format of action research had been shared with them earlier, as then, they would have proceeded accordingly. Since the creation of new activities was difficult, they would have appreciated help in this area from the facilitators. The teachers found class management to be a challenge.

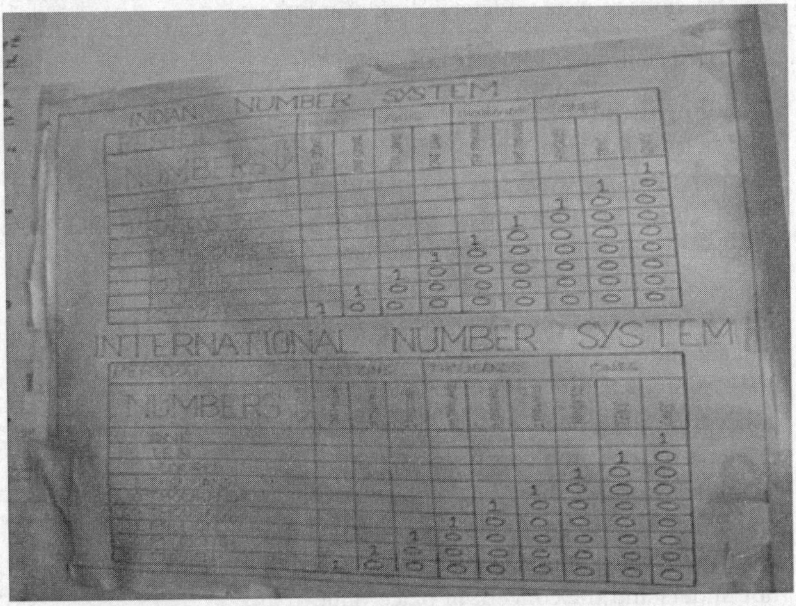

Action Research (AR) Document – Shakuntala and Saud

Names of Teachers: Saud and Shakuntala
AR Topic: To ensure children of Class VI understand the concept of 'place value' up to 3-digit numbers.

1. Identifying the Problem
Listing out problems faced • Some students could not understand the numerals and quantities at the level of their class/age. • Many levels of learning and understanding existed in one class • Lack of interest in studies and self-confidence • Due to wide range of abilities in the class, it was difficult to see success with any of the plans.

Identifying one problem, which is most important

- We chose *Understanding the concept of 'Place Value'* as the most important problem because this was one of the most basic concepts, and without it they would not be able to understand concepts of Class VI. Other concepts like multiplication and fractions require understanding of numbers.

2. Analysing the Problem

Detailing the problem

We held discussions with children and conducted assessments at intervals of two days at the beginning of the academic year in April. These assessments were both in oral as well as in written form. We did this so as to understand the learning levels of all children and thus decide where to begin teaching.

We found that the level of most children was much lower than what could be expected from Class VI children. Several children could not recognise digits, numbers and did not understand the concept of place value. (Since there was a problem even at this basic level, no further problems were explored).

Basic work on these concepts was done for 2–3 days with all children. After that, we found that most children understood at least digits, face value and place value. However, nine children still could not understand the concept of place value at all.

Assessments and work with the class helped us to identify the specific children who were still unable to understand the concept, even after teaching them.

Possible reasons

- Illiteracy of parents and parents being busy with work
- Children having to help with household chores and with occupational work of parents
- Disinterest in the subject leading to lesser understanding of Mathematics (and vice versa, because of inability to understand easily, having less interest in the subject)
- Students were enrolled from other schools where enough attention had not been paid to studies.
- Not understanding mathematical terminology (i.e. words like subtract, greater than, '*sainkda*', hundreds, etc.)
- Mother tongue of several children was Bengali, making it difficult for them to understand what the teacher was saying and

what was written in the book (e.g. difficulty in understanding 'problem sums' where a question is given in words and not numbers).

Efforts made by us to tackle the challenge

Since these were Class VI children, they had some understanding of the subject. So after talking to them, we designed activities and learning material based on the prior understanding of the students.

We decided to start at the very basic level with all the children of the class. After working for 2–3 days, we found that many children of Class VI were able to catch up with the basics. However 9 children were still facing difficulty.

First, we taught all children using the 'traditional method'. We did this mainly to save time and quickly move to the course of Class VI. Since we ourselves had learnt using that method, and it had been effective enough, we believed that the traditional method is not wholly ineffective. However, when we found that children did not learn, then we resorted to other methods.

Key observations

We realised that it is very difficult to instill an understanding about digits and numbers in children, especially when the concept is too abstract for them and they are unable to connect numbers with their daily lives and unable to appreciate their importance. So we concluded that it may be important to have some activities where children are given real-life problems and they can be actively engaged in making efforts themselves.

3. Identifying Alternative Approaches

Identifying and listing alternative approaches to deal with the situation

- By drilling method – Traditional method of rote-memorising
- By using number line – Children can be taught the concept of number line and how to move forward or backward on it.
- By using activities – A combination of activities could be used – objects or matchstick bundles to understand numbers, strips of paper for units, tens and hundreds concept and then cards with digits to understand place value better.

Identifying the best possible approach

- By using activities – We made up different activities on our own or used those from Mathematics textbooks of other schools. We identified a combination of three activities as the best possible approach. This was because we felt activities would help children engag and hence pay more attention; different activities address different competencies more effectively; and if activities are changed, the interest levels of children will be maintained and they will not get bored.

4. Developing a Strategy to Implement the Identified Approach

- A crucial point that we noted was that children were at two different levels – after working for 2–3 days on the basics, some children had caught up, but some children still needed more efforts. Hence, there was one specific group with whom the action research was needed and hence, separate planning for two groups was required.
- An advantage was that since we were two teachers taking the class, we could divide the groups amongst ourselves.
- We identified activities, decided their sequence based on what needed to be learnt first, and also prepared required TLM. (TLM was prepared along with children because then we felt they would take more interest in the work).
- We decided to also cover a little of the Class VI course with the action research children, so that they would not lag behind the rest of the class too much.

5. Implementing the Identified Approach

First, to teach digits and counting from 1 to 9, we asked children to pick different numbers of things from the school garden. Then we used matchsticks for the same thing. Children learnt the concept of 0 too. Three children were able to learn it faster but the rest got it after some repetition. This work took us about two weeks.

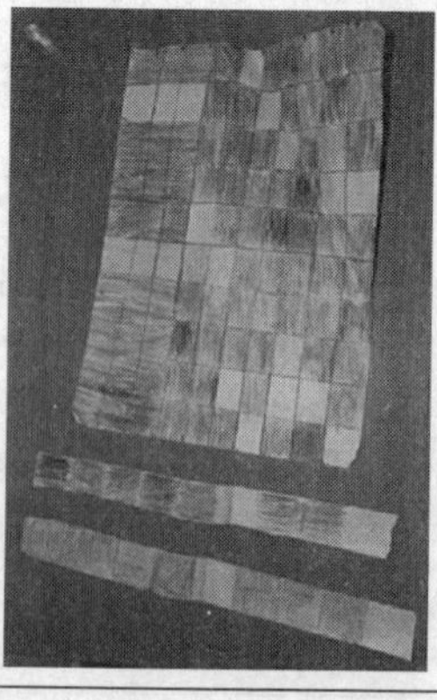

For the next two weeks, we dealt with the concept of 'tens' and their place value. This began with bundles of ten matchsticks each.

We told them that one bundle meant 10 and two bundles meant 20, etc. To bring some variation to the activity, instead of using sticks, we used strips of paper with 10 boxes drawn on each strip. Children made these strips and coloured the boxes on their own. Hence, one strip meant 10, two strips meant 20, etc. After working on the concept of 'tens', we introduced the concept of 'hundreds'. For this, we used a sheet of paper with 100 boxes (10 × 10).

Then, after this, we introduced three-digit numbers. A box with several cards – with one digit written on each card – was taken and three cards were distributed to each child. Each card had one digit (from 0 to 9) written on it. Each child had to make the smallest possible three digit number with the digits that they had. We then moved from one child to the next, checking the number they had created and asked them to say and write the number in words. Then they had to write the same number in expanded form. Similarly, they had to form the largest possible number with the digits they had, write it in words and in expanded form.

Key observations

Within the group of nine children too, we found that different children took different amount of time to learn. So we formed smaller groups and pairs within them and noticed that a lot of learning took place through children learning from each other. One child was still unable to catch up because he was irregular in attending school. We identified the need to work with this child and eight other children who are not at the level of the rest of the class. It will take time for us to bring them to the level of the rest of the class.

Classroom Observation

Saud and Shakuntala

They had divided their class into two groups. One set of nine children comprised those who needed more practice in number recognition and place values. These were the children with whom action research is being carried out. One of the teachers began to work with these children in a group. The other group did not need more practice in this topic and had moved to addition and subtraction with integers. The other teacher began the class with these children. Both groups were sitting in the same classroom.

Number recognition group – Saud was working with these children. He was repeating an activity that he had done with them earlier. From a box, he took out several small cards and distributed three cards to each child. Each card had one digit (from 0 to 9) written on it. He asked each child to make the smallest possible three-digit number from the digits they had. The teacher then moved from one child to the next, checking the number they had created and asked them to say and write the number in words. He tried to give hints to children who could not say the number by telling them to recollect where the *units place, tens place* and *hundreds place* were. He pointed out to one child and said (to the observer) that he is the one lagging behind the most but the teachers are unable to work with him because he does not come to school regularly. He then asked them to write the same number in expanded form. He reminded them that they had done it earlier and so they just had to remember how they had done it. After that, he asked them to form the largest possible number with the digits that they had, write it in words and in expanded form. Again he went to each child individually to see if they were facing any problem and tried to explain to them again. After this, he repeated the entire exercise by giving them four digits instead of three.

Addition and subtraction with integers – Shakuntala was working with the remaining children. She divided the class into three groups and wrote some problems on the board which each group had to solve. She tried to encourage them by saying, 'Let us see which group gets the maximum number of questions correct.' She moved around the groups to see what the children were doing. Bottle caps of two different colours had been distributed to each group as an aid for them to form a number line to do their calculations. Caps of one colour indicated positive integers and those of another colour indicated negative integers.

At one point, when the answers were being discussed, an argument broke out when a child refused to agree with the answer given by the teacher. He said, *'Madam ji, aisa kaise ho sakta hai? Dekhiye main number line par dikha sakta hoon.'* (How is this possible, madam? See, I can show you on the number line.) A crowd gathered around him. Some children agreed with him, while others agreed with the teacher. The teacher encouraged other children also to attempt to explain the answer in their own ways. Then the teacher also explained it a couple of times. Then she gave another question of a similar nature and asked the children to solve that. It was observed that instead of providing the solution to the problem directly, she gave a similar problem, helped them solve it and then compared the process with the original problem). There was no time for further discussion and the class ended with this.

SECTION III

ANALYSIS AND CONCLUSION

A study such as this can be analysed from many angles. With a detailed profile of each teacher, the document of her AR work, a classroom observation and finally, a post-study interview, there is rich, ample material to draw from. The contributors to this book lay no claims to a complete analysis, as there will always be room to better understand the work of these teachers and the reasons for their successful action research. In this concluding section, an attempt is made to examine the extent to which the objective of the study (as given on page 39) was indeed fulfilled.

In Section I, we attempted to connect across teacher profiles (as collated using the **Teacher Profile** questionnaire) and also across **Classroom Observations**. We made an attempt to see if and how some of the assumptions/understanding articulated in each Teacher's Profile translated into (or conflicted with) practice during the (single) classroom observation as well as through the entire period of action research.

In Section II, the **Action Research documents** showed each teacher's reflection *in* and *on* action.

In this section, we analyse how the sub-elements of each Teacher's Profile (and, to a limited extent, the CRO) gave some idea of each teacher's appreciative system, overarching theories, role frame and repertoire (these terms are explained later in this section). Their **video-recorded interview** after the completion of an AR cycle provided them with an opportunity to *reflect on* their reflection-in-action, and also allowed some of their overarching theories to emerge.

Extracts from this interview have been interwoven with relevant extracts from Teacher Profile documents, Classroom Observations and AR documents in the Overview that follows the analysis.

We finally look at the shifts in thinking experienced by the teachers and the implication of these shifts on their practice, as we go into the second spiral of research.

1. Action Research and Reflections of Teachers

> *No man ever steps in the same river twice, for it's not the same river and he's not the same man.*
> ***Heraclitus, 6th century BCE***

Kearsley (2010) says that the principles of andragogy 'can be applied regardless of age and could be considered good teaching practice' and these may also be taken to represent the principles of facilitative practice. The parallels among and the effectiveness of these principles of learning were experienced at three levels:

- with the teachers,
- with the students, and
- with the facilitating team that helped the teachers through the action research project.

The experiences of teachers were valued by facilitators, and the former were given full charge of their analysis, understanding and strategies. The teachers felt motivated and ready enough to carry out the study as they were concerned about their students and could articulate the problem at hand. As they worked through their identified problems and addressed them with the resources available, they tried out 'good' teaching practices and also gained some new insights. They were most successful in this when they, in turn, valued the students' contexts and prior knowledge. Thus, teachers learnt the importance of valuing each child's current location, even as their own was valued by the facilitators. The facilitators too, were engaged in such work for the first time. So they learnt on the job, juggling with the impulse to intervene and not intervene, engaging with the teachers so that they pin down the unique situation that is causing some uncertainty or disturbance, while allowing the teachers to emerge as the problem-solvers. The facilitating team was thus engaged in acquiring skills of good facilitative practice, and the facilitators' observations in Section II offer us a glimpse of their thinking.

> *To maintain the state of doubt and to carry on systematic and protracted inquiry – these are the essentials of thinking.*
> ***Dewey (1933)***

As can be seen from the narratives contained in Section II, when teachers connected with students, accepting their shortcomings and celebrating their strengths, they found that this gave children a great deal of self-confidence. When they helped their students connect their learning with their own environment and day-to-day experiences, the children found the learning meaningful and thus engaged with it enthusiastically. Children even began to take responsibility for their own learning and acquired skills of reading, writing, comprehension and expression in a remarkably short time. For instance, Shipra, Narendra and Sahabuddin recorded that when they started their action research, the number of words that children could read were very few. However, after working with the children for three months, they found that the children could read a significantly greater number of words. Neeraj found that the children who had quietly (and blindly) accepted what was given in the Science textbook or told to them by the Science teacher, were now

- asking relevant questions in science,
- attempting to explain the likely cause of their observations,
- designing experiments to test their own hypotheses and
- learning through experiments about, for example, germination.

Similarly, Shakuntala and Saud found that children's understanding of mathematical concepts crystallised when

a. they used examples from the children's immediate environment to illustrate a concept,
b. involved children in the making of teaching–learning materials (instead of merely handing them these materials ready-made), and
c. encouraged them to create their own problem sums. Particularly in a context where most teachers' own experience (as school-goers) was one where the textbook (and the exercises contained therein) were treated as sacrosanct, this was a remarkable move.

Did the Reflective Practitioner Truly Emerge from Within these Teachers?

In the second spiral of this study, the following question needs to be answered: How do we know that the teachers showcased here did indeed grow more reflective? We draw from their own observations and professed insights, their revisiting (and shift in some) assumptions, perceptions of each other and/or visibly increased peer interaction, as we also resort to 'concrete' evidence like changed lesson plans and teaching practice. While a spread of information was thus gathered, a select subset of all the issues is scrutinised here, where relevant to the work done by each teacher. This is followed by an elaboration of the four constants identified by Schon and shifts, if any, in each of them.

In Argyris and Schon's (1974) single and double loop model, a distinction is drawn between two levels of reflection. A single loop reinforces actions taken. It does not involve the examination of underlying beliefs. However, in a double loop, underlying principles and beliefs are examined:

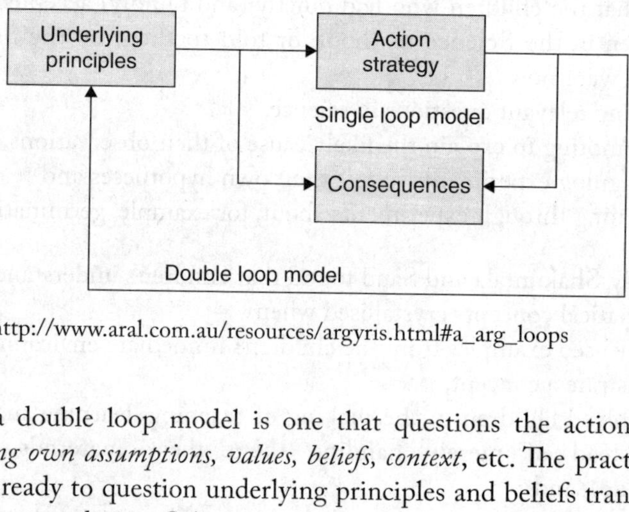

Source: http://www.aral.com.au/resources/argyris.html#a_arg_loops

Thus, a double loop model is one that questions the action taken *including own assumptions, values, beliefs, context*, etc. The practitioner who is ready to question underlying principles and beliefs transforms practice, according to Schon.

In this study, all the teachers reflected as per the single loop model. This becomes clear in the chapters that follow.

We take a look now at those who also practised double loop reflection. This is elaborated further in the chapter *Reflection on Reflection-in-action*.

Mohit clearly questioned the assumption underlying the bias towards the written and verbal modes of assessment, when he attempted to include the less articulate children in his class. In revisiting the belief (upon which his own school education was based) that *children who do not speak or write do not know anything*, he broke away from it in his eagerness to address his action research problem. Neeraj questioned the assumption that teaching science content from a textbook is adequate – a method which was used by his teachers when he was a student. In wholeheartedly adopting the Whole Language Approach, Narendra, Sahabuddin and Madan overthrew their assumptions about how languages are learnt. They admitted to this in their post-AR cycle interview and in their own documentation.

While Shipra mainly altered her strategies to improve English vocabulary in her students, she later showed a progression in her framing of the problem. As this book is being written, Shipra is working on assessment methods that are in alignment both with the nature of the language as well as the children's own context. Thus, the underlying exploration of cohesion between chosen methods of assessment and the nature of the subject implies the surfacing of (as yet unarticulated) assumptions.

As will be seen (in chapter x), several teachers revisited their former assumptions (perhaps as a result of participating in action research) and examined them critically.

We begin by connecting a data point of the Teacher Profile – length of teaching experience – to the experience of conducting action research.

Did a Teacher's Length of Teaching Experience Help or Hinder in Reflecting Through Action Research?

In-service teacher training is a challenge in itself, more so when teachers are highly experienced. As the years of teaching increase, it is more likely that the teacher settles into patterns of thinking and behaviour. For this very reason, it could be expected that teachers-in-the-making are more likely than moderately or highly experienced teachers to show an openness to change. Effecting a change in classroom practices often requires revisiting one's appreciative system, and sometimes even requires a change in values. This is by no means an easy task.

> *Experience is not what happens to you, it is what you* ***do*** *with what happens to you.*
> ***Aldous Huxley***

Rodgers (2002) refers to Dewey's (1916/1944) definition of education as 'that reconstruction or reorganisation of experience which adds to the meaning of experience, and which increases [one's] ability to direct the course of subsequent experience.' Rodgers also draws our attention to Dewey's description of the two elements that constitute experience: interaction and continuity. Through interaction, the person undergoing the experience both changes the world and is changed by it. Continuity, Rodgers notes, can narrowly be conveyed to be 'something very close to what Piaget meant by schema building'. Building upon prior experiences, we glean meaning from new ones. 'Interaction and continuity, the elements of experience, are the *x* and *y* axes of experience.'

This naturally leads to the inference that years of professional experience can add richness and depth to the practice of the professional. This is as true of teaching as any other profession. With every additional year of experience, a teacher can add to her repertoire and understanding. While content to be transacted may not change significantly over the years, each batch of students brings fresh opportunities for exploration and innovation. And yet, this very length of experience can pose a barrier to fresh learning – if the in-service teacher has (unconsciously) settled into a predictable pattern of replicable behaviour and classroom practice. As Dewey (1916/1944) points out, routine habits tend to possess us, instead of *our* having control over them.

Obviously, then, experience alone – however educative – is not enough.

What, then, could be the trigger for change? Osterman (2010) asserts that 'Without reflection, theories of action are not revised and, until new concepts, ideas, or theories of action begin to influence behaviour, learning will not occur.'

Repeated encounter with similar situations that demand the same content knowledge or similar skills result in the employment of certain practices that crystallise over the years into habits – which begin as mental habits. Dewey (1933) observes:

> Most persons are quite unaware of the distinguishing peculiarities of their own mental habit. They take their own mental operations for granted, and unconsciously make them the standard for judging the mental processes of others. Hence, there is a tendency to encourage everything in the pupil which agrees with this attitude, and neglect or fail to understand whatever is incongruous with it. The prevalent overestimation of the value, for mind-training, of theoretic subjects as compared to practical pursuits, is doubtless due partly to the fact that the teacher's calling tends to select those in whom the theoretic interest is specially strong and to repel those in whom executive abilities are marked. Teachers sifted out on this basis judge pupils and subjects by

> a like standard, encouraging an intellectual one-sidedness in those to whom it is naturally congenial, and repelling those in whom practical instincts are more urgent.

How can the rich experience borne of years of professional practice be leveraged so as to generate rather than pose a barrier to further learning and reflection? York-Barr et al (2006) offer:

> Reflective practice offers one powerful way for educators – individually and collectively – to stay challenged, effective, and alive in their work. The greater the number of people involved, the greater the potential to significantly improve educational practice, and, therefore, the greater the potential to enhance student learning.

Ghaye (2011) is of a similar view, when he asserts that 'Reflective practices also help us understand the links between feeling, thinking and doing. How we feel affects how we think. This affects what we actually do.'

Therefore, a pertinent question that we now ask is: to what extent did the length of teaching experience impact the teacher's readiness to reflect and then, act on the new understanding so as to bring about some change? Of all the teachers, Mohit and Neeraj are the least experienced, and we found that these teachers-in-the-making displayed a great willingness to revisit their own assumptions. In fact, even in their problem-setting, they showed a tendency to question their own overarching theories, as is evident from their AR documents. But this does not imply that being more experienced was an obstacle to change. The moderately experienced teachers, Shakuntala, Madan, Sahabuddin and Narendra, showed a remarkably fresh approach in the way in which they looked at the problem at hand, and did not respond in a mechanical manner. Deepak, Shipra and Saud are very experienced, and their responsiveness to the power of action research has belied the common expectation that experienced teachers find it more difficult to change.

In short, the teachers who participated in this study did not show any correlation (reverse or otherwise) between length of teaching experience and extent of shift in thinking or practice.

The structure of the action research template is now revisited in the light of literature as well as teachers' experiences in this study.

Action Research Template

By far, this document was found to have had the most impact upon teachers' thinking. Most of them acknowledged that this template lent structure to their thought processes – and consequently their documentation. The document (see template in Appendix) requires the teacher to mull over the action research problem and thus prevents him/her from rushing headlong into it. At the start, the teacher has to identify the problem, analyse it and think of reasons why some children are facing the problem while others are not, how the teacher knows this for sure that this is the case, and so on. McIntosh[1] points out that 'Asking the right questions – similar to the way in which physicians ask questions in order to make a diagnosis – is fundamental to creating the dialogue.'

Based on this, the AR template was designed such that the teacher mulls over the identified problem for quite a while before addressing it. The teacher is encouraged – through filling in the AR template – to first sift through *several identified problems* before zeroing in *one* researchable problem, then analysing it to understand its ramifications, and *only then* to go on to think of likely strategies to address it. Unless the right question is asked, it is unlikely that significant progress will be made.

The template goes on to nudge the teacher into detailing out the problem, by having the teacher examine the evidence for claiming that certain children face the problem while others do not. Specifically, it asks:

- How many children face the problem?
- Efforts made by the teachers to tackle the challenge.
- Key observations – How many children learnt it well, what method of teaching–learning was useful to some extent, etc.

It is only after conducting the above analysis that the teacher is led to proposing alternative strategies to address the issue. Thereafter, the teacher is encouraged to select the best of these as the first approach to be tried out in class.

Before implementing the selected strategy, the document asks the teacher to think through the resources needed for its implementation, the likely time frame and possible outcomes. The intent here is to ensure that the teacher carefully plans the classroom transaction before implementation of the selected strategy. Naturally, it then demands *evidence* for the effectiveness of the implemented strategy – if indeed it was perceived as being effective.

> *The problem fixes the end of thought and the end controls the process of thinking.*
>
> **Dewey (1933)**

In this insistence, we align ourselves with McIntosh's 'practice-based evidence' rather than 'evidence-based practice'. As stated by many researchers (like Johns [2007]), the auditing of reflective qualities like wisdom and greater mindfulness through concrete measures is avoided by the stark admission that reflection 'is not scientific in its approach'. Control groups and statistics are thus done away with in this approach, which posits reflection as 'a form of human inquiry that can grow'.

We now proceed to look at each step of the Action Research across the set of participating teachers, in the context of the work of Schon and Dewey.

Framing of the Problem

As Schon (1983) points out, the framing of the problem is a critical step as it then lends itself to the development of strategies. So an attempt is made here to understand the problem-framing exercise by the teachers.

In Schon's terminology, inquiry can lead to a 'frame experiment', which happens when the

> inquirer remains open to the discovery of phenomena, incongruent with the initial problem setting. What allows this to happen is that the inquirer is willing to step into the problematic situation, to impose a frame on it, to follow the implications of the discipline thus established and yet remain open to the situation's back-talk.

Deepak Dixit manifested the above quality, when he set aside his agenda to teach the class about transparent, translucent and opaque objects and addressed, instead, their shaky understanding of the process of vision. As children's 'absurd' hypotheses about vision unfolded, he remained open to them – even as he struggled to find ways to deal with them respectfully.

How did teachers frame their research problems? Were they digging into their (perhaps unarticulated) overarching theories (Schon 1983) while framing their problems? Did they take reality as a 'given', or did they experience the need to change the perceived reality? Or were they restricting themselves to devising new strategies to address the unique case at hand? As Schon says, in an 'effort to solve the problem as initially set', the practitioner could investigate a problem of making something or of understanding something. For ease of reference, the table presenting the problems chosen by the teachers is reproduced in the next page.

> *The situation is complex and uncertain and there is a problem in finding the problem.*
>
> ***Schon (1983)***

Teacher(s)	Action Research Problem
Shipra	English: reading and writing skills of some students in Class V below expected level
Mohit	How to teach EVS to students of Class IV who cannot comprehend the language (Bengali students in Hindi state)
Madan	Reading of the Hindi alphabet by four students of Class IV below expected level
Shakuntala and Saud	Math: some students of Class VI do not understand place value
Neeraj	How to develop scientific temper in students of Class V and VI
Narendra and Sahabuddin	Hindi: reading of some students in Classes V and VI below expected level
Deepak Dixit	Children of Class VI do not understand vision: how to teach them in an organic manner

It can be seen that barring Neeraj and Deepak, all teachers were *seeking effective strategies* to bring about a certain understanding in their students, be it in Language, Science, Math or EVS. Their concern was with the *transaction of content in an effective manner*. Taking the reality (content, curriculum, students' learning levels) as a given, these teachers went about finding suitable strategies to enhance the learning of their students. For example, Shakuntala and Saud were team-teaching Math to Class VI, and had identified some concerns well before the idea of Action Research was mooted in their school (see their AR document). The bounds that had been set by the curriculum determined the setting of the problem, in this case, as these teachers could clearly see that such fundamental aberrations needed urgent attention.

In contrast, Neeraj's aim of developing scientific temper in his students reflects an *attitude* that he wishes to see in his students, and it could have stemmed from his – probably unarticulated – overarching theory of the *nature of Science*. 'Not only in scientific experiments, but whatever the subject, even if it is something about Art, *every human being must have a scientific temperament*, … I was thinking that children…whatever they see, should investigate the truth – not just believe it, *because someone says so*,' he said as he reflects on his reflection-in-action in the final interview. It evidently had a bearing upon the framing of his action research problem. Similarly, in Deepak's articulation of teaching children 'in an organic manner', it is likely that his pedagogical approach is embedded in his vision of the subject, an overarching theory that he has about Science. As already noted, his professed intent to make children independent thinkers comes through clearly in his AR document. During his interaction with the students, he felt 'stuck' on one occasion, and made a telephone call to the Principal Investigator, asking how he should proceed as the children were putting forth some bizarre hypotheses. 'I don't want to tell them the right answers, but I don't know how to get them to think in the right direction without telling them…'. When he was asked to demand from children evidence or logic to support their hypotheses, Deepak was still unsure of how to proceed. However, he slowly led them into animated discussion and debate, as is evident from his documentation.

Having framed the problem, Schon emphasises that the 'inquirer remains open to the discovery of phenomena, incongruent with the initial problem setting'. This could well result in a re-framing of the problem. Thus, Neeraj began by listing out several issues:

- Poor self-study habits in children for science
- Inadequate connect between science and the local environment
- Problem of non-completion of homework in the case of some children
- Children's low level of interest in science

and then, as he scrutinised the situation more deeply, zeroed in on the problem: *Inadequate scientific aptitude of children, which he later reframed as: development of scientific temper in children.*

Teachers who wish to embark on action research for the first time after reading this book would do well to take cognizance of the *journey* that the *framing and reframing of a problem* often turns out to be. Similarly, Deepak had been called to assist a teacher in explaining the concepts of transparency, translucency and opacity, but found he could not embark on this until the students first got a grip on the process of seeing things.

Another interesting lens through which problem-framing can be viewed is a question we raised earlier in this section: did the teacher take the reality as a given and frame the problem *within that perceived reality*? Or did she make an attempt to change the reality through framing of the problem? No doubt, in focusing on the poor understanding of some children, *every* teacher is displaying a desire to change the situation. While it can be argued that every teacher wished to change the situation through identifying a problem, there is more to it than that. For instance, Neeraj showed an urge to change the reality ('children simply accept whatever the teacher says, they ask no questions') in the problem that he framed. In his mind, this passive acceptance of facts was misaligned with the nature of science and scientific thinking. After completion of one AR cycle, Narendra and Sahabuddin realised that the route to better language learning in their students would be through their mothers, and so have, since then, begun including the mothers of the children in their language classes. Here, a social reality was seen as the main cause, and it was this that the teachers then began to tackle.

Mohit took some time to understand his action research problem, spurred as he was by the pointed question from Vipin Chauhan, his facilitator: 'What exactly is your *point of dissatisfaction*?' Although he was concerned about the difficulty experienced by children (who did not speak Hindi) in understanding EVS lessons, he realised that as their EVS teacher, he could not possibly set about teaching them Hindi – learning languages, he knew, took time. Besides, he was aware that Language teachers were working separately with these very children, in an attempt to improve their comprehension of Hindi, the medium of instruction. He consulted his peers and also talked to children, and realised that while these children could understand Hindi to some extent, their main obstacle was lack of self-confidence. He swiftly factored this into his (now altered) method of assessment by refraining from demanding written answers from these children: he gave them the option of drawing as a means of answering a question. Keeping in mind the possibility that this could result in their feeling segregated from the rest of the class, he sensitively maneuvered this shift by giving the *entire class* the *same set of questions* to answer, and throwing open the option (*to all*) of answering these questions in written form, pictorial form or both. For the same reason, he ruled out the possibility of taking extra classes for these children after school hours, because he felt this would surely reinforce their feeling 'lesser' than the rest of the class. Interestingly, his colleagues, Narendra and Sahabuddin did take classes after school hours

> *The situation talks back, the practitioner listens…*
>
> ***Schon (1983)***

for their 'action research' students, and managed to give these students the feeling that they were getting something special!

Analysis of the Problem

While analysing the problem, and also while implementing their identified strategy, it is pertinent to focus on the following aspects, drawn from Dewey (1933):

1. Did teachers become cognizant of their own 'mental habits'?
2. If yes, did they try to alter that habit/those habits?
3. Did they draw a distinction between 'memory' and 'thinking'?
4. Did teachers become (increasingly) aware of their own learning needs, for example, ideas for classroom strategies, resources, etc.?
5. Did teachers revisit their prior pedagogy and recognise it in the terms Dewey uses: '... to many persons, "pedagogy" means precisely a set of mechanical, self-conscious devices for replacing by some cast-iron external scheme the personal mental movement of the individual'? If yes, did this lead to an altered pedagogy?

Interestingly, several teachers did display many of the above shifts. While the distinction between memory and thinking was drawn by all these teachers well before they embarked on action research, several teachers did reflect on, and then alter, their pedagogy. For instance, Neeraj reflected on his earlier pedagogy, during the final interview, when he asserted: 'Before this ... I used to get the answers from the children, then have a discussion, then tell them the principle.' From telling them the principle (which he found dissatisfying), he turned the process around to one of having them arrive at the principle themselves. He therefore first set about working towards evoking inquiry from his students, by putting up a chart for them to ask questions, and for making systematic observations. What is remarkable is that his repertoire thus far did not include this practice: 'Earlier, I used to think about it, but I never applied it in this way ... (I never thought about) how I should take it forward practically.' Yet, he swiftly moved into it, urged as he was by the impetus of his identified problem. That he continues to be concerned about the alignment of his classroom pedagogy with the nature of Science is evident from his own documentation: 'I have realised several times in class that children often narrate the definitions/theories but they are not able to discuss the rationale behind the theory. They hardly entertain any 'why' and 'how' questions. There are

> *Reflective thinking is always more or less troublesome because it involves overcoming the inertia that inclines one to accept suggestions at their face value, it involves willingness to endure a condition of mental unrest and disturbance.*
>
> ***Dewey (1933)***

rare cases of giving live examples. The children neither make observations in detail nor do they maintain their records. There is no practice of noting down observations or to use these observations whenever needed. It is therefore common that children do not pay much attention to the process of observation and its documentation.'

Schon (1983) pointed out that when a new situation or event occurs and teachers' established routines do not work for them, teachers use reflection-in-action to cope. Mohit did exactly this when he found that children who were not comfortable with Hindi were the same ones who were not participating in the EVS class. He found that the usual method of teaching worked for the other children – but not for these. This prompted him to reflect in action, and the rest of the story is told by him in his AR document.

Schon (1983) stresses the role that overarching theories play in the thinking (and therefore action) of the practitioner. As Madan analyses his AR Problem, he touches upon his (as yet unarticulated) overarching theories thus: 'Before starting action research, I was turning over in my mind the following question: "What does it take to read a word?" If I see a word and I am not able to connect this word to something concrete, then this word has no value for me and this word does not provide any meaning. To provide meaning to words is called reading. We use symbols to provide hints for words. These symbols are an integral part of language. So I decided to teach these children, keeping this understanding as the base.' The identification of the problem led Madan on a deep enquiry into the way in which a language is learnt. Turning the problem over in his mind, Madan also arrives at another insight: 'Most of the students in our school are from the Bengali community. Hindi is a new language for them. The difference in sound system of these two languages could be one of the reasons for the observed problem.' Indeed, the mismatch between the mother tongue and language of instruction is seen as an impediment equally by the Math teachers, Shakuntala and Saud, who add a couple of other causes as contributing to the difficulty experienced by the children:

- Illiteracy of parents and parents being busy with work
- Children having to help with household chores and with occupational work of parents

Identifying Possible strategies to address the problem While entering this step of the AR cycle, creativity is demanded of teachers who have themselves seldom been taught creatively, when they were students. We found that this resulted in some interesting consequences. Madan Mohan Joshi, a teacher who considered himself to be a Science teacher was called upon to teach Hindi. In his carefully considered employment of a combination of the Whole Language Approach and the Traditional Approach to teaching Language (the latter being the way in which he had been taught), he displayed his willingness to be guided by theory in his reflection-in-action, without being totally bound by it. Using coloured strips, matchstick bundles and Teaching–Learning Materials (TLMs) prepared by the children, Shakuntala and Saud straddled the gap between the children who have yet to understand place value in Class VI, and those who are in a position to grasp the course content. To quote from their documentation:

- *TLM was prepared along with the children because then they would take more interest in the work.*
- *It was decided to also cover little bit of the course with the action research children, so that they would not lag behind rest of the class too much.*

While reflecting on his reflection-in-action Neeraj acknowledged the impact of the workshops that he attended in the Foundation, on his own thinking: 'it was quite an interesting phase, that … we were getting curious as to how to do things in the future … So after training, when we came back, then we saw that this is also possible in the class … and in what way can we apply this.' Dismayed by the listlessness of his students in the Science class, he set about initiating discussions, prompting them to ask questions and note down observations systematically. To his delight, the very children who would not show any interest earlier, now began to participate actively in discussions and conduct experiments. Admitting that he was not taught to question, and that Science is usually taught by rote, he says: 'If children are doing something, then they should arrive at the principle on their own.' In these admissions there is evidence of questioning of assumptions about the nature of science, traditional pedagogy and an appropriate pedagogy of science.

Selection of Suitable Strategy to Address the Problem

During this step, it was found that many processes described by Schon occurred, in whole or in part, amongst these teachers:

1. Some teachers **became aware of their frames**, that is, they took note of the values and norms to which they gave priority thus far. Mohit acknowledged the bias to written and oral modes of assessment that he had harboured thus far, and it was the unique situation that he found himself in which brought this bias to the fore. Madan became aware of his frame of thinking in teaching EVS, and was surprised at the results when he adopted similar methods for teaching Hindi.
2. Some **assumptions surfaced**: As already described, Mohit admitted that in the past, like most other teachers, he had assumed that if a child does not write or speak, then 'he does not know anything'. When he found that the silent children in his class began to answer questions which the articulate ones could not, after their self-confidence was enhanced, this assumption was turned on its head. It led to a very valuable insight for Mohit – that every child does observe, regardless of whether or not the child articulates that observation. Shakuntala and Saud realised that their assumption that only the traditional way of teaching place value worked, was erroneous.
3. Some **unanticipated learnings/changes/dilemmas emerged**. Mohit gained an unexpected insight: he was surprised when his quiet 'action research student' pointed out how fish breathe – and the rest of the otherwise articulate class could not figure this out. When asked what could be the reason for this unexpected turn of events, he declares: 'I felt that it is something to do with observation … this boy's mind opened up … he could be seeing other things, too, without doubt … but he hadn't the opportunity to express it earlier … Somewhere it could be our fault that we think that in the class because he can't write or read, he doesn't know anything. But when he felt confident and we asked him, "Did you see anything?" his raising his hand was a great thing for me – because, earlier, he would never raise his hand …' Elliott (1991:51) points out the difference between the kind of reflection that is required here and means-end reasoning. In a particular set of circumstances, choosing a course of action demands a scrutiny of one's values – and this lends an ethical character to the reflection. However, 'since ethical choice implies an interpretation of the values to be realised, reflection cannot be separated from reflection about ends.' Again, Madan admitted to an increase in his own interest in Hindi, after teaching the language for the first time.

Sahabuddin admitted that he realised how even adults read a text, as he employed the Whole Language Approach: 'It is very interesting…this entire process as I saw it working. Even we read, without reading the full word; we often read based on guesswork.'

4. The **difference between memory and thinking** clearly emerged for Madan as he found children initially reading the hidden word purely from recall, thus indicating an absence of meaningful reading. Again, he found that by the end of the action research, children could even read the entire story in reverse sequence and he thus affirmed that they were now *not* reading from recall. Similar was the experience of Narendra and Sahabuddin, who distinguished between children reading the text from recall and reading it meaningfully.

Implementation of Identified Strategy

During this stage, almost all the teachers *became aware of their own learning needs*, ideas for classroom strategies and/or their need for more resources. For instance, Shakuntala confessed to a need for ideas to develop appropriate teaching–learning materials, for 'there is only so much we can do. If we even got a hint of some new ideas from somewhere else, we could work on it,' she declared.

Sahabuddin felt a lack of resource material and wished to gain more insights by reading. 'I would like to read the works of other writers and understand their thinking regarding children…because we may have studied Psychology in BEd. But we have not studied Psychology to this level.'

One teacher showed cognizance *of his own mental habits*: Madan stated, 'Through action research … I got an opportunity *to think about those children in a different way* … The main point is … that on those problematic issues … I got an opportunity to think differently. I thought about it and spoke about it to my group, analysed these issues and tried to find a solution.' Interestingly, even as he adopted a new pedagogy, Madan also acknowledged the power of the traditional method of teaching and learning language, as that is how *he was taught*. However, he realises that this worked with him because there was an opportunity for reinforcement of his learning at home, something his present students (many of whom are first-generation learners) sadly lack.

Even as Mohit devised an activity to teach animals' habitats to these children, he broadened the scope of the activity to include the entire class so that the possibility of these children feeling inferior would not arise. Like Shakuntala and Saud, he had the children prepare the necessary resources for conducting the activity, which has been described by him in detail in his AR document. The noteworthy point here is that Mohit did not plunge into the activity. He spent a few classes discussing animals and their habitat with the entire class, and ensured that the five children also participated in the discussion at least to some extent. He noticed that while all of them listened carefully, only two actually spoke. Even as he took note of the voluble articulation by the rest of the class of the habitat of various animals, he could see that their felicity of expression was not accompanied by a sound knowledge of classification of animals based upon their habitat. Thus, Mohit's concern for the five children who were facing a language issue did not blind him to the knowledge base of the rest of the class. His activity was designed to ensure an opportunity for every child to participate, and he quietly accepted a *partially* correct answer from one of the five children as a way of encouraging her. [To his delight, four of the five children got the right answer, only one of them after an unsuccessful attempt.] What is remarkable is his reflection on his prior understanding of these children, which was based upon the assumption that children who do not speak or write do not know anything. He now asserts that if we give that child sufficient self-confidence to express himself, then there is no reason why that child will not speak/write.

Further, he noticed that the children whom he regarded as being 'above average' could not figure out how fish breathe, while one of these five children pointed out the bubbles which he had seen emanating from the fins. MacNiff (2003) states that action researchers see knowledge as *what they do*. 'It is never complete and it is constantly shifting and developing as new and different understandings emerge. It becomes a way of being that is full of potential, surprises and unpredictability, so absolute answers to questions become meaningless, because whatever is found becomes a new question.'

> *Reflection is turning a topic in various aspects and in various lights so that nothing significant about it shall be overlooked – almost as one might turn a stone over to see what its hidden side is like or what is covered by it.*
> ***Dewey (1933)***

Another teacher, Saud, began to *realise how documentation is so critical*, for he acknowledged thus: 'Had we also from the beginning, gained access to another teacher's documentation, then we would have seen … has someone done this kind of work and if so, what is the result? So, in that sense, we would have benefitted from another teacher's documentation of similar action research ... perhaps we could have done the design in a better manner ...'

Neeraj understood the fine difference between the context of textbook content and that of his own learners. Being very connected to the local and personal context of the children in his class, he recounts how he realised while teaching them about food that the information contained in the book pertained to eating habits of people in Uttarakhand. It would have been easy to regard such content as being contextual. However, Neeraj was alert to the fact that most of his students hailed from *Bengali families* whose eating habits are very different. Eating local cuisine is not a part of their day-to-day experience. So, he began by discussing specifically the kind of food that they liked or that is cooked in their homes. He broke free from the textbook even as it purported to be contextual. By constantly connecting with what is happening and taking cues for the next step from what is happening, he reinforces Farrell's observation: 'The metaphor of reflection as a compass enables teachers to stop, look, and discover where they are at that moment and then decide where they want to go (professionally) in the future.'

During this step of implementing the identified strategy, all the teachers consciously altered their pedagogy. Shakuntala and Saud dropped the traditional method of teaching place value and resorted to the use of abacus, TLMs, etc., while Shipra used word-and-picture cards in graded levels of difficulty to slowly challenge her young readers. As she noticed the visible enjoyment of the children, she introduced another game to elicit reading of words on cards. Narendra and Sahabuddin moved entirely towards using the whole language approach after they found that simply mixing the phonetic and Whole Language Approach did not work well. Madan, too, analysed the children's difficulty in reading and adopted the Whole Language Approach after careful deliberation. Deepak Dixit probed the root of children's responses to how they see things, and with the understanding that children held incorrect beliefs due to the structure of the language used to describe sight, he proceeded to tackle this as described in his document. Mohit altered his pedagogy as well as assessment methods to factor in the inability of some of his students to express themselves orally (or in writing) in Hindi. Neeraj relied heavily on discussion as an entry point to the lesson; after he found that children displayed little or no curiosity when lessons were transacted in the traditional way. In other words, there was considerable reflection-in-action that is evident from all these strategies.

2. Reflection on Reflection-in-action

Across this set of teachers, there was almost unanimous agreement during the final review that they made significant gains through the entire process of conducting action research. In other words, the result of the second spiral revealed itself to some degree *even to the teachers* – who were ostensibly engaged only in the first spiral! The specific insight that they gained varied with each teacher, but there were some common benefits. Much of this was articulated during their final interview, when they reflected on their reflection-in-action. We summarise below the findings from the interviews.

Change in Understanding and Its Impact on Practice

This happened in two ways:

- revisiting of the teacher's own pedagogy, and subsequent altering of the pedagogy (Schon's single loop model), and
- revisiting of an understanding about children and/or how they learn, followed by a changed classroom practice (Schon's double loop model).

Mohit acknowledged that like many teachers, he probably believed that children who do not express themselves verbally or in writing 'do not know anything'. His experience of conducting action research forced him to revisit and dispel this belief. Clearly, this changed belief has affected his practice as shown by his altered assessment strategy.

Madan's changed practice of using a combination of phonetic and Whole Language Approach resulted from his questioning the efficacy of a single approach to teaching language. Neeraj's adoption of an altered pedagogy that relied heavily on discussion, exploration and inquiry by students was a result of his questioning the assumption that mere transaction of textbook content would bring about the learning of Science. Sahabuddin revisited his pedagogy of teaching Hindi, and in so doing, gained fresh insights into how children – and even adults – learn a language.

Schon (1983) suggested a sequence of steps: a situation triggers routine responses by the teacher, but to the teacher's surprise, these do not produce routine responses from the students. Now the teacher wonders why this is the case. Reflection then gives rise to on-the-spot experimentation by the teacher.

This is exactly what happened to Deepa (a non-participating teacher who was away on maternity leave during the entire period of action research) who found Shipra's novel way of increasing children's English vocabulary exciting. She then began to wonder why she could not adopt this method in Hindi too. She provides a handwritten account of the rest of the story, where she records with delight the animation with which her students' vocabulary in Hindi grew in leaps and bounds. She also recalls with humour how during her own student days, the example of a clock (*ghadi*) that was used by the teacher to introduce words beginning with the sound 'gh' never made sense to her, for the simple reason that there was no clock in her house. Had her teacher also employed the method of looking for alternative words that began with the sound 'gh', she would not have had to struggle as she did to learn words beginning with 'gh'. Implicit in this altered practice is Deepa's questioning the assumption that the textbook has the perfect example, as also her insight into the need to bring in contextual examples.

Perceived Change in Students

Shakuntala and Saud adopted the novel practice of getting the children to design their own problems, instead of simply giving them problems to solve. This resulted in a dramatic increase in motivation of a formerly non-participative student: 'There was a child, who, in the beginning, would neither listen nor do his homework. Now while we did action research, he began taking a notebook and chasing me around school, demanding, "I want homework" .... The same child who used to run away from Math or any subject, was after me ... even if the rest of his class was playing outside, he would insist: "I want homework". I would try to put him off saying, "I am going to another class; I will give it to you after school is over." I would think that he would forget and come only the next day. Instead, there he would be around at closing hour, reminding me, "You said you would give me homework." So I would give him two or three questions, and ask him to design his own problem sums. He would bring two whole pages of sums the next day. This child's eagerness definitely increased.' Mohit had a similar experience, when he found that after action research, 'these children can understand ... they are filled with confidence.' Neeraj echoes this sentiment as he remarks on the marked change that he sees in his class: 'Whenever I would be overseeing the process of activities that children were engaged in I would find that children were animatedly talking to each other. Discussions would take place continuously amongst the children. So, though, it was very noisy, it was good that they were talking to each other. As soon as I would come in, all of them would start saying, "Sir, can I say something? Can I say something?" so there was a quite a lot of noise from the children.' Narendra and Sahabuddin lamented that, in the beginning, children did not take much interest, and would run away home, saying they wouldn't study. But when different types of work were given to them by these two teachers, they began to get interested. While doing action research, when he and Sahabuddin began to take extra classes after school hours for them, and eventually stopped these classes upon completion of the action research cycle, they began to ask: 'Sir, why don't we have extra classes today?'

Modifying Teaching Strategies

Shipra admitted that action research gave her an opportunity to focus in a structured manner on children who had been her concern even earlier. Mohit confessed that formerly, his lesson plans would not address those 4 or 5 students who were 'below average', 'but now I include strategies for these children as well.' Sahabuddin experienced a shift in his stance from always being a teacher to now adopting the role of a learner as well. Shakuntala acknowledged that the timeline brought an urgency to complete the cycle even though her co-teacher, Saud, and she were anyway addressing 'below average' kids even before starting AR. Neeraj valued the framework provided by action research, which, he claims, 'would help us to think like this in future. It is my first experience where my effort is to see that children reach a scientific principle *by themselves*. Earlier we used to just tell them, and move on.' He admitted to a change in his classroom pedagogy. Where he would formerly plunge straight into the lesson, he now makes an effort *before* teaching any subject to provoke discussion, 'so that, in children, curiosity is awakened. This kind of process ... I did not follow earlier.' Schon (1983) says that overarching theories do not supply rules that can 'predict or control a particular event'; instead, they supply 'language from which to construct particular descriptions and themes to develop particular interpretations.'

Neeraj's focus on scientific temper and his concern over the absence of curiosity and enquiry in his class stemmed, more likely than not, from his overarching theory of the nature of Science. That he was himself not taught through inquiry is a fact he admits to – and yet, that he resorted to addressing this as his action research problem speaks of the robustness of this theory for him. This connects to what Schon says: 'If a practitioner has such a theory, he uses it to guide his reflection-in-action.'

In his sustained efforts to systematise the observation, enquiry and thinking of students, Neeraj showed a tenacious unwillingness to let go of his objective. This brings to mind what Dewey (1933) has said:

> Any teacher who is alive to the modes of thought naturally operative in the experience of the normal child will have no difficulty in avoiding the identification of the logical with a readymade organisation of subject matter, as well as the notion that the only way to escape this error is to pay no attention to logical considerations. Such a teacher will have no difficulty in seeing that the real problem of intellectual education is the transformation of natural powers: the transformation of more or less casual curiosity and sporadic suggestion into attitudes of alert, cautious and thorough inquiry.

Neeraj enabled the shift of his class from a bunch of mute, passive learners, to lively, curious and logically thinking students, and he describes the routes he used in his AR document. In grappling with this issue, Neeraj appears to have extensively employed discussion as pedagogy. He admits that he now seldom rushes into any topic; instead, he begins with animated discussions and questions that pertain to the topic to be taught. Mohit also displays extensive use of discussion in responding to students' query as to how fish breathe.

Why is discussion not used often enough by teachers? Indeed, both Neeraj and Mohit admit that they have adopted this practice only as a consequence of action research. 'Earlier,' Mohit confesses, 'I used to be the sole person talking. Now I find I listen more and talk less.' Mohit has perhaps placed his finger on the common reason for this difficulty, articulated by Loughran (2002) – 'Student teachers often find it difficult to conduct an interpretive discussion (Baird and Northfield 1992, Barnes 1975) because they struggle with their use of 'wait time'.'

Perhaps this is a pointer for facilitators of teachers' action research: to aid teachers in getting more comfortable with this inevitable 'wait time'.

Schon (1983) advocates a reflective conversation between the professional and his clients. Narendra and Sahabuddin engaged in one such conversation when they were faced with a listless group of students. They met this situation by turning around and asking their students to state what it was that *they* would like to see happen in class. As students' suggestions flowed, both Narendra and Sahabuddin took note of them and began implementing these in class. To their satisfaction, the participation of the students visibly increased. Had any of their own school teachers ever asked *them* such a question? 'No one asked me this question in my school life,' Sahabuddin confesses.

Increased regularity in documentation and peer discussion were other after-effects of action research. This was noticed by Deepa, the non-participating teacher, as she returned from maternity leave. She notes: 'The changes I saw in the teachers was that *they regularly started writing reflections* … they shared their writing and discussed many issues with each other …' Peer interaction thus increased visibly as a consequence of action research.

Several teachers admitted that formerly, they used to depend on others' (resource persons') suggestions and advice 'for solutions to our problems; now we have started thinking by ourselves through discussion with peers. We get ideas, pin down reasons and meet resource persons'. In addition, some of the teachers began to interact more intensely with the local community. Some teachers met parents regularly (to ask their permission to teach their children extra hours) and the attendance of the children also improved. Many teachers began to enquire deeply into the source of children's problems, and even traced them to their homes. There was also a noticeable increase in frequency of peer-to-peer discussion of classroom problems after AR began.

Deepa noticed several changes when she returned from maternity leave (just as teachers were drawing to the end of their first action research cycle): 'I saw that teachers who were part of this were writing … about how they should proceed, what improvement was noted … and I also noticed that they were very connected to their team. They shared things like how many words the children could read at first, and now, what words they are able to read, etc. 'Earlier when I used to make a lesson plan, I would write self-observations. I would list out what I did, what my weaknesses are …. When I returned from maternity leave, I saw each teacher was writing a 'Reflection'. So I asked them what Reflection was. At first, I didn't understand. Now I write more *about the children as well, and not only about myself*. It has now become a weekly habit.

Impact of Documentation

Loughran (2002) notes that 'writing an anecdote enhances the meaning-making from the action in the practice setting and can unsettle some of the taken-for-granted assumptions about teaching that student teachers have developed (are developing) and increase the likelihood that new ways of seeing might emerge.'

It was found, during the course of this study, that all the teachers benefitted enormously from the act of documenting their action research in the format provided. Their thinking flowed in a structured manner, they stepped back and looked at their action research with an element of objectivity, and time-consuming as the process was, none could deny its critical significance in their development. Some of them, like Narendra, would document on occasions 'when there was something we really liked'. However, AR has now brought about the routine practice of documentation, which, Narendra admits, shows greater reflection. 'For instance, if this thing has not worked we state that we could make other changes.' Saud is of the view that his earlier practice did not call for documentation, as '….what we had to do, we would plan it and start doing it.' Here, he learnt how to document, something he confessed that he could never do properly earlier, but which he can now do in detail.

Ghaye (2011) points out that 'Looking back on your experiences and learning from them is important – but reflecting on the past can be limited by what we can remember and by what has happened. It is also important to reflect on the here and now – to reflect not only on what has happened or what we would like to happen, but on what's happening now.'

Sahabuddin experienced exactly this realisation when he conducted action research on students who could not read and write Hindi properly. While reflecting on his reflection-in-action, he asserts that during action research, he gave a lot of importance to documentation because his earlier writings would focus on what had gone by: 'If I talk of the earlier times, I would write: "I went to school and today I had a plan and I taught according to the plan and plan was carried out well." It was … like, "*in my class, this happened, this happened, this happened*" …. It was the word "*happened*"' … but now, it is "what is *happening*?". Between "*happened*" and "what is *happening*?", a big difference came about.' So he now takes pains to record what worked, what did not, how children enjoyed his class and what his own learning was from the class. Madan says something similar when he admits that before doing action research, he would anyway document, but documentation increased while doing action research. 'Now, we had to think more and write *about the children* ...'

We now draw from Schon's (1983) four 'constants':

1. The media, languages and repertoires that practitioners use to describe reality and conduct experiments
2. The appreciative systems they bring to problem setting, to the evaluation of inquiry, and to reflective conversation
3. The overarching theories by which they make sense of phenomena
4. The role frames within which they set their tasks and through which they bound their institutional settings

While Schon emphasises that these 'constants' are not 'unchanging', and that in fact, they do sometimes change 'in response to reflection', these four constants lend that solid reference 'from which, in reflection-in-action, [the practitioner] ... can allow his theories and frames to come apart.'

Repertoire

Most teachers experienced the limitations of their repertoire as they tried to pull out the appropriate strategy from their bag of tricks, as it were, to address their particular problem. Madan acknowledged the enhancement of his own knowledge base as he learnt to tackle the problems faced by his students. In so doing, he realised that '*our* knowledge too is created...' Narendra, Sahabuddin, Shakuntala and Saud acknowledged their felt need for more ideas to tackle the issues faced by them in the classroom. Shipra, Neeraj and Mohit experienced visible enhancement in their repertoire, as they gained confidence in implementing their altered strategies. Deepak felt encouraged as well as uncertain, after he tried addressing students' misconceptions through discussion. Overall, as already described, there was a visible increase in the repertoire of all teachers.

Appreciative System

Schon emphasises the importance of constancy in a practitioner's appreciative system, as without a robust set of values, he points out that the practitioner will neither be able to frame the problem at the start, nor 're-appreciate the situation in the light of its back-talk'. Values are not pre-ordained constructs in action research. Elliott (1991:51) states:

'Values as ends cannot be clearly defined independently of and prior to practice. In this context, the practice itself constitutes an interpretation of its ends in a particular practical situation. The ends are defined in practice and not in advance of it.'

For instance, Mohit acknowledged an increased sensitivity to students whose mother tongue is not Hindi and realised how he may well have assumed that their silence earlier was indicative of ignorance. While his emphasis on choosing a strategy that did not divide the 'action research students' from the rest of the class showed how strongly he valued inclusion, his action research (the 'back talk' of the situation) resulted in his acknowledging (and questioning) the prevalent bias towards written and spoken means of expression.

We can also see this in the case of Shipra, who shifted what she valued thus: 'Before doing AR, my focus was more on covering a particular topic in a fixed time, and I would assume that children would more or less 'get it' in that fixed time. But while doing AR, I perceived that it is not as important to cover a certain topic as it is to ensure that every child has learnt, and if so, how much?' In Schon's (1983) framework, this translates into a shift in the teacher's appreciative system. What is especially noteworthy here is that Shipra has been teaching for seventeen years – and this realisation has come to her now, after completing just one cycle of action research. Surely, this reveals the power of action research in triggering a change in an experienced in-service teacher! Neeraj finds his classes far noisier now than before, but has come to regard this as a good thing: 'This, I see as being positive ... as, that if it is noisy, children are talking ... discussing ...' In Schon's terminology, Neeraj has experienced a shift in his appreciative system: he now sees the value of a noisy class.

Overarching Theories

Both Dewey's and Schon's work suggest that

> Teachers can compare what is actual and occurring (theories in use) in their practice with their own beliefs (espoused theories) about learning and teaching. This productive tension between actual experience and espoused theories provides teachers with an opportunity to systematically look at their practice so that they can deepen their understanding of what they do and thus come to new insights about their students, their teaching, and themselves.
>
> [Farrell 2012]

Indeed, this tension was experienced by several teachers: when Neeraj found children not taking any interest in Science and not asking questions, he experienced a conflict between his understanding of science as a subject and the manner in which children were 'learning' it. Shakuntala and Saud were forced to examine their faith in the traditional way of teaching place value, again because their experience held a mirror before them: and they describe their journey eloquently in their AR document. Narendra and Sahabuddin revisited their understanding of how children learn to read, and what prompted them to do so was their actual experience of how children *used memory to read*, rather than letter-by-letter recognition. This gave them new insights which they have documented in their AR template.

Similarly, Madan's use of different diagnostic techniques (like having children read the story in reverse, to see if they are reading it from memory or truly reading with understanding) to ascertain the reading ability of the students was remarkable in its scientific rigour. As pointed out earlier, this could have stemmed from his prior experience of being a teacher of Environmental Studies. He, too, experienced a tension between different approaches to teaching language and felt the need to combine the traditional approach with the whole language approach, when he found that children could not read the story from a random point – which meant that they read it in sequence mainly from memory. Madan has also shown a willingness to view his role frame flexibly – from a teacher of Environmental Studies to one of Hindi (he had even been called upon to teach Mathematics in his previous school). Madan's reliance on overarching theories of language teaching-and-learning (like the Whole Language Approach and the traditional approach) has been balanced by his willingness to release himself from the grip of both and devise his own activities that combine the two approaches. Thus, these overarching theories, while guiding his reflection-in-action, do not restrict him tightly.

Institutional Context

How did the teachers treat their institutional contexts? Several teachers (Neeraj, Madan, Saud and Sahabuddin) admitted that their work was enhanced by the environment in the Foundation, and in their school. Shipra acknowledged drawing ideas from peer discussion, something that her colleague Deepa (non-participant in the AR study) perceived as an increase in discussion amongst teachers. Madan consulted the Principal, while trying to address his AR problem, and Deepak gave him the idea of getting the children to try and read a story in reverse sequence, to check if they were reading it from memory or genuinely decoding the letters. Quite clearly, here was an environment where the exchange of ideas was possible between teachers, as well as between teachers and Principal.

Quoting Johns and McCormack (2002), McIntosh infers that 'In effect, it means a 'letting go' of traditional hierarchies and outcome orientated activities and moving towards entering into the learning experience. Ultimately, in order to engage effectively in a reflective conversation of whatever shape and form, there needs to be an organisational system which allows this to occur.'

As described in chapter II. x *Teacher Snapshots*, the deliberate inclusion of the *teachers' views on the school curriculum* in the Teacher Profile document was in order to probe the grip on the minds of teachers of something that is handed down by the authorities: seldom is it questioned by the teacher who is under pressure to 'cover' the syllabus. As Oberg and McCutcheon (1987) state, most teachers take parameters like curriculum, textbook, etc. as given:

> Perhaps this is because teachers are conditioned to follow and not to lead, to obey and not to question the authority of the school bureaucracy, even though the curriculum guidelines, textbooks, and testing policies authorities prescribe could be seen as the root of many problems teachers encounter. Perhaps teachers see such matters as outside their arena, or perhaps they are conscious of job security and they do not see questioning authority as part of their role.

[In Schon's (1983) terms, this translates into the role frame of the teacher, through which she sets boundaries for her institutional settings.] As can be seen from their responses, only two teachers (Mohit and Neeraj) were openly critical of the curriculum, with most others taking it as given. [One or two of the others bemoaned its 'vastness'.] Despite this, as can be seen from their work, these teachers have worked innovatively within the constraints of the curriculum. The teachers have kept within the institutional context, and only in rare instances, have moved beyond covering the syllabus and teaching the prescribed course. Yet, their simple strategies have proved powerful enough to address the identified problems in *all* the cases.

The overall simplicity of approach is remarkable both in its efficacy as well as in its potential for adoption by other teachers who read this set of cases. In the words of the facilitator Tapasya Saha: 'These teachers were more focused; they pinpointed the problems of individual students and were actually working around them at different levels in their classes within a time frame. I could also see that the activities they designed were not very difficult or critical but were very simple, effective and innovative, and could keep the children engaged and engrossed. Action research not only makes the teaching–learning more enjoyable and meaningful, but the practice of action research itself can make a good teacher an even a better one.' It is also likely that the practice of action research can turn a not-so-good teacher into a good one! That it can make a teacher reflective has indeed been borne out by a great deal of research.

Changed Lesson Plans

One of the tasks of a school Principal is to oversee lesson plans of teachers. Deepak Dixit has found a marked change in the lesson plans of teachers after they embarked upon action research. This has been corroborated by both participating as well as non-participating teachers.

Deepak says, 'The teachers definitely became reflective. I say this on the basis of their lesson plans. When I look at their earlier lesson plans and the ones now … just looking at them you can say there is a marked difference … because now the lesson plans have to be aligned with their reflections … Earlier the lesson plans would get over and they would move on to the next week's lesson plan … But now they write their reflections in them … what their experience was and if they have to modify something why they have to do so … So they started doing needs analysis of the children … I have noticed a difference in the quality of reflection in the lesson plans of the non-participating teachers too. It may be noted here that Prachie did not participate in AR, but still she was able to reflect because she gained initial exposure to the process and was always present during discussions within the team members, and also when the facilitators visited the school. To me, it seems that just providing a conducive atmosphere and maintaining a constant connect to the idea enabled Prachie to be reflective.'

Fig. III.1 shows a sample of a teacher's lesson plan before starting action research. Conspicuous by their absence are any reflections by the teacher of the teacher–learner exchanges, the basis for adopting the chosen pedagogy, or even any observations about the nature of

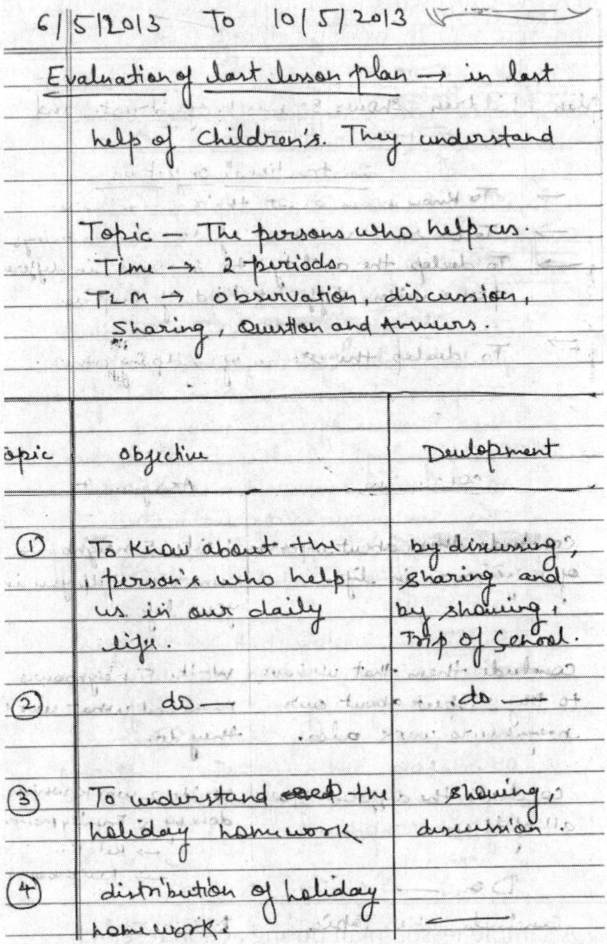

6/5/2013 To 10/5/2013

Evaluation of last lesson plan → in last

help of Children's. They understand

Topic — The persons who help us.

Time → 2 periods

TLM → observation, discussion, Sharing, Question and Answers.

opic	Objective	Development
1	To Know about the person's who help us in our daily life.	by discussing, sharing and by showing, Trip of School.
2	do —	do —
3	To understand ~~eaed~~ the holiday homework	showing, discussion.
4	distribution of holiday homework.	←

Fig. III.1 A sample lesson plan before starting action research

engagement of the children after this plan was transacted. It is a point-wise plan of what is to be done in class.

In contrast, Fig. III.2 shows the same teacher's lesson plan *during* action research, where the flow of thought under 'evaluation' is not only a new element, but it clearly shows the quality of reflection, as it notes the manner in which the children responded to the teacher's pedagogy. 'They asked many questions and found the answers themselves through discussion. The session was very interactive, and being a teacher,

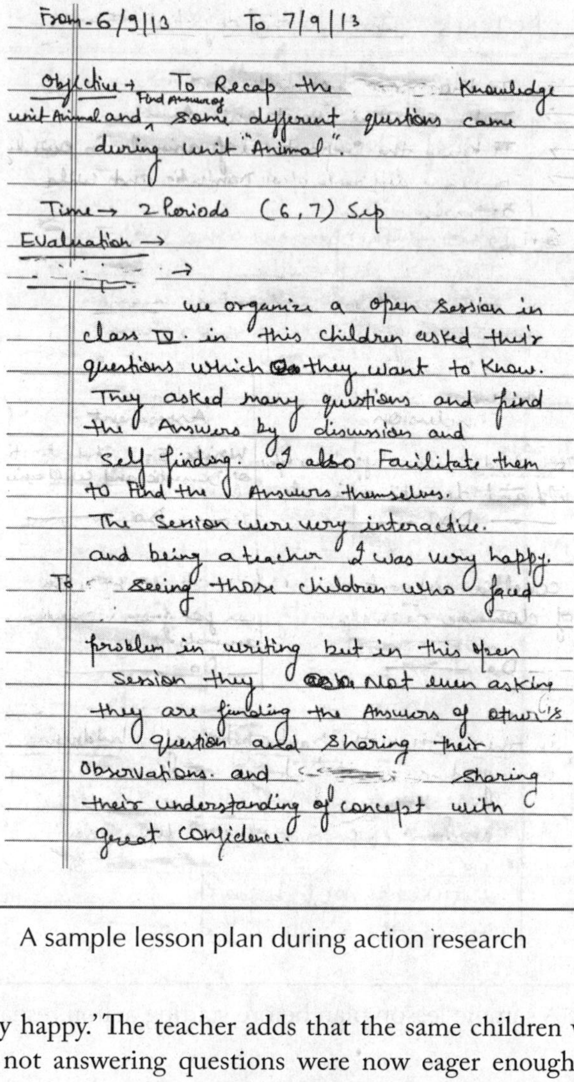

From-6/9/13 To 7/9/13

Objective → To Recap the Knowledge unit Animal and Find Answers of some different questions came during unit "Animal".

Time → 2 Periods (6, 7) Sep

Evaluation →

→

we organize a open session in class IV. in this children asked their questions which they want to Know. They asked many questions and find the Answers by discussion and self finding. I also Facilitate them to find the Answers themselves. The session were very interactive. and being a teacher I was very happy. To seeing those children who faced problem in writing but in this open session they Not even asking they are finding the Answers of other's question and Sharing their observations. and Sharing their understanding of concept with great confidence.

Fig. III.2 A sample lesson plan during action research

I was very happy.' The teacher adds that the same children who were formerly not answering questions were now eager enough to share their observations and even try and find answers to questions that had been posed to *other* children. The teacher ends by recording his delight at the increased self-confidence of these children. [Other lesson plans are not included here, due to lack of space.]

3. Overview

This section consolidates the essence of each teacher's action research, and its effectiveness in promoting reflection. The profile of each teacher is summarised, and a glimpse offered of their action research work as well as their final *reflection on reflection-in-action*. 'Anticipatory, retrospective, and contemporaneous reflection demand different skills and framing abilities and interact with experience in a variety of ways.' (Loughran, 1996)

This could be seen in the quality of inputs that the authors of this book gained from the three instruments: CRO, AR document and post-AR cycle interview. During the CRO, the manifestation of inherent assumptions and attitudes came to the fore, as has been described in the section on CROs. In the AR document, the teacher's reflection-in-action was sometimes obvious, and at other times, an undercurrent. In the post-AR cycle interview, the teacher was encouraged to look back, make meaning of the action research and reflect upon his/her reflection-in-action. This afforded an opportunity for the articulation of hitherto unarticulated shifts and insights. For instance, when Mohit Sharma was asked why his 'action research student' could articulate an observation about the way fish breathe (which his 'above average students' did not), he eloquently observed that this could be because their minds had opened up now, and it could well be that they had actually been observing things all along, but due to diffidence, had refrained from expressing it. This is exactly what Loughran (2003) refers to when he advocated that teachers' experiences be 'presented back to them in ways that might be helpful and offer insights that they had not previously recognised.'

Facilitating the emergence rather than articulation by the facilitator of such insights is critical to the development of reflexivity. As Loughran (2003) says, in the two methods 'the knowledge developed may well be the same, but the process in developing the knowledge is very different. Who is doing the learning really matters and is directly related to where the effective reflective practice occurs.'

Indeed, Loughran goes on to point out that in this process, a teacher 'could see things that were hitherto tacit, or implicit, in his practice and begin to articulate them in ways that carried meaning not only for himself but also for others.'

In a school with a vibrant and reflective atmosphere, such insights could even emerge from peer discussions. Indeed, this sort of facilitative reflection through action research, if sustained, should eventually culminate in the creation of precisely such an ambience in a school.

Summary of Teachers' Action Research

Of the twelve teachers including the Principal in this school, two teachers chose not to participate, and a third is still working on his action research. One teacher left on maternity leave as soon as the study started and returned to work when it ended four months later. The other teacher did not perceive any problem in her class, and so she chose not to carry out action research. [How her Principal handled this is described later.] The third teacher is continuing to engage with his first cycle of action research and his work will find a place in a later publication.

For ease of reference, we present again the summary of the action research problems selected by each teacher:

Teacher(s)	Action Research Problem
Shipra	English: reading and writing skills of some students in Class V below expected level
Mohit	How to teach EVS to students of Class IV who cannot comprehend the language (Bengali students in Hindi state)
Madan	Reading of the Hindi alphabet by four students of Class IV below expected level
Shakuntala and Saud	Math: some students of Class VI do not understand place value
Neeraj	How to develop scientific temper in students of Class V and VI

Teacher(s)	Action Research Problem
Narendra and Sahabuddin	Hindi: reading of some students in Classes V and VI below expected level
Deepak Dixit	Children of Class VI do not understand vision: how to teach them in an organic manner

In the descriptions, the following nomenclature has been adopted:

- teachers with less than five years' teaching experience are termed 'teacher-in-the-making',
- those with five to ten years' experience are called 'fairly experienced' and
- those with more than ten years' experience are termed 'very experienced'.

Shipra Agarwal is a very experienced teacher, having taught for seventeen years, but still displays a willingness to look at her classroom practices. She is not critical of the curriculum, accepting it as a 'given'. Training programmes do not seem to have impacted her very much thus far, but she likes the opportunity to attend such programmes. During her classroom observation, her sincere attempt to connect with each child was evident. Shipra confessed that she welcomed the idea of action research when she realised that it would open up a way to work with the children she had been concerned about for some time. Some children in her English class (Class IV) had difficulty in reading and understanding words in English, and their vocabulary was much below that expected of nine-year-olds. She first attempted traditional methods of teaching English words before resorting to activities and games, since the traditional methods did not work. She consulted peers on how to tackle the problem, showing her openness to suggestions. She also dipped into TLMs made by her colleague so that she did not get weighed down by the work of single-handedly preparing resources for her class. She noted with care whether or not children were merely decoding words or actually reading with understanding. Shipra devised several games and activities to draw out the children who had difficulty with English words, while retaining her concern for the rest of the class as well in this effort. She did this by mixing words (of varying difficulty) in the game, so that children were challenged according to their level. She also admits that she managed to do this work as part of her regular routine, and did not experience any extra pressure because of action research. She was visibly happy when she could see the results of her games and activities, and the same children who could not read earlier were now reading words. The children had improved somewhat after her work with them, though they still need help. In her post–AR-cycle interview, she acknowledged that action research has given her a structured way to think about problems faced by her students, to systematically arrive at a solution. That action research actually opened up a door for this highly experienced teacher is evident from the fact that she continued to conduct action research even after this study was completed.

Mohit Sharma is a teacher-in-the-making, and yet (or perhaps, because of this!), is refreshingly free of the grip of the curriculum. 'We decide their curriculum!' he declares. Training programmes appear to have impacted him to a fair extent, if the enthusiasm with which he recounts them is an indication. He is gratified by the change seen in his students at the end of an action research cycle. '*At the beginning of the year many students were not able to write, to express themselves but they are confident now. They can stand up and speak and express their thoughts*.' Mohit's classroom observation revealed his penchant for off-beat ways of getting children to revise their lesson. Mohit disagrees strongly with the notion that some children are gifted. This probably stems from his concern for equality in the classroom. Upon seeing that the five students who faced a difficulty in expressing themselves in Hindi (the medium of instruction) seemed to feel 'lesser' than the rest of the class, he took care during his action research to devise means of assessment which would *not* demand their oral or written expression in Hindi. Instead of demanding that all students write out their answers, therefore, he threw open the options of drawing a picture, writing an answer or doing both – in response to the same question. Thus, all students answered the same set of questions in the way that each found easiest – and some even chose to use both methods. Had Mohit been rigid about the ends that he was 'supposed' to achieve, it is unlikely that he would have hit upon this method of allowing students the space to be assessed in their chosen way. A valuable insight that Mohit appears to have gained, as he reflects on his reflection-in-action, is best expressed in his own words: '... this boy's mind opened up ... he could be seeing other things, too without doubt ... but he never got the opportunity to express it earlier ... Somewhere it could be our fault that we think that in the class because he can't write or read, he doesn't know anything.' The realisation that he had in the past relied too heavily on conventional modes of assessing students' learning has impacted him so deeply that it spurred him to sustain this alteration of his methods of assessment. Hidden in this realisation also is the latent admission that this belief was part of the general ambience: more likely than not, this was what his own teacher assumed about him and his schoolmates. He could break away from long-practised patterns of assessing children's understanding (founded on an archaic belief that the written or spoken answer is the only one that is worthy of consideration) only when the incongruence of that belief stared Mohit in the face.

Madan Mohan Joshi is a fairly experienced teacher who, like Mohit, dismisses the belief that some children are gifted. Even though he did not really opt for this profession, he has grown to like the work. What is even more noteworthy is the fact that he sees himself as a teacher of EVS (environmental studies), but he was asked to teach Hindi, a subject that was not in the domain of his core expertise. As often happens in many schools, this teacher had to draw upon as yet unused – and, perhaps, yet to develop – expertise. Instead of balking at the attempt, he took pains to probe into the structure of language, how children learn it and how they can be enabled to learn it better. He appears to have used his diagnostic skills – perhaps from his experience of teaching EVS – in trying to fathom how children read words and then comprehend them. For instance, he noticed that even if he hid one word, children read the text as if that word was present. 'My belief was that the word structure was something which the children fixed in their mind and kept on repeating as it is written there .... Even if I were, by the way, to hide one word, *even then* they would say it ...' He clearly articulates his belief and tests it out in a scientific manner.

His measured and low-key demeanour belies his tenacity to go to the root of the problem faced by his students in reading and understanding Hindi words. [With persistence, he visited the homes of his students to understand why they were finding it so difficult to understand the language – and discovered that exactly those children whose parents were away for the entire day (as daily wage labourers) were the ones who faced a problem in understanding Hindi.] During his classroom observation, Madan's sensitivity to each child's unique environs came through. Despite the noticeable absence of impact of training programmes on his expertise – from his own response to such a question – Madan displays a willingness to explore different approaches to teaching language: other than the traditional approach that he was himself taught through.

Reflecting on his reflection-in-action, Madan echoes Shipra's sentiment when he admits that he gained something very valuable from action research: 'I got the opportunity to think about those children in a different way … that on those problematic issues … I got an opportunity to think differently. I thought about it and spoke about it to my group, did an analysis of such children – why do they have problems?... and tried to find the solution…'

Saud is a highly experienced teacher who took to the profession when he found that he enjoyed offering tuitions for a child in the neighbourhood. Despite having other options, he made teaching his career choice. While he does not profess that training programmes had a great influence on his teaching practice, he does enjoy the workshops that he has attended after joining this school. He shows a great degree of concern for students in his anxiety about their mixed learning levels. He takes the curriculum as given, even as he admits that it is vast. He taught Math to Class VI along with Shakuntala; they identified their problem long before this study was launched in their school. 'We didn't give it the name – action research. But we found that there were a few children in Class VI who did not know *place value*, and so we were thinking about addressing this issue.' He expresses the importance of documentation when he admits: 'If someone wants to do work in this area, our documentation will help them. Why, we, too, would have benefitted if we could have asked – has someone done this kind of work and if so, what was the result?' His words resonate with McIntosh's declaration: 'It is through finding the right words that an understanding occurs.' At the same time, McIntosh acknowledges that the shift from thoughts to words can be difficult, for attaching words to feelings can be uncomfortable. [Almost all the teachers found documentation to be a challenge, and yet almost all of them acknowledged the usefulness of this step of their research work.]

> *Moving from thoughts to words can sometimes be difficult, for attaching words to thoughts and feelings can be troublesome and uncomfortable. Finding the right word can be a challenge. However, moving from the private to public through this process can be enlightening, for it emerges out of unconscious into conscious forms of knowing.*
>
> ***Polanyi (1958)***

Saud admits that team-teaching with Shakuntala helped them to address the different levels of the twenty-nine children in Class VI. 'In the class there were twenty-nine children and we were able to manage the other children as well in a relaxed manner … The other teacher could work with the other half and alternately, amongst ourselves, we would shift. …We used to also try that, whatever they do, they should not see themselves as separate … When there was a group activity, these children were included in the group …' He shows his commitment to understanding the children's level of understanding when he points out that even in the group that had not quite grasped place value, there was a heterogeneity in terms of understanding. He takes care to discuss any new initiative with his co-teacher, Shakuntala, before implementing it. When the two teachers adopted the novel step of having their students develop teaching–learning materials to understand place value, they found that the students enjoyed this so much that they did not want to stop making these materials. Saud adds: '…. the children didn't want to stop it….we allowed them so that – in this, they would make something challenging…' However, he points out that this was not at the cost of the teachers completing the task that they had planned for that day. While he did perceive an improvement in the learning levels of these students, he thinks they have a long way to go before they reach the expected level of Class VI. His commitment is evident both from the manner in which he was seen attending to individual children during his classroom observation, and from his declaration that this sort of work would have to be done, regardless of whether or not it was called 'action research' – '…. whether we give it the name action research or not, we have to do the work ….'

Shakuntala is a moderately experienced teacher who opted for teaching as her vocation, and would not change her profession even if given a chance. She confesses that the insulting and humiliating behaviour of some of her own school teachers made her resolve to become a teacher who did not treat her own students thus. Like Saud, she takes the curriculum as given, even though she admits that it is vast. She cannot recount any training programmes that impacted her. She enjoys teaching Math, but is comfortable teaching other subjects as well. She deems it important for children to study their lessons at home, and bemoans the fact that this is seldom possible for first-generation learners.

It is evident that she takes pains to identify the learning level of her students, and admits, like Saud, that *Action Research* was a mere name that was given to a process that she had anyway been following. At the beginning of term with Class VI, she says: 'I did normal revision as it is done with Class III or Class II children ... on the blackboard and in their notebooks .... I didn't do it with separate assessment or worksheets. At the beginning of the academic year we realised that we could not do much for these children ... till they have knowledge of place value and numbers ...' [The action research project did not take off until August.] For her, therefore, the only new element that was introduced by taking up action research was documentation, which she shared with her co-teacher, Saud. In order to transact the content, she uses dice, abacus, TLMs developed by the students, etc. While she did see improved learning levels, she admits that there is a great deal more to be done with the children who could not understand place value.

Her strategy of getting children to develop their own problem sums excited one child so much that he followed her around pestering her to give him homework. Shakuntala also admitted that the need to complete a cycle of action research brought in a certain urgency to solving an issue which she had anyway set out to solve. Shakuntala and Saud confirmed the importance of documentation.

Neeraj Kothari is a teacher-in-the-making whose family background (his father is a DIET faculty member) appears to have spurred his interest in education. He recounts several training programmes with zeal – and is one of the few teachers who admits to implementing what he learnt in the summer training programme that was conducted by the Foundation: 'It was quite an interesting phase ... We were curious as to how to do things in the future ... so we felt quite good ... When we came back after training ... we saw in what way we could apply this .... That in the class too it was to try these strategies' Like many of his peers, he did not opt for this profession but has now grown to like it considerably.

He believes that learning need not happen only through teachers, textbooks and schools; his penchant for using discussion as pedagogy is evident from his CRO as well as his post–AR cycle interview. He now takes the trouble to always begin his classes with a lively discussion, something he did not do earlier. He admits that when he went to school, he was taught Science by rote; he decided not to teach his students similarly. 'We have also received education like this, as it usually happens – but after coming here I noticed quite a few changes. I saw that in Science, children were not very serious; they would ask a few questions ... I did a study of the children and I found that the children's homework would not get completed. I wondered why.' This is how he arrived at his AR problem: how to develop scientific temper in students of Class VI and VII.

For a teacher who was taught Science by rote, he displays a remarkable freedom from the compelling urge to 'tell' students the 'right' answer. His facilitation of collaborative enquiry by students of the cause of germination is described in his AR document. As a result of this approach: 'They do not now believe something straightaway but they see for themselves, and only then, they believe. Secondly, if they have a question, they are able to identify and phrase it and they are then able to satisfy their curiosity to reach their goal.' He confesses that his classes have now become noisier, with children constantly talking to each other and to their teacher about their eagerly articulated doubts, but he sees this 'noise' as being very productive. From a teacher who faced a class of mute, unresponsive learners who passively accepted whatever the teacher said, Neeraj has now turned the situation around so dramatically that his students rush up to him with numerous things that they wish to discuss – as soon as he enters the class. Neeraj is energised enough by the results of his first cycle of action research to carry it further in another topic: properties of matter.

Narendra Kumar Joshi is a teacher-in-the-making; he appears to think a lot about his classroom practice and does not make claims. He deems most of the training programmes that he has attended to be relatively insignificant, but for one that actually connected with classroom processes. He used to believe that learning happens only in schools, but after becoming a teacher, he realised that this was not true. 'They learn a lot from their surroundings ....' Since he has noticed that working with children has challenged many of his former beliefs, he finds the work to be worth his while.

Narendra is one of the many teachers who did not really opt for this as a profession, but have grown to like it. He is acutely conscious of the social concerns which are inextricably tied to this profession, and this is borne out by his post-AR cycle work where he has begun working with the parents of the children who find Hindi difficult. He keenly observes the degree of participation and learning of each child in his class, as evidenced from his CRO and more so, from his post-AR interview. Together with his co-teacher, Sahabuddin, he identified his AR problem: *to improve the Hindi reading and comprehension skills of some students of Class V and VI.* There were about twenty children across these two classes, who read Hindi haltingly and incorrectly. 'And Sahabuddin and I would constantly think about how we should work with them.'

Indeed, he and Sahabuddin had identified this as an area that they needed to work on long before the action research project was launched in this school. 'I started discussing with these students on various points like their interests, their families; games that they like to play, etc...so as to establish a good rapport with them. When they started talking freely with me, I started working on their known vocabulary like making words with given letters, writing words from their language, rhyming words, using word cards, taking sentences from familiar stories and using words from the sentences to make new sentences, etc.' Using various novel strategies like word strips, sentence strips and story cards, the two teachers managed to bring about a marked shift. The results of their joint efforts are tabulated in Section II, showing a significant improvement in most of the students' reading and comprehension skills.

However, Narendra admits that there are still some students who have not improved significantly from their earlier level, and is concerned that the strategy which worked with the others did not work with these. Narendra thinks that the space for leisurely cogitation over the issue at hand is an imperative, because 'only when we actually think about something, write it and *then* reflect upon it and do the work, *then* we do something new ...' Narendra also realises that for a teacher who is already reflecting about the issues in his class, action research may not be necessary as a formal strategy but if they practice it by naming it as such, there would be benefits. Systematic documentation that the practice of AR brought into their work has brought new benefits for both him and Sahabuddin. They now write documentation as a routine, and it shows greater reflection than before.

Sahabuddin Ansari is a moderately experienced teacher who constantly reexamines pedagogy and his students. He recounts with zeal several training programmes that he attended, and declares that he gave up a lucrative post as a General Manager because he did not find the numerous learning opportunities in it that he is now constantly offered as a teacher. His experience with action research has made him even more aware of his own training needs, and he now wishes to learn more about child psychology. He took care to consult the parents of the children who were facing reading difficulty in Hindi before taking extra classes for them. He is critical of the textbooks used, because of poor layout and presentation. 'Children are attracted to books that are well laid out and illustrated, even if they are difficult to read.'

> *Thinking begins in what may fairly enough be called a forked-road situation, a situation which is ambiguous, which presents a dilemma, which proposes alternatives.*
>
> ***Dewey (1933)***

He also invests time and effort in understanding his students better: 'To understand children better I play and chat with them. I also visit their homes in order to find out the sources of their mistakes/any pattern.' In working with Narendra on the AR problem described above, he chose to adopt the Whole Language Approach, which gave him new insights. 'In action research we think we are learning from students; we are facilitators, and we are facilitating.'

Since he had taught Language through the Traditional Approach, he was intrigued by the Whole Language approach, 'It is very interesting … this entire process as I saw it working …. Sometimes, without reading the full word, we read based on guess work.' He intuited that this approach would probably work with these children, as they were slightly older than those who commonly begin to learn language, and the remarkable results that he and Narendra achieved are tabulated in Section II.

Deepak Dixit is the Principal of the school and a very experienced teacher as well. Despite his years of experience, he displayed a readiness to take a fresh look at his classroom practices and implement what he learnt from the Foundation's summer training programme. He is one of three teachers in this school who actually opted for the teaching profession, despite temporarily succumbing to social pressures and completing an MBA to work briefly in the corporate sector. He found his calling in teaching. He is of the view that the curriculum needs to be constantly evaluated and is unhappy that both the content and the method of teaching it has remained largely unchanged since his own schooldays.

He takes an active interest in self-development and recalls attending training programmes from which he drew some learning. His detailed account (see Section II) of the lesson that he was invited to assist teaching – *transparent, translucent and opaque objects* – reveals the thoroughness of his approach. When he found that the students did not have a clear understanding of the process of vision, he postponed teaching them about transparent, translucent and opaque objects, and addressed the former concern first. His professed intention to make children independent thinkers is borne out by the manner in which he leads children into enquiry and discussion but steadily refrains from giving them the 'right answer'. His style of leadership appears to be one that allows expression from his teachers, while at the same time, one that takes note of complacency.

In dealing with a teacher who claimed there was no real problem in her class, he displayed a mature realism by avoiding confrontation even as he was nudging the teacher to reflect and actually perceive a problem. His support of the action research study was critical in its sustained execution and completion. His cognizance of teachers' changed lesson plans, non-participating teachers' shifts and participating teachers' impact on improved learning of students shows his genuine concern for effecting an improvement in the quality of teaching and learning that happens in his school.

Deepa did not participate in the action research because she was away on maternity leave. Upon her return to school she noticed several changes. There was a noticeable increase in discussion amongst teachers, and there was also far more detailed documentation, she records. Lesson plans were now accompanied with teachers' reflections about themselves, their students and classroom processes, and Deepa slowly began to adopt this practice too.

When she joined her colleague, Shipra, in teaching English to students of Class I, she was intrigued by Shipra's practice of drawing out from students familiar English words beginning with a specific sound. She notes that this was a novel exercise, especially as it evoked multiple responses from children. 'When I was taught English, 'c' could only be for 'cat', but here, I found children coming up with so many words that started with that sound.'

She enjoyed helping Shipra facilitate these interactive classes so much that she tried this practice out in her Hindi classes and was delighted with the results. Deepa has documented her own learning and practice in great detail.

> *As long as our activity glides smoothly from one thing to another or as long as we permit our imagination to entertain fancies at pleasure, there is no call for reflection. Difficulty or obstruction in the way of reaching a belief brings us, however, to a pause. In the suspense of uncertainty, we metaphorically climb a tree; we try to find some standpoint from which we may survey additional facts and, getting a more commanding view of the situation, may decide how the facts stand related to one another.*
>
> ***Dewey (1933)***

Prachie chose not to participate in the AR study. She did not perceive any deep-rooted problem worth conducting action research on, as her students understood whatever she was trying to convey. Deepak Dixit, the Principal, received this quietly, but 'was looking for something which could draw the attention of the teacher and help her to reflect on to her class and classroom practices. I decided to have a conversation with the concerned teacher and try to investigate the issue without pressurizing her. We had a discussion, in which I asked her some questions based on her classroom processes. The emphasis was on the learning outcome of the class, as whole. I also helped her analyse the status of all the students in the class, in English language. Some of the questions guided her to move in the desired direction.'

What he did was to present a challenge to her in a very novel manner. He deftly posed (see text boxes that follow) an action research problem to a teacher who formerly could see none. He asked her: 'How many familiar two-letter words can be decoded as well as understood by a Class III student?' While working with the students of her class, the teacher realised that there are certain words which are being used repeatedly and are simple for their level. The two-letter words used were easy to read and recall, so a set of 21 such words was drawn by the teacher from the text previously covered in class.

Prachie found the following:

Student No.	1	2	3	4	5	6	7	8	9	10
Words read correctly (out of 21)	7	16	11	2	19	15	21	20	21	19
Words read incorrectly (out of 21)	14	5	9	19	2	6	0	1	0	2

Student No.	11	12	13	14	15	16	17	18	19
Words read correctly (out of 21)	14	20	19	0	18	16	21	21	16
Words read incorrectly (out of 21)	7	1	2	21	3	5	0	0	5

She was already aware that these children would find English difficult, since their mother tongue was not even Hindi (the medium of instruction); the above results therefore did not surprise her. However, they did lend a structure to her thinking. Now she could clearly distinguish between three categories of words:

1. Words which the children decoded without understanding. They were only able to pronounce them.
2. Words which they understood based on the context. Examples of such words were *up, us, me, no, do, go, and we.*
3. Words which had been taught in the class and that they had worked on in a worksheet (Prepositions) in the current and previous classes. [For instance, to check if they knew the meaning of the preposition 'on', the teacher drew a cup and asked them to fill in the blanks for: *The (picture of a) cup was ...... the table.*] So these were familiar words which could be decoded as well as understood.

She had initally said that she had not been interested in action research because she felt she had found solutions to the problems she could see. She later admitted to benefitting from the structure that Deepak Dixit lent to her examination of a problem that she was already aware of. Her openness to receiving the Principal's suggestion aided her in reflecting constructively.

How critical was the trigger provided by the Principal? The Principal now concludes: 'It was only a matter of helping her see a problem through and assuring her that all the possible help in documentation would be provided to her when needed. As she is a teacher of the class and maintains a daily record of the students of her subject or class she knew the level of the students. After the discussion, she herself concluded that there are students in the class who need some attention/ time etc. She then felt that the previous impression which she carried was incorrect.' Deepak is willing to assist Prachie with developing a template for action research if she is interested.

'It is Prachie who will be taking the process forward; I will just be there in case she needs any assistance or support. It may be in documentation or in the actual process. I understand that a teacher may run out of time and thus may not be able to document the work on the template. So this could possibly be the place where I *may* pitch in depending on Prachie's requirement.'

Loughran (2002) describes the situation where a teacher cannot see that any problem exists at all. He argues for the importance of developing a range of ways of seeing a problem. It is this skill that a facilitator needs to develop. The teacher who could formerly not see any problem was skilfully led into perceiving one that had thus far escaped her notice. Deepak had found a non-confrontational way of creating an environment conducive to reflection.

Deepak Dixit said, '*Towards the end of the data collection, the teacher looked a bit confused. She was asked to review the reflection and come up with a plan on how to tackle this situation.*'

Limitations of this Study

Like any study, there were certain unfulfilled aims and many points to take away from this study for future work.

a. It was noticed that several teachers expected support from facilitators in identifying alternative strategies for the classroom. It was in this regard that some teachers felt that the facilitation was inadequate. The Principal Investigator explains why this may have been so: 'As an anchor who was facilitating the entire team, I fell into a trap: because there were so many tasks to complete, I was *constantly ticking things off the list*: has every teacher's Teacher Profile been completed? Has every Action Research Template been filled? Has every teacher's class been observed? etc. So my focus was more on what's *been done*, rather than "*What is happening here and now*?" I realised this mistake when I finally reflected on what many teachers shared at the end of the study: they bemoaned the lack of ideas, and expressed the need for greater support from facilitators in giving them leads on strategies to address their problems. When I reflected on why this had not happened enough, I realised that my focus on what's *been done* had prevented me from looking at what was needed *at each moment*.'

b. Another error that any practitioner of action research can easily make is *mechanical reflection*. The phrase is something of an oxymoron, but in their zeal to turn reflective (or reach the end of the road), practitioners may well find that their focus on the end result blinds them to what is happening right under their noses. Action research, if it is to be done well, *can only happen in the here-and-now*. Repeatedly drawing one's attention away from the present and towards the desired goal (to the extent that one misses the current events), will only defeat the purpose of the entire exercise.

c. A thorough review of the literature on facilitation at the start of the project would have offered the opportunity to ground the facilitation in methodology that has proven successful. In this regard, Zhang, Lundeberg and Eberhardt (2011) have examined the strategies that six facilitators used to promote discussion amongst 35 in-service teachers. This was done as part of a professional development programme which used problem-based learning approach for teacher learning.

> Data analysis showed that experienced facilitators used a variety of strategies in their facilitation, including questioning, revoicing, making connections, clarifying, reframing, summarizing, role playing, meta-talk, and modeling. In particular, questioning and revoicing were the most important strategies in all sessions studied, accounting for about half of the facilitators' talk.

Such intense engagement of facilitators with teachers could, however, also have posed problems: their dependence on the facilitator may have increased radically! Therefore, a tempered aproach which balances facilitation with teacher autonomy would need to be adopted.

d. As described, this was the second spiral of action research, with the action research problem now being how best to facilitate the teacher in her action research. Apart from the diary jottings (contained herein in the interleaves) there was no record of the facilitator-teacher interactions. By adopting a Facilitator's Template for recording this action research (rather like the template given to teachers for the first spiral of action research), a major gap in this study could have been filled, that is, inadequate documentation by the facilitators in their approach to facilitation. Had this been done in a detailed and structured manner, future studies such as this could have been better informed.

e. Another obvious limitation lies in the fact that just a single CRO was conducted for each teacher. While several classroom observations would possibly have brought out more tangible evidence for teacher beliefs playing out (or not) in practice, they would have also probably hampered the teacher's smooth facilitation of the class. A balance was struck by observing a single classroom transaction, but naturally, this had its consequences. In this regard, tighter documentation of perceived shifts in children could have enhanced the richness of the study. If, for instance, a teacher noted enhanced animation in classroom discussion as action research proceeded, detailed documentation of this change (qualititative as well as quantitative) in children's participation would have rendered such a shift more palpable. The absence of children's voices is another gap: which, if present, would have added another dimension to this study.

f. The carrying out of just one action research cycle to enhance reflection can also be viewed as a limitation. Often, this may not suffice to produce a meaningful change.
g. Yet another gap (which should be addressed in similar work in the future) is the lack of recommendation of appropriate readings for teachers to enrich their action research. Facilitators would have greatly enhanced the emergence of the reflective practitioner from these teachers, had this been done even in small measure.
h. There was also lack of rigour in the second spiral of research. Had there been a detailed structure for facilitators not just to facilitate action research, but also to observe and examine shifts in teachers' thinking and practice (through the course of action research) the second spiral would have been far more explicit than it appears to be.
i. If there is a 'distant' feel to this study, that, too, is a limitation worth acknowledging. The lack of frequent and intense engagement within the team of facilitators also proved to be problematic. Since they were geographically located in different places and were simultaneoulsy engaged in many other projects, they met as a team only once – at the beginning of the study. Thereafter, their interactions were mostly through telephone or email, with some sub-groups of a team meeting in person every now and then. Cohesiveness that could have resulted from a focused engagement of a facilitating team with the teachers (cumulatively) is missing in this study.

Has Reflective Practice been Sustained in this School After the Study Ended?

The aim of this study was to allow the emergence of the reflective practitioner from each teacher, using action research as one possible means. It cannot therefore be deemed 'complete' with the successful completion of just one action research cycle by each teacher. Nor is it realistic to tick off the aim as ever being 'met', since reflection is an ongoing practice.

There have been several efforts that have continued in this school after January 2014, when the final interviews were conducted with all the teachers. At the time of writing this book, Narendra has chosen an alternative approach 'to help children realise their potential'. He is working with five children and he will keep his focus (in the new approach) on the *parents* of these identified children and will sensitise them for the education of their wards. Narendra has begun working with the mothers of the students whose mother tongue is not Hindi, so that the children get a chance to reinforce their learning at home with their mothers. These parents frequently come to school and the teacher has continual interactions with them in a planned manner.

Sahabuddin has begun exploring the use of mushroom farming to teach various subjects like Math, EVS, Language, etc., even as it offers the children work experience. He is trying to integrate Work Education with other subjects.

Shipra has begun questioning the mode of assessment in English – which is an alien language for these children – and is working on assessment methods that are in alignment both with the nature of the language as well as the children's own context. Her problem-framing has thus shifted from devising new strategies (for transacting given content), to one that is situated in her – as yet – unarticulated overarching theories about language learning and assessment.

Neeraj is continuing with his past action research on 'How to develop scientific temper among children'. This time, he has chosen the topic 'Properties of Matter'.

Deepa has identified a problem and has begun working on it. She was so inspired by Shipra's method of enhancing the English vocabulary of children, that she is now exploring ways of doing the same in Hindi.

Shipra in a video-recorded interview in August 2014 said, 'Doing action research is not as important as becoming a reflective teacher. In my view, even if a teacher does not conduct action research, it is okay. But a teacher needs to reflect on her teaching practice in some way or the other.'

Guidelines for Conducting Similar Action Research

For the reader who wishes to take forward this work by initiating it in another school, we suggest (but do not prescribe!) certain ways to do this –

- An initial orientation of the staff of the school into the concepts of (a) action research and (b) reflective practice would be a good place to start. This should include discussion, readings, and some actual case studies emphasising the effectiveness of action research in enhancing reflection.

- Following this, the teachers should be given the *option* of engaging in action research. It is important that a teacher *opts* for (rather than is 'told' to do) action research. By the very act of stepping forward to engage with an issue that she faces, a teacher takes upon herself the onus of seeing it through. Ownership is very important.
- Framing the problem often needs a good deal of facilitation. Indeed, it is in this step that the stage is set, so to speak. The facilitator could begin by asking the teacher to list out all the problems that (s)he faces and would like to address. Some may be systemic issues (e.g. why is the syllabus so vast?), others may be philosophical (e.g. what is worth learning?) and yet others may be practical, day-to-day issues like those described in this work. Sifting the action-researchable problems from those which cannot be addressed in a four-to-six month time span is the first challenge for the facilitator. [The teacher also needs to be made aware that certain issues are within her control, and others are not.]
- Assist each teacher to pick out *a burning issue (for that teacher)* from a set of problems that the teacher articulates. Therefore, the facilitator needs to be alert and resist the temptation to step in and frame the problem for the teacher. If this is done, it becomes the facilitator's action research and not that of the teacher! Therefore, just like a teacher of children has to hold back from providing the right answer, a facilitator of action research has to refrain from jumping into the arena and suggesting an action researchable problem. Questions that could nudge the teacher towards phrasing the problem are: *Which of these issues would you like to see resolved at the earliest? Which of these problems, if left unsolved, would seriously hamper your work?* etc.
- Following this crucial step of framing the problem, the flow of the action research template given in this work could be followed by the facilitator and teacher. Other templates could be developed as well. Some structure is advisable so as to maintain a certain rigour; in rare instances, dropping all structures may yield better results.
- During facilitation, the facilitators should not yield to temptation and step in and solve the problem. It is important to bear in mind that the role of the facilitator is simply *to facilitate* – that is, direct the teacher to sources of ideas, like books, research papers, resource persons, relevant websites, etc.
- Throughout the action research cycle, the facilitator can provide appropriate support to the teacher in documenting the entire

research. Again, the documentation need not be done only in the form of a structured template, as in the current work.

- All the above guidelines are for the first spiral of action research. When it comes to the *facilitator's* action research (the second spiral) examining if and how action research is enhancing reflection in the teacher, it is important to first be clear if this is collaborative action research or not. In other words, if the facilitator is participating in the effort to enhance reflection in the teacher, then there is room for the facilitator to encourage the teacher in his efforts, recognise and share shifts even as they occur and nudge the teacher on to the desired end. However, if the study begins with a question: *Can action research allow the emergence of the reflective practitioner from the teacher?* then, it is important that the facilitator maintains a neutral stance, only stepping in to facilitate, but not participate in, the action research of the teacher.
- As already mentioned, it is important that the second spiral is also documented in a structured (or unstructured) manner, so as to have a picture of the emerging reflective practitioner, throughout the study.
- The facilitator (and/or Principal Investigator) should take note of tangible as well as intangible changes in the schools' ambience as the action research proceeds. This can be done in several ways: through regular classroom observations, scrutiny of lesson plans, listening to children's exchanges outside the classroom, interviewing children at intervals during the period of action research, sitting in on staff meetings, and noting ripples (if any) to non-participating teachers. Increasing reflection is bound to show up in many ways – only some of which can be evidenced concretely.

Way Forward

This study gave many insights to both teachers as well as facilitators. The most critical supporting element that was cited by some as 'missing' in this study is the regular and sustained support for teachers with a greater spectrum of resources and ideas (even content knowledge) than their present repertoire allows for. To quote Dewey (1933):

> Education that takes as its standard the improvement of the intellectual attitude and method of students demands more serious preparatory training, for it exacts sympathetic and intelligent insight into the workings of individual minds, and a very wide and flexible command of

subject matter – so as to be able to select and apply just what is needed when it is needed.

Sometimes, the facilitator may not be in a position to help the teacher 'select and apply just what is needed when it is needed.' In such a situation, the facilitator can and should enable the teacher *to ask* for this specific sort of assistance, and then direct the teacher to the appropriate source of such assistance.

It is now pertinent to ask what such a study of action research conducted by teachers can lead to: both in this particular school and elsewhere. The developments in this school are being followed by a subset of the facilitating team that did this study. A few presentations have been made by four teachers in an internal research conference Manthan held at Azim Premji Foundation.

For readers who would like to work towards the emergence of effecting reflective practice in their schools after reading this book we suggest the following:

- If you are looking for ideas and activities to trigger such thinking amongst your teachers, there is a plethora of literature available. To begin with you could use *Teaching and Learning through Reflective Practice: A Practical Guide for Positive Action* by Tony Ghaye (Routledge, 2011). This book describes how reflective conversations can be initiated and sustained, and is of interest to teachers, teacher educators as well as those pursuing professional development courses.
- Triggering reflection is only the start. It will need to be sustained if transformation is to be achieved. As Chambers and Clarke (undated online publication) state: 'Professional support networks across workplaces and between organisations, including higher education need to be used or formed.'

> *The extent of our capacity for reciprocal reflection-in-action can be discovered only through an action science which seeks to make what some of us do on rare occasions into a dominant pattern of practice.*
>
> **Schon (1983)**

Therefore, the attempt to initiate reflection should find fruition in a sustained effort which can best happen if the ownership of the effort spreads to those who were initially just 'participants' in the project. One way of bringing about this 'flip' is to get teachers who conducted action research (and showed indications of reflective thinking) to share their work with other teachers who are still new to the idea of action research. In convincing other teachers of the value of their research work, these teachers will begin to experience a greater ownership of their efforts and themselves emerge as 'champions' of action research, and eventually, of reflective practice.

Adkins Coleman (2010) emphasises the importance of such a partnership (between teachers who have embarked upon the journey of facilitation and teachers who have not yet embarked upon it): 'To prepare future teachers more adequately for urban schools, therefore, teacher educators need to provide the opportunity for them to learn from teachers who successfully facilitate engagement.'

As Lieberman (1995) points out, teachers can do this in a number of ways –

- by building new roles (e.g., teacher leader, peer coach, teacher researcher);
- by creating new structures (e.g., problem-solving groups, decision-making teams);
- by working on new tasks (e.g., journal and proposal writing, learning about assessment, creating standards, analysing or writing case studies of practice); and
- by creating a culture of inquiry, wherein professional learning is expected, sought after, and an ongoing part of teaching and school life.

Lieberman (1995). Reprinted with permission of Phi Delta Kappa International, www.pdkintl.org.

It is with the vision of such a culture of inquiry developing in schools that this work is being compiled. Tandon (1989) has emphasised the collaborative nature of action research, which can hone the capacity of a person to conduct their own research. It can also free minds for critical reflection so as to bring to the fore that which did not lie within the realm of *conscious* knowledge. Once this happens, the knowledge becomes available for use in daily life.

And finally, a note to teacher educators: Schon (1983) has made the interesting statement: 'The teachers are astonished by the sense behind a student's mistake.'

Can we, as teacher educators, be as astonished by the sense behind *a teacher's* mistake?

There is no such thing as an unreflective teacher.
Ken Zeichner (1996)

REFERENCES

Adkins-Coleman, T. A., and J. E. Lyons. 2010. 'I am not afraid to come into your world': Case studies of teachers facilitating engagement in urban High School English classrooms. *Journal of Negro Education* 79(1): 41–53.

Argyris, C., and D. A. Schon. 1974. *Theory in practice: Increasing professional effectiveness.* San Francisco: Jossey-Bass.

Bandura, A. 1986. *Social foundations of thought and action: A social cognitive theory.* New Jersey: Prentice Hall.

Batra, P. 2005. Voice and agency of teachers. *Economic and Political Weekly* 40(40): 4347–56.

Berghoff, B., S. Blackwell, and R. Wisehart. 2011. Using critical reflection to improve urban teacher preparation: A collaborative inquiry of three teacher educators. *Perspectives of Urban Education* 8: 19–28.

Biggs, J. B. 2003. *Teaching for quality learning at university: What the student does.* 2nd ed. Buckingham: SRHE and Open University Press.

Boud, D. 1994 *Conceptualising learning from experience: Developing a model for facilitation.* Proceedings of the thirty fifth annual adult education research conference, ed. M. Hymans, J. Armstrong, and E. Anderson, 49–54. Knoxville: University of Tennessee.

Boud, D., R. Keogh and D. Walker, eds. 1985. *Reflection: Turning experience into learning.* London: Kogan Page.

Brock, Mark N., Bartholomew Yu and Matilda Wong. 1991. *Journaling together; collaborative diary-keeping and teacher development.* Paper presented at the International Conference on Second Language Teacher Education, City Polytechnic of Hong Kong, April 1991.

Carr, W. and S. Kemmis. 1986. *Becoming critical: Education, knowledge and action research.* Lewes: Falmer.

Chambers, P. A. and B. L. Clarke. Using case studies for implementing reflective practice in in-service teacher education. http://tntee.umu.se/lisboa/papers/full-papers/pdf/F4PAChalmers.PDF

Corey, S. 1953. *Action research to improve school practice.* New York: Teachers College, Columbia University.

Costa, A. and R. Garmston. 1994. *Cognitive coaching: A foundation for renaissance schools*. Norwood: Christopher-Gordon.

Costello, P. 2011. *Effective action research: Developing reflective thinking and practice.* New York: Continuum International Publishing Group.

Danielson, Charlotte. 2007. *Enhancing professional practice: A framework for teaching*, 2nd ed. Alexandria, Virginia: ASCD.

Darling-Hammond, L. 2006. *Powerful teacher education*. San Francisco: Jossey Bass.

Dewey, J. 1933. *How we think.* New York: Heath & Co.

Elliott, J. 1991. *Action research for educational change.* Milton Keynes: Open University Press,

Farrell, Thomas S.C. 2012. Reflecting on reflective practice: (Re) Visiting Dewey and Schon. *TESOL Journal* 3.1.

Fazio, X. 2009. Teacher development using group discussion and reflection within a collaborative action research project. *Reflective Practice-International and Multidisciplinary Perspectives* 10(4): 529–41.

Gerald, S., and R. D. Evered. 1978. An assessment of the scientific merits of action research *Administrative Science Quarterly* 23(4):582–603.

Ghaye, T. 2011. *Teaching and learning through reflective practice: A practical guide for positive action*, 2nd ed. Oxford: Routledge.

Gibbs, L. M. 1998. *Love canal: the story continues*. Stony Creek: New Society Publishers.

Glanz, J. 1999. A primer on action research for the school administrator. *The Clearing House* 72(5): 301–4.

Gore, J. M. 1993. *The struggle for pedagogies: Critical and feminist discourses as regimes of truth.* New York: Routledge.

Guba, Y. S., and E. G. Lincoln. 1985. *Naturalistic inquiry*, Beverly Hills: Sage.

Hatton, N., and D. Smith. 1995. Reflection in teacher education: towards definition and implementation. *Teaching and Teacher Education* 11(1): 33–49.

Houston, W. R. 1988. Reflecting on reflection in teacher education. In H. Waxman, H.J. Freiberg, J. Vaughn and M. Weil (eds.) *Images of reflection in teacher education,* 7–8. Reston: Association of Teacher Educators.

Hughes, I. 2008. Action research in healthcare. In P. Reason and H. Bradbury (eds) *The Sage Handbook of Action Research: Participative Inquiry and Practice*. London: Sage.

Irvin, J. L., and D. C. Daniels. 2002. What research says: Becoming a reflective practitioner. *Middle School Journal* 33(5): 52–56.

Johns, C. 2007. *Becoming a Reflective Practitioner.* Oxford: Blackwell.

Kearsley, G. 2010. Andragogy (M.Knowles). *The theory into practice database*. Retrieved from http://tip.psychology.org

Kemmis, S., and R. McTaggart. 1996. *The action research reader,* 3rd ed. Geelong: Deakin University Press.

Knowles, M. 1980. *The modern practice of adult education from pedagogy to andragogy*. Chicago: Follett.

Knowles, M. 1984. *Andragogy in action: Applying modern principles of adult learning.* San Francisco: Jossey-Bass.

Krishna Kumar. 1988. Origin of India's textbook culture. *Comparative Education Review* 32(4): 452–64.

Krishna Kumar. 2008. *A Pedagogue's Romance: Reflections on schooling*. New Delhi: Oxford University Press.

Latour, B. 1988. The politics of explanation. In S. Woolgar (ed.), *Knowledge and reflexivity: New frontiers in the sociology of knowledge,* 155–76. London: Sage.

Lewin, K. 1948. Resolving social conflicts. In Gertrude W. Lewin (ed.) *Selected papers on group dynamics.* New York: Harper & Row.

Lewin, K. 1952. Group decisions and social change. In G. E. Swanson, T. M. Newcomb, and F. E. Hartley (eds.) *Readings in social psychology*. New York: Holt.

Lieberman, A. 1995. Practices that support teacher development: Transforming conceptions of professional learning. *The Phi Delta Kappan* 76(8): 591–96.

Lingard, L., M. Albert, and W. Levinson. 2008. Grounded theory, mixed methods, and action research. *British Medical Journal* 337: 459–61.

Lock, R. H., G. Conderman, and J. Morin. 2004. Reflect upon your practice. *Intervention in School and Clinic* 40(2): 111–15.

Loughran, J. J. 1996. *Developing reflective practitioners: Learning about teaching and learning through modeling*. London: Falmer.

Loughran, J. J. 2002. Effective reflective practice: In search of meaning in learning about teaching *Journal of Teacher Education* 53: 33.

MacNiff, J., and J. Whitehead. 2002. *Action research: Principles and practice*, 2nd ed. London: RoutledgeFalmer.

Mahapatra, Amukta. 2004. Transformation and tinkering. *Seminar* 536.

May, Wanda T. 1993. Teachers-as-researchers or action research: What is it, and what good is it for art education? *Studies in Art Education* 34(2): 114–26.

McCutcheon, G. 1989. Teacher deliberation. In M. Apple and L. Beyer (eds.) *Curriculum: Problems, politics, possibilities.* Albany: SUNY Press.

McIntosh, P. 2010. *Action research and reflective practice: Creative and visual methods to facilitate reflection and learning*. London: Routledge.

McNicoll, P. 1999. Issues in teaching participatory action research. *Journal of Social Work Education* 35(1): 51–62.

McNiff, J., and J. Whitehead. 2005. *Action research for teachers: A practical guide.* London: David Fulton Publishers.

McQuist, P. 1978. The epistemology of action research. *Acta Sociologica* 21(2): 143–63.

McTaggart, R. 1994. Participatory action research: Issues in theory and practice. *Educational Action Research* 2: 313–37.

Merleau-Ponty, Maurice. 2003. *The Structure of Behavior*. trans. Alden L. Fisher. Boston: Beacon.

Mezirow, J. 1978. *Education for perspective transformation: Women's re-entry programs in community colleges*. New York: Teacher's College, Columbia University.

Mills, Geoffrey E. 2006. *Action research: A guide for the teacher researcher* New Jersey: Pearson Merrill Prentice-Hall.

Nisbett, R., and L. Ross. 1980. *Human inference: Strategies and shortcomings of social judgment*. New Jersey: Prentice-Hall.

Nunan, David. 1997. Developing standards for teacher-research in TESOL. *TESOL Quarterly* 31(2): 365–67.

Nyquist, J. D., and D. H. Wulff. 1996. *Working effectively with graduate assistants.* Thousand Oaks: Sage.

Oberg, A., and G. McCutcheon. 1987. The potential and practice of action research: Part 1. *Peabody Journal of Education* 64(2): 116–27.

Osterman, K. 1990. Reflective practice: A new agenda for education. *Education and Urban Society* 22: 133–52.

Osterman, K. F., and R. B. Kottkamp. 2004. *Reflective practice for educators: Professional development to improve student learning*, 2nd ed. Thousand Oaks, California: Corwin Press.

Ozanne, J. L., and L. Anderson. 2010. Community action research. *Journal of Public Policy & Marketing* 29(1): 123–37.

Pajares, M. F. 1992. Teachers' beliefs and educational research: Cleaning up a messy construct. *Review of Educational Research* 62: 307–332.

Pak, J. 1985. *Find out how you teach.* Adelaide: National Curriculum Resource Centre.

Perrett, G. 2003. Teacher development through action research: A case study in focused action research. *Australian Journal of Teacher Education* 27(2): 1–10.

Polanyi, Michael. 1958. *Personal knowledge.* Oxford: Oxford University Press.

Powell, J. P. 1985. Autobiographical learning. In Boud, D., R. Keogh and D. Walker, eds. *Reflection: Turning experience into learning*, 41–51. London: Kogan Page.

Richards, Jack C., and Charles Lockhart. 1992. Teacher development through peer observation. *TESOL Journal* 1(2): 7–10.

Riel, Margaret. 2010. *Understanding action research.* Pepperdine University: Center For Collaborative Action Research. http://cadres.pepperdine.edu/ccar/define.html

Rodgers, Carol R. 2002. Defining reflection: Another look at John Dewey and reflective thinking. *Teachers College Record* 4: 842–66.

Rokeach, M. 1968. *Beliefs, attitudes, and values: A theory of organization and change.* San Francisco: Jossey-Bass.

Sagor, R. 1992. *How to conduct collaborative action research.* Alexandria: Association for Supervision and Curriculum Development.

Schon, D. 1983. *The reflective practitioner: How professionals think in action.* London: Temple Smith.

Schon, D. 1987. *Educating the reflective practitioner.* San Francisco: Jossey-Bass.

Shulman, L. 1992. Ways of seeing, ways of knowing, ways of teaching, ways of learning about teaching. *Journal of Curriculum Studies* 28: 393–96.

Smith, M. K. 1996; 1999, 2010. 'Andragogy', *the encyclopaedia of informal* education. [http://infed.org/mobi/andragogy-what-is-it-and-does-it-help-thinking-about-adult-learning/. Retrieved: 13 August 2015]

Sriprakash, A. 2011. Being a teacher in contexts of change: Education reform and the repositioning of teachers' work in India. *Contemporary Education Dialogue* 8(1): 5–31.

Stanley, Claire. 1998. A framework for teacher reflectivity. *TESOL Quarterly: Research and Practice in English Language Teacher Education* 32(3): 584–91.

Susman, G. I., and Evered, R. D. 1978. An assessment of the scientific merits of action research. *Administrative Science Quarterly* 23(4): 582–603.

Tandon, R. 1989. Participatory research and social transformance. *Convergence* 21(2/3): 5–15.

Ulmer, C., and M. Timothy. 2001. How does teacher reflection affect teaching practices? Follow-up study. Paper presented at the 12th European reading conference, Dublin, Ireland.

Vaino, K., J. Holbrook, and Miia Rannikmae. 2013. A case study examining change in teacher beliefs through collaborative action research. *International Journal of Science Education* 35(1): 1–30.

Van Maanen, M. 1990. Beyond assumptions: Shifting the limits of action research *Theory into Practice, Teacher as Researcher* 29(3): 152–57.

Waxman, H., H. J. Freiberg, J. Vaughn, and M. Weil (eds.) *Images of reflection in teacher education*. Reston, Virginia: Association of Teacher Educators.

Whyte, W. F. (ed.) 1991. *Participatory action research*. Sage Focus editions, Book 123. Thousand Oaks: Sage Publications.

York-Barr, J., W. A. Sommers, G. S. Ghere, and J. Montie. 2006. *Reflective practice to improve schools: An action guide for educators*, 2nd ed. Thousand Oaks: Corwin Press.

Yost, D. S., S. M. Sentner, and A. Forlenza-Bailey. 2000. An examination of the construct of critical reflection: Implications for teacher education programming in the 21st century. *Journal of Teacher Education* 51(1): 39–49.

Zeichner, K. 1996. Teachers as reflective practitioners and the democratization of school reform. In K. Zeichner, S. Melnick, and M. L. Gomez (eds.) *Currents of reform in pre-service teacher education*, 199–214. New York: Teachers College Press.

Zeichner, K., and D. Liston. 1996. *Reflective teaching: An introduction.* Hillsdale, New Jersey: Lawrence Erlbaum Associates.

Zeichner, K., and K. Y. Liu. 2010. A critical analysis of reflection as a goal for teacher education. In N. Lyons (ed.) *Handbook of reflection and reflective inquiry: Mapping a way of knowing for professional reflective inquiry*, 67–84. Dordrecht, The Netherlands: Springer.

Zhang, Meilan, Mary Lundeberg and Jan Eberhardt. 2011. Strategic facilitation of problem-based discussion for teacher professional development. *Journal of the Learning Sciences* 20(3): 342–94.

Appendix

Teacher Profile

The facilitator is advised to collect it at any stage of the study in a sensitive manner; some part of it may be collected through interviews. It can also be gathered in parts/installments.

Name Age (approx., in years)
Gender
Educational qualifications
Professional qualifications
Years of teaching experience
Father's profession
Mother's profession
Husband's occupation
No. of family members No. of children No. of dependents
No. of trainings that you've attended in last three years (provide details of type of training, topics dealt with etc.)
Hobbies, areas of interest
Grades that are being taught by you
Class and subject you are most comfortable teaching

Teacher as a Professional

1. What is your goal as a teacher?
   (a) What do you see as obstacles to reaching the goal?
   (b) What keeps you motivated to move towards the goal?
2. What are you currently doing that is helping you to achieve the goal?
3. Why did you choose teaching as a profession?
   Keeping your professional qualifications in mind, if you are now given an opportunity to choose any profession, what would you choose and why?

4. What according to you is the most satisfying/rewarding part of being a teacher?
5. Narrate any one incident from your teaching career that you remember. Why do you remember it?
6. Narrate an incident when a child in your class learnt something well.
7. What is the biggest challenge of being a teacher?
8. Who are the people who can support you to teach better? Why and how?
9. What are the possible material resources that can support you?
10. If there was any one thing about schools that you could change, what would that be? Why?
11. What is the breakup of your engagements in school in day-to-day life?
12. Describe how you spent the entire day yesterday. Mention those things which you do every day but did not do yesterday and those that you did yesterday but do not do generally.

Answers to questions 1–4 and 12 can be collected through interview and the rest through informal discussion.

Teacher as a Facilitator/Views on Learners and Learning

1. Do you think some children are more gifted than others?
2. When do you think children can learn best?
3. When do you think children don't learn?
4. What motivates children to perform better? Reasons?
5. Do you think children should be given feedback on their work? If yes, what kind of feedback?
6. Do you think children should be ranked/compared with each other? Why/why not?
7. Do you think girls are better in some subjects than boys? If yes, which and why?
8. Do you think boys are better in some subjects than girls? If yes, which and why?
9. Are there some things/subjects that only some can learn? Are there some none can learn, and you have to be born with it? Are there some which all can learn? Give examples for each.

10. Can you learn at any age? Is there any age limit to learning? Do you like to give/be given feedback? To/by whom?
11. What do you observe about children in your class during the teaching-learning process?
12. What do you do to pay attention to each child in the class?
13. Is the curriculum of all subjects class/age appropriate?
14. Do you think that the textbook is the only source for teaching–learning?
15. Do you think children can learn only in schools?
16. Do you think learning can happen only through teachers?
17. Do you think children from illiterate families cannot learn easily?

Answers to all questions should be collected through interview; answers to questions 1, 14, 15, 16, 17 should be marked on a 5-point scale in the questionnaire [1 – Strongly disagree, 2 – Disagree, 3 – No opinion, 4 – Agree, 5 – Strongly agree].

Observation may be additionally used for questions 11 and 12.

Teacher as a Reflective Practitioner

1. What are the sources you can gain knowledge from? Share the sources.
2. What would you like to learn, if given a chance?
3. What are you trying to learn and (how) is it helping you understand your children better?
4. Do you like to give feedback? To whom?
5. Do you like to be given feedback?
   By whom? How do you think you can get it?
   What do you do with the feedback?
6. What kinds of feedback will make you a better teacher?
7. Do you see any change in your students after they've spent a year with you? Describe the change, if yes.

Answers to questions 1–3 can be collected through interview and the rest through informal discussion.

Action Research Template

Name of Teacher:

Identified AR Problem: <To document in detail under the following heads:>

1. **Identifying the Problem**
• Listing out problems that teacher is facing • Identifying one problem, which s/he feels, is most important
2. **Analysing the Problem**
• Describing details of problem ○ How many children face this problem? ○ Efforts made by the teachers to tackle the challenge ○ Key observations – How many children overcame the problem, what method of teaching–learning was useful to some extent etc.
3. **Identifying Alternative Approaches**
• Identifying and listing alternative approaches to deal with the situation • Identifying the best possible approach
4. **Developing Strategy to Implement Identified Approach**
• Developing a plan to implement the strategy ○ What will the teacher do? ○ How will it be done? ○ What resources would be required to implement the approach? ○ What duration would be enough to deal with the problem? ○ Possible outcomes
5. **Implementing Identified Approach**
• Implementing approach as per the plan • Reflecting upon processes at regular intervals • Making on-site change in the efforts, as and when needed • Listing challenges faced by the teacher ○ Change in learning of children

6. Reflection of Teacher on the Processes

- Reflection by teacher on her/his practice
- Reflection of facilitator on teacher practice

- How effective was the process?
- What insights did you get from this entire plan?
- What was your key learning from this action research?
- What things will you continue to do?

Index